New in this Edition

The fourth edition of *Five Steps to MadCap Flare* has been updated to include features changed in Flare Versions 9 and 10 as well as several new features. You'll also find new and updated images of screens, minor revisions to procedures, and new notes and tips throughout the book.

Here's a summary of what's new in this edition:

New content	Where to find it
Characters and Symbols. New procedures and enhanced functionality for inserting and working with symbols and special characters.	Step 3
EPUB. Includes information and instructions for creating an ebook in MOBI format.	Appendix H
Filtering condition tags in the XML Editor. Working in the XML Editor when you have multiple condition tags applied to content is now much easier with the new Flare feature that lets you hide content tagged with selected condition tags so you can work with your topics as they will look in the finished output.	Appendix F
FrameMaker import. FrameMaker import has been enhanced. You can now import images with callouts in a format that you can maintain with MadCap Capture, and master pages are automatically imported as Flare page layouts.	Appendix B
New page types. Flare includes new page-layout page types for first and empty pages to support right-to-left languages. Step 5A includes information about the new page types and when to use them.	Step 5A
Preview topics with specific page layout. You can now preview topics in Print Layout mode with a particular page layout that you select from the XML Editor's toolbar.	Step 2
Responsive output. Create "smart HTML5 output" that can be viewed on different devices like tablets, smart phones and web browsers from one set of output files and one target and skin.	Step 5B

New content	Where to find it
Right-to-left languages. Contains information about Flare's support of RTL languages in outputs and in the XML Editor.	Document Basics
Undefined condition tags. Flare now has a method for fixing undefined condition tags — condition tags specified in targets and then deleted. Appendix F describes why they occur and how to fix them.	Appendix F

For a full list of features in various versions of Flare, see "What's New in This Version" in Flare's Help.

What readers are saying

"Five Steps to MadCap Flare is a must-have for any serious Flare user. If you're just starting out, *Five Steps* will give you the confidence and direction you need to get going. Even expert users will find useful tips and tricks in these pages. Whether used as a reference or training book, *Five Steps* has the essential information you need to make using Flare easier."

> — *Paul Pehrson, MadCap Flare Certified Instructor, DocGuy Training*

"This book provides a guided, controlled introduction that will help new authors get out of the starting blocks and quickly become productive. An excellent addition to an online developer's library."

> — *Neil Perlin, Madcap Flare Certified Instructor, Hyper/Word Services*

"This book focuses more deeply than any other resource on the importance of understanding a project as the foundation of success with Flare. Written in plain, conversational language, the book helps readers determine project needs by asking questions—plus it supports Flare's own increased emphasis on templates and how you can use them at many levels."

> — *Eddie VanArsdall, MadCap Flare Certified Instructor, VanArsdall InfoDesign, Alexandria, VA*

"The hardest part about learning Flare is figuring out where to start. It's overwhelming! This book is a wonderful guide through the maze of Flare features."

> — *Cheryl Landes, Tabby Cat Communications, Seattle WA*

"Typically, I've only focused on one type of output from Flare—help systems. Using this book, however, I would be well equipped to try other output formats since the detail given in the book leaves no room for guesswork or error. When you are under pressure of deadlines, this book is the helping hand you need!"

> — *Brian Laing, Documentation and Training Analyst,*
> *Xerox Corporation*

"The 'learn and do' approach significantly cuts the learning curve. The roadmap and project forms alone are worth the cost of the book!"

> — *Susan Huckle, Freelance Technical Writer, Irving, Texas*

"This book provides a real jump-start on the Flare learning curve, and the step-by-step tutorial for creating print output is worth the price of the entire book."

> — *Ginny Reynolds, Bridge-Tek Services*

"I wish I could have tapped into the advice on multi-level numbered lists when I began using Flare—plus the appendix on building context-sensitive help is terrific. This information would have saved me hours."

> — *Doug Eaton, Technical Publications Lead, Sensis Corporation*

"This book is exactly what I need to get jump-started using Flare!"

> — *Jeff O'Gorman, Specifications Writer, InterSpec*

"This book is incredible! It's designed for new users in a way to help them get a handle on how to use Flare and does so quickly with just enough detail. If you're new to Flare, you'll want to read this book. If you've used Flare for a long time, keep this book on your bookshelf as a quick reference."

> — *Deb McNally, Technical Communications Specialist*
> *Dover, NH*

Five Steps to

madcap software

FLARE

Use it to learn
—keep it for reference!

Lorraine Kupka

fiddlehead publications

a division of
NorthCoast Writers, Inc.
Fairport, New York
USA

Five Steps to MadCap Flare™

Fourth Edition, for Flare Version 10

ISBN-10: 098520592X
ISBN-13: 978-0-9852059-2-8

Fourth Edition, March 2014.

Printed in the United States of America.

Warranty and Disclaimer

Although every effort has been made to make this book as complete and as accurate as possible, the author, the publisher, and NorthCoast Writers, Inc. assume no responsibility for errors or omissions. The information provided is on an "as is" basis; no warranty is implied. Neither the author, nor the publisher, nor NorthCoast Writers, Inc. shall have any liability or any responsibility to any person or entity with respect to any loss or damages arising from the information contained in this book.

Publisher

Fiddlehead Publications, a division of NorthCoast Writers, Inc.
Fairport, New York, USA

Order additional copies at: www.NorthCoastWriters/FiddleheadPubs.com.

For information about discounts, bulk and special orders, contact **info@northcoastwriters.com** or call **1-585-223-6323**.

Foreword

By Anthony Olivier, CEO of MadCap Software

We developed MadCap Flare in part because we believe that good documentation shouldn't be hard—and it all begins with content management. To that end, Flare uses a native XML architecture that enables you to reuse content and publish in online, desktop and print formats.

Five Steps to MadCap Flare is a great resource, especially if you're new to Flare and topic-based authoring. It uses a step-by-step approach to unravel the complexities—and flexibility—of the user interface so that you can determine how best to use the product in your environment.

At MadCap Software™, we liken learning Flare to "peeling back the layers of an onion." This book helps you take the first step and realize success with an initial project so that you're ready to take on more. Best of all, it describes the concepts behind the procedures and many of the interdependencies that are not always obvious to new users.

Acknowledgements

My sincere thanks to:

The dedicated readers of previous editions of *Five Steps to MadCap Flare*, who have given me helpful feedback, thanked me for writing this book, and encouraged me to keep updating it. Thank you! You make this "labor of love" a worthwhile endeavor.

Joy Underhill for her contributions to the first two editions of this book, including helping to get them to market, editing, design ideas, setting a friendly tone with a fabulous introduction, taking the perspective of a new topic-based author, and also for her friendship. Best of luck as you pursue other ventures!

Brian Laing, Creative and Technical Communications, Xerox Corporation, for assistance with DITA import and export.

Cheryl Landes, Tabby Cat Communications, (www.tabbycatco.com), for indexing assistance.

Cindy Harris, Harris Studios, Inc. (www.HarrisStudios.com), for a wonderful cover design and business graphics.

My family for their support and encouragement. Writing and publishing this book has been a major undertaking, which would not be possible without their support.

Lorraine Kupka

Contents

Introduction 1

Welcome! 2
Why I wrote this book 2
Who this book is for 2
What this book discusses 3
What this book does not discuss 3
How this book is organized 4
A step-by-step approach 5
A strategy for learning Flare 6
    First, learn the basic Flare workflow 6
    Next, expand your knowledge 7
    Then try formatting 7
    Finally, use more advanced features 8

Document Basics 9

Overview 10
What is topic-based authoring? 10
    How traditional and topic-based authoring differ 10
    What Flare does for you 11
Terms to understand 11
    Build, generate, compile: What's the difference? 12
    Primary targets 12
About print documents 13
About online documents 13
    Help systems 13
        Context-sensitive help 13
    Knowledge bases 14
    Types of online documents 14
        Choosing the right type 15
    How online output looks (skins) 16
About DITA documents 18
    What is DITA? 18
About EPUB documents 18
About right-to-left languages 18
    Selecting the language 19
    Editing RTL language content in the XML Editor 19
    Supported outputs 19
What's next? 20

A Quick Tour 21

Overview 22
The Flare workspace...22
   About active panes and windows...22
Left pane 24
   Accordion bars..24
   Project Organizer 25
   Content Explorer 26
Middle pane 27
   XML Editor 28
   TOC Editor 30
Right pane..31
Ribbons and toolbars 31
   Ribbon groups..32
   Minimizing the ribbons 32
   Changing to toolbars 33
   Ribbon button menus 33
   Quick Access toolbar 33
Status bar...33
What's next? 34

Step 1: Get Started 35

Overview 36
Planning and managing your Flare project.....................................36
   Do you have existing source content? 36
   What kind of output do you want to create?...............................37
   What are the similarities and differences between outputs? 37
   How will content be managed and shared? 38
   What reports do you need?..39
   How will you track content development? 39
   How will content be reviewed?..39
   What's next? 39
Roadmap for using Flare...39
   How to use this roadmap 40
   Basic tasks...41
   What's your input? 41
   What's your output?..43
Common tasks 47
   Creating a Flare project 47
      Using the Start New Project Wizard...................................48
      Binding your project to a source control application...................50
   Opening a Flare project 53
   Adding a topic 53
      Methods used to add a topic...54
   Previewing a topic...57
   Opening a topic...59

Checking spelling.. 60
   Checking spelling as you type 61
   Checking spelling manually 62
   Adding terms to the dictionary 64
  Adding a target 65
  Saving your work 66
Working with templates... 68
  Recommendations.. 68
  Before creating your first template 69
  Creating a template for a Flare topic or project file 69
  Creating a project template... 71
  Using the Template Manager... 72
What's next? 74
  Recommendation.. 74

Step 2: Learn the XML Editor... 75

Overview... 76
  What is XML? 76
Tutorial setup 77
Task 1: Simplifying your workspace... 77
Task 2: Entering text 78
Task 3: Viewing the code 80
Task 4: Viewing cursors and text blocks 82
Task 5: Manipulating text 84
Task 6: Formatting text 85
Task 7: Viewing layout modes 91
  What are mediums?.. 93
Task 8: Adding another topic 93
Task 9: Saving a project 94
Learn more.. 94
  Using XML Editor toolbars 95
  Using structure bars.. 95
   Structure bars show table structure 96
   Toggling tag and span bars on and off 97
   Structure bar menus 97
  Viewing markers 98
Using Auto Suggestion 99
  Changing and disabling Auto Suggestion 100
Rulers 101
What's next? 102

Step 3: Develop Content 103

Overview... 104
Copying and pasting content into a topic 105
Deleting a topic 106
Checking for links to a topic 108

Working with lists 109
    Creating a list 110
        Creating a single-level list 110
        Creating a multi-level list 111
    Inserting paragraphs between list items 112
    Changing lists 112
        Rearranging lists 113
        Sorting a list 113
        Re-numbering a list 114
        Merging lists 116
Working with tables 117
    Inserting a table 118
    Showing grid lines 118
    Using structure bars to manipulate tables 119
        Selecting rows and columns 119
        Inserting rows and columns 120
        Deleting rows and columns 120
        Resizing rows and columns 121
        Moving rows and columns 122
    Converting tables to text and text to tables 122
    Cutting and pasting table rows, columns, and cells 123
    Merging tables 123
    Sorting table contents 124
Working with images 124
    Image thumbnails 125
    Where are images stored? 125
    Flare manages image file changes 125
        An example 125
    Adding an image 126
    Adding screen captures with Madcap Capture 127
    Resizing an image 128
        Resizing and image quality 128
        Resizing images locally 129
        Resizing images with styles 131
Showing images as thumbnails 131
    Why show images as thumbnails? 131
    Showing images as thumbnails while editing a topic 132
        Example 132
    Showing images as thumbnails in online output 133
        An example 133
        How to show thumbnails in online output 135
        Applying local formatting to images 135
        Applying styles to images 137
        Other options 139
    Problems with thumbnail settings 139
Inserting QR codes 139
Adding symbols and special characters 140
    Setting the default quick character 140

Formatting your content 141
  Ways to format content 142
  What's the difference? 142
    Local formatting 142
    Formatting with styles 142
  Local formatting vs. styles: which to use 143
  Formatting tables 143
  Recommendation 144
  Applying local formatting 144
    Applying local formatting to tables 145
  Applying styles from a stylesheet 146
    Where do styles come from? 147
    Applying styles to text 148
Customizing styles 149
  Cascading stylesheets 149
    Style classes 149
  Ways to change styles 150
  Changing styles with the Stylesheet Editor 151
  Adding a style class 154
Marking text for redaction 155
    You choose when to conceal and when to reveal text 155
    What you can redact 156
    Formatting 156
Learn more 158
  The Insert Table dialog 158
    The General tab 158
    The Borders tab 161
What's next? 162

Step 4: Create Navigation Aids 163
Overview 164
Creating a Table of Contents 164
  Multiple TOCs 165
  Master TOC 165
  What can a TOC item link to? 166
  Linking TOCs 166
  Creating a TOC 167
  Opening a topic or the Properties dialog 169
  Creating new books in a TOC 169
  Creating new TOC items 170
  Renaming a TOC 171
  Rearranging items and books in a TOC 171
Creating links 172
  Types of links 172
  Creating text hyperlinks 173
  Creating related topics links 176
  Creating bookmarks and linking to them 177
  Testing your links 180

Adding cross-references 180
  About commands 180
  Cross-references in print and online output 181
  Inserting a cross-reference 182
  Changing cross-references..184
    Changing a single cross-reference 184
    Changing the format of a cross-reference style 184
  Updating cross-references manually..187
  Advanced features 188
Creating index entries 188
  Adding index keywords 188
  Applying condition tags to index entries...................................194
  Viewing index keywords..195
  Changing and deleting index keywords 195
  Deleting index markers 195
  How index entries appear in online output 196
  How index entries appear in print output..................................196
  Formatting a print index 197
What's next? 200

Step 5A: Create Print Output 201
Overview 202
Keeping track of print output 202
Types of print output 202
  Microsoft Word output...203
    Distributing Word output 203
  Adobe FrameMaker output 203
    Distributing FrameMaker output..204
  Adobe PDF output 204
    Distributing PDF output 204
  Microsoft XPS output 204
    Viewing XPS output 204
    Distributing XPS output..204
  XHTML output..205
    Distributing XHTML output 205
Before creating print output...205
What you can include in a print document 205
Recommendation..206
Creating a simple print document..206
Creating a more complex print document 208
  How to use this tutorial...209
  Sample document 209
  Tutorial tasks...212
Tutorial setup 213
Task 1: Create placeholder topics 213
Task 2: Create a topic outline 216
Task 3: Add page layouts...219
Task 4: Delete pages from page layouts......................................221

Task 5: Customize footers 223
Task 6: Customize headers 227
Task 7: Link page layouts to topics in the TOC.. 230
Task 8: Set up the print target... 233
Task 9: Build the print output 235
Learn more... 236
    Page layouts 236
        Page layout templates 237
        Page types.. 238
        Page buttons 239
        Page frames 239
    Options for accessibility 241
What's next? 242

Step 5B: Create Online Output 243

Overview 244
Keeping track of online output... 244
Types of online output.. 245
    About responsive output 248
The basic steps.. 249
    About breadcrumbs 250
Adding a master page.. 251
Adding and editing skins 252
Setting up an online target 253
Building online output... 256
    What content is included in output? 256
        Options for excluding topics from output and search 257
        Procedure for building output... 257
Testing and troubleshooting... 258
What is publishing?.. 259
Distributing online output 259
    How to distribute 259
    What to distribute 260
        Where are the project's output files? 260
        About the Output File... 261
What's next? 262

Appendix A: Planning Worksheets 263

Part 1: Source of content 264
Part 2: Type of output 265
Part 3: Content reviews.. 267
Part 4: Content structure and management 268
Part 5: Project conventions and documentation... 268
Part 6: Start new project 269
Part 7: Target settings.. 270
    Sample target settings form (two products) 271

Appendix B: Import Content 273

Overview 274
What you can import 274
What this appendix includes 275
What this appendix does not include...275
Getting started..275
Importing from Word and FrameMaker files.................................276
    A bird's-eye view of the import process 277
        Before importing 277
        Prepare your content 277
        Import tasks 278
        Recommendation...279
    Dividing one document into many topics................................279
        An example 280
    Choices for importing styles 280
    Choices for maintaining content..281
        About Easy Sync 282
        What if you change your mind after importing the content? 282
    Importing a Word document 283
        About Word drawing objects and images...............283
        How Flare creates TOCs from a Word document 284
        How to import content from Word documents...........284
        Where are my imported topics? 291
        Re-importing content..292
    Importing a FrameMaker document 292
        About FrameMaker images...................................293
        Before importing FrameMaker documents...............293
        How to import content from FrameMaker documents 294
        Where are my imported topics and images?............301
        Re-importing content..302
Importing CHM files..302

Appendix C: XML Editor Reference 303

Top toolbar...304
Bottom toolbar..306
Cursor types...308
Shortcuts when working with text 309
    Selecting text 309
    Deleting text 310
    Copying and pasting text 310
    Moving text within a topic...310
Shortcuts for inserting content..311
Navigational shortcuts..312
Miscellaneous shortcuts 312

Appendix D: Context-Sensitive Help 313

Overview 314
What is context-sensitive help? 314
    Header file 314
    Alias file 315
    an example of mapping 316
    How Flare uses context-sensitive help 316
    Your tasks 317
Creating a header file 318
    Adding a header file to your project 319
    Adding content to the header file 320
Adding an alias file 320
Setting up an alias file 321
    Multi-select and assign identifiers 324
    Auto-generate identifiers 324
Setting up the target 325
Testing your context-sensitive help 325
    Testing context-sensitive help from Flare 325

Appendix E: Track and Troubleshoot 327

Overview 328
Broken links and unlinked items 328
    How broken links and unlinked items appear in the TOC ... 329
Unlinked TOC items 330
Image issues 331
Build errors 331
    Opening the log file 332
    Fixing bad links 333
Analyzing your project 333
    What you can analyze 334
    Selecting Analyzer scanning options 334
    Analyzing your project 336
Assigning file tags 337
    Flare's default file tags and tag sets 337
    Other tasks 339
Creating project reports 340

Appendix F: Single-Sourcing 343

Overview 344
Using condition tags 344
    An example 345
    Terms you should know 345
    Creating condition tags 346
    Applying condition tags 347
    Filtering by condition tags in the XML Editor 350

Undefined condition tags 351
    Fixing undefined condition tags 352
Using snippets...353
  Conditional snippets...353
  Snippet formatting..353
  Creating snippets 353
    Creating snippets from scratch 354
    Creating snippets from existing content..................................356
  Methods for inserting snippets 357
    Inserting a snippet on a blank line 358
    Inserting a snippet inside a text block with existing text............358
  inserting snippets 359
  Changing snippets 359
Using variables..360
  An example 360
  Conditional variables..360
  Variable formatting..360
  Variable sets 360
  Types of variables 361
  Inserting variables 362
  Highlighting variables 363
  Adding and changing variables 363
Using global project linking 365
  What should a global project contain? 365
  your tasks...365

Appendix G: DITA Import and Export 371
Overview 372
About importing..372
  About condition tags 372
  The import process 373
    Recommendation...373
  Choices for maintaining content..373
    About Easy Sync 374
    You can change your mind after importing the content..............374
Importing DITA files...375
  Examples 375
  Before importing DITA files 375
  How to import content from DITA files 376
  Where are my imported topics? 381
  Where are my DITA topic types? 381
Exporting to DITA..382
  Keeping track of DITA exports 382
  The basic steps..382
  Setting up your DITA target...383
  Building DITA (code) output..384
  Testing and troubleshooting...386

Distributing exported DITA output.. 386
    Where are the project's output files? 386
    About the DITAMAP file... 387
A few caveats about exporting to DITA.. 387

Appendix H: Create EPUB Output 389

Overview... 390
Before creating EPUB output.. 391
What you can include in an EPUB document.. 391
    Front and back matter.. 391
    Content 391
    Navigation links... 392
What you can't include.. 392
Creating an EPUB document... 393
    Creating MOBI output.. 395
Distributing EPUB output 396
Viewing EPUB output... 396

Appendix I: The Next Step 399

Now it's up to you.. 400

Index 403

Introduction

In this chapter ...
> Welcome
> Why I wrote this book
> Who this book is for
> What this book discusses
> What this book does not discuss
> How this book is organized
> A step-by-step approach
> A strategy for learning Flare

WELCOME!

Welcome to the fourth edition of *Five Steps to MadCap Flare*. Keeping this book current due to MadCap Software's continued development of Flare is no small task; but MadCap's commitment to developing Flare and to implementing enhancements based on user feedback are just two of the reasons why I love this product. I hope you find *Five Steps to MadCap Flare* informative and useful; and just like MadCap, I'm interested in your comments and suggestions so I can continually improve this book. Please contact me at **Info@Northcoastwriters.com**.

WHY I WROTE THIS BOOK

I wrote this book because I needed it when I was learning Flare!

Flare is a progressive and powerful authoring tool, but one with a steep learning curve. Although the Flare Help system is extensive, I wanted a book to help me get started so that I would be more comfortable exploring its many features on my own.

But there was no book about getting started with Flare in the bookstores, so … time to write one!

WHO THIS BOOK IS FOR

This book is intended for new and experienced Flare users. If you've never used Flare, this book will get you through the basics. If you're an experienced Flare user, this book will help expand your knowledge of Flare and refresh your memory when needed. Best practices, found throughout the book, are helpful for both new and seasoned users.

By stepping through this book, you should be able to successfully plan for and create a Flare project. You won't know everything there is to know about Flare; but you'll be able to create online, print, EPUB, and DITA output that follows industry best practices.

Once you've mastered the Flare user interface—and have a good idea of how to build a project using Flare—you'll be able to learn more as you use Flare to create more complex projects.

Flare is like an onion. You learn it by peeling back layers one a time as you gain experience. The goal of this book is to help you peel back that first layer—without any tears!

WHAT THIS BOOK DISCUSSES

Five Steps to MadCap Flare describes how to get started using Flare. You will learn how to:

- Plan your Flare project

- Create projects and topics

- Develop content that includes lists, tables, and images

- Format content with styles

- Use features for navigating in output (Table of Contents, links, cross-references, indexes)

- Create context-sensitive help

- Use Flare features for reusing content (condition tags, snippets, variables)

- Create targets for online, print, EPUB, and DITA output

- Build and distribute your output

This book also provides details about many useful features, such as importing content and troubleshooting your project.

WHAT THIS BOOK DOES NOT DISCUSS

This book does not contain comprehensive information about Flare. The extensive documentation provided by the Flare Help system provides a wealth of information, and I encourage you to use it frequently. (Throughout this book, I'll tell you where to find specific topics in Flare's Help.)

This book's intent is to provide enough information to familiarize you with Flare concepts and procedures so you're comfortable using the user interface and creating a basic project.

HOW THIS BOOK IS ORGANIZED

This book contains the following chapters:

- **Document Basics** — Provides an overview of topic-based authoring and the types of documents you can create with Flare.

- **A Quick Tour** — Explains the primary components of the Flare user interface.

- **Step 1: Get Started** — Details how to plan a Flare project and complete the plan using a task roadmap. This chapter also explains common tasks you'll do with your Flare projects.

- **Step 2: Learn the XML Editor** — Provides a step-by-step tutorial for using features of the XML Editor and includes supplemental information ("Learn more").

- **Step 3: Develop Content** — Describes how to create lists and tables, insert images, symbols, and special characters into your content—plus how to use image thumbnails, mark text for redaction, create and change styles, and format your content with and without styles.

- **Step 4: Create Navigation Aids** — Describes how to include features, such as links, Tables of Contents, indexes, and cross-references, that let users navigate in output.

- **Step 5A: Create Print Output** — Details how to create simple print output and provides a tutorial for creating more complex print output. This chapter also describes how to build and distribute print output and use page layouts.

- **Step 5B: Create Online Output** — Describes how to create and distribute online output (Help systems and knowledge bases).

- **Appendix A: Planning Worksheets** — Provides worksheets for planning your project and tracking multiple targets.

- **Appendix B: Import Content** — Explains how to import content from Microsoft® Office Word, Adobe® FrameMaker®, and CHM files.

- **Appendix C: XML Editor Reference** — Provides supplemental reference information about the XML Editor.

- **Appendix D: Context-Sensitive Help** — Describes how to create context-sensitive help.

- **Appendix E: Track and Troubleshoot** — Details how to troubleshoot your project and use the internal analyzer provided with Flare. Also describes how to track project status with file tags and create various reports that show project information.

- **Appendix F: Single-Sourcing** — Explains Flare's features for reusing content from a single source, including how to use condition tags to create customized output, how to create and insert snippets and variables, and how to link a global project to other Flare projects.

- **Appendix G: DITA Import and Export** — Explains how to import DITA content into Flare and export DITA code from Flare.

- **Appendix H: Create EPUB Output** — Describes how to build and distribute EPUB output (.epub and .mobi).

- **Appendix I: The Next Step** — Lists some of the Flare features you might explore on your own after completing your first project.

This book also contains an index.

A STEP-BY-STEP APPROACH

This book is organized sequentially, meaning you should start at the beginning and proceed forward. Once you are more familiar with Flare, you can use the Table of Contents and index to jog your memory about certain features.

How you will use this book depends on your experience.

- **If you haven't used a topic-based authoring tool**, read the Document Basics chapter first, followed by the Quick Tour and each of the five steps.

- **If you're familiar with topic-based authoring tools**, scan the Document Basics chapter to learn basic Flare terminology. Then begin with the Quick Tour, followed by each of the five steps.

> **Note** — Depending on the type of output you are creating, you will use Step 5A: Create Print Output, Step 5B: Create Online Output, Appendix G: DITA Import and Export, or Appendix H: Create EPUB output. However, if you want to produce all types of output from a single project, you will use all of these steps.

A STRATEGY FOR LEARNING FLARE

For your first Flare project, consider creating a small "throwaway" project. You can make mistakes without worrying how it will affect your real work.

Use this project to develop the styles you'll use later. If your throw-away project is bloated with local formatting, it won't hurt anything. By the time you're ready to work on a real project, you'll be more comfortable using styles and your XML code will be much cleaner.

FIRST, LEARN THE BASIC FLARE WORKFLOW

- Create a new project and add 5 or 6 topics.

- Copy and paste text into each topic so you have some content to work with. You can use content from a Word document, a FrameMaker document, or even a text file.

- Create two lists and insert a table.

- Create a TOC. Drag a few topics from the Content Explorer into the TOC to add them. Then add one or two topics to your project and TOC simultaneously.

- Set up WebHelp and PDF targets (without any page layouts).

- Build and view output.

- Save your project.

NEXT, EXPAND YOUR KNOWLEDGE

- Learn to use the XML Editor. Enter and change text in a topic or two.

- Check spelling. Create a spelling error in a topic and learn to spell-check a topic and your entire project.

- Insert an image.

- Create a few text hyperlinks that are linked to other topics in your project.

- Create a few index entries.

- Apply a condition tag. Mark some text with the default condition tag "PrintOnly" and set up the WebHelp target to exclude the PrintOnly condition tag. Then build and view the output to see that the marked text is excluded.

- Add your own condition tag and apply it to text.

- Insert a variable. Use one of the default variables (CompanyName or PhoneNumber).

- Add your own variable and insert it into a topic.

- Build and view WebHelp output. Click an index entry after clicking the Index bar, and click a hyperlink or two. Make sure the index entry and hyperlinks open the correct topics.

THEN TRY FORMATTING

- Learn to use local formatting. It's not bad to use local formatting in a few isolated places; but as a best practice, you should use styles instead.

Note — To see what local formatting does to your XML code, open a topic in Flare's XML Editor and click 🔲 in the XML Editor's top toolbar to see the XML code *before* adding local formatting. Then click 🔲 to switch to the XML Editor again. Apply some local paragraph formatting and save the topic. Look again at the topic's XML code to see the extra code that local formatting adds.

- Learn to use styles. Apply styles from the default stylesheet (Styles.css).

- Change styles. Use the Stylesheet Editor in Simplified View to change the formatting applied to the "p" and "h1" styles.

- Add your own styles. Add a class of the "p" style and change its formatting. Apply the class you created to text in a topic.

FINALLY, USE MORE ADVANCED FEATURES

What you do next depends on what you want to create.

To ...	Do this ...
Create context-sensitive Help	Read Appendix D.
Create print output	Learn about cross-references (Step 4). Complete the tutorial in Step 5A.
Import Word, FrameMaker, or CHM files	Read Appendix B.
Import or export DITA content	Read Appendix G.
Create ebooks	Read Appendix H.

Document Basics

In this chapter …
- ➤ About topic-based authoring
- ➤ Terms to understand
- ➤ About print documents
- ➤ About online documents
- ➤ About DITA documents
- ➤ About EPUB documents
- ➤ About right-to-left languages

OVERVIEW

This chapter provides an overview of topic-based authoring and how Flare is used to create documents that are topic-based. It also describes terminology and capabilities that will familiarize you with some of the language and concepts used in the remainder of this book.

WHAT IS TOPIC-BASED AUTHORING?

According to a recent Wikipedia post, topic-based authoring is:

... a modular content creation approach (popular in the technical publications and documentation arenas) that supports XML content reuse, content management, and makes the dynamic assembly of personalized information possible.

Let's clarify that.

- **Modular content creation** — As simple as it sounds, the heart of topic-based authoring is creating topics. Modular simply means that content exists in units—called topics.

- **XML content reuse, content management** — Topics are discrete units of information, which makes them easy to reuse and maintain.

- **Dynamic assembly of personalized information** — Because topics are discrete units of information, they can be combined in various ways for customized results.

HOW TRADITIONAL AND TOPIC-BASED AUTHORING DIFFER

When you use traditional word-processing tools to write, you organize information—**content**—in a linear fashion. The resulting print-based output is often read front to back. You use various **navigational aids** to help readers find information quickly, such as a Table of Contents, index, and cross-references.

When you use a topic-based tool to write, you organize content into several units of information—called **topics**. You'll arrange the topics into outlines (tables of contents) to produce output tailored to different needs. You can still produce linear print documents; but you can also create online documents from the same content. With online documents, readers point-and-click to obtain information when they need it, instead of reading in a linear fashion.

WHAT FLARE DOES FOR YOU

Here's a brief sampling of what Flare lets you decide:

- Which topics to include in a document

- How topics will be assembled and organized

- The navigational tools used to help readers find what they need

- How content will be reused in the print and online worlds

- What content will be included in various topics (You can exclude content from a topic as well as exclude topics from output.)

The important thing to take away is that when you work with Flare, you will be working with topics, not linear content. With Flare projects, you'll be able to reuse content and maintain it much more easily.

TERMS TO UNDERSTAND

Topic-based authoring and Flare itself both have unique terminology that you'll see throughout this book. Take a moment to review this list so you won't be caught off-guard when you see these terms.

- **Output** — What is created after you build a Flare target. This will be a print document (e.g., Word, FrameMaker, PDF file), an online document (Help system or knowledge base), an EPUB document, or DITA code. Output consists of one or more files and folders, depending on the type of output you build.

> **Note** — Although a PDF file is delivered online, it is considered a print document.

- **Target** — A Flare file you create that defines settings used to build output. When you build your output, you select the target to build it from. Typically, a project has many targets. For example, you might have two PDF targets for two different levels of software, such as a regular and light.

> **Best Practice** — Create one target for each different deliverable output.

- **Build** — The process of creating output for the selected target using Flare project files.

- **Distribute** — Giving Flare output to others. The output type determines the files you need to send. You might distribute Flare output to colleagues, users, software developers, or your IT staff.

- **Publish** — Copying online output to a location such as a website, a network, or a hard drive. Publishing does not create the output; it simply transfers it. However, for new users, I discourage this practice until you're more familiar with Flare.

BUILD, GENERATE, COMPILE: WHAT'S THE DIFFERENCE?

You're likely to see several terms that mean the same thing when you use the Flare Help system. I've tried to remain consistent in this book. This formula might help:

Generate = Compile = **Build** (my term)

Just remember: **build** is the process of creating your **output**, based on the **target** you select.

PRIMARY TARGETS

Your project can have many targets, but one target is always designated as "primary." "Primary target" is Flare's way of singling out one target so you can use toolbar buttons to open, build, view, or publish that target. You may find this easier if you work more with one target than others.

> **Note** — To change which target is primary, right-click the target in the Project Organizer and select **Make Primary** from the menu.

ABOUT PRINT DOCUMENTS

You can create these types of print documents with Flare:

- Microsoft Word

- Adobe FrameMaker

- Adobe PDF

- Microsoft XPS

- XHTML

Step 5A: Create Print Output, describes in detail these types of print documents and what you need to do to create them. Step 5A also contains instructions for creating a simple print document and a tutorial for creating a more complex print document that includes a Table of Contents and alternating headers and footers.

ABOUT ONLINE DOCUMENTS

Online documents typically refer to Help systems and knowledge bases. You can create both types of online documents with Flare.

For detailed information about creating online documents after you have finished developing your content, see Step 5B: Create Online Output.

HELP SYSTEMS

A Help system is a method of delivering topic-based information to users from within a software application. When a user clicks the application's Help menu, the Help system opens.

A Help system typically includes a Table of Contents, an index, and the ability to search for words in help topics.

Context-sensitive help

A context-sensitive help system is one in which topic-based information is accessed from buttons placed on dialogs and windows in a software application. In such systems, a software developer places a button on a window or dialog for which a writer has written a help topic. When a user clicks the button, it opens a help topic that provides information about the window or dialog.

Flare includes context-sensitive help on some of its dialogs as shown next.

Figure DB-1:
Help button in Flare Help

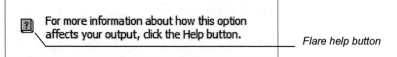

For more information about how this option affects your output, click the Help button.

Flare help button

KNOWLEDGE BASES

Knowledge bases are collections of information, often used to share knowledge in an organization or to supplement a Help system. The contents of a knowledge base are documents, such as frequently asked questions, user documentation, and articles.

The primary differences between a knowledge base and a Help system are:

- A knowledge base is not opened from within a software application.

- A knowledge base cannot contain context-sensitive help topics.

Knowledge bases are stored online and are searchable much like Help systems. Users may also browse through topics to find what they need.

TYPES OF ONLINE DOCUMENTS

Flare can create the following types of online documents:

- DotNet Help

- Eclipse Help

- HTML5

- Microsoft HTML Help

- WebHelp

- WebHelp AIR

- WebHelp Mobile

- WebHelp Plus

Each of these types is described in Table 5B-1 on page 245.

Choosing the right type

Your work environment may only support certain online document types. It's a good idea to contact technical personnel in your organization to understand which format they expect you to create.

The following table briefly outlines when to choose each online document type. The Flare Help system contains additional information about these types.

Table DB-1:
Choosing
online
document
types

Choose this type ...	When ...
HTML5 (also called "WebHelp 2.0" in Flare)	<ul><li>You want the more modern appearance of HTML5.</li><li>Output must support the HTML5 specification.</li><li>Output should be optimized for search engines.</li></ul> **Note** — Some browser versions, especially older versions might not support all features of HTML5.
Eclipse Help	<ul><li>You need a Help system plug-in that is compatible with an Eclipse environment.</li></ul> To create Eclipse Help you must install some additional Eclipse components.
WebHelp	<ul><li>You need output that opens in a browser window and users have different browsers.</li><li>You want to create output in various languages (by using language skins).</li><li>Help will be opened from a desktop application.</li><li>Users are using different Internet browsers or platforms.</li></ul>
WebHelp Mobile	<ul><li>Your users need to access documentation from various mobile platforms (such as iPhone, iPad, MS Mobile, Blackberry, Palm WebOS and Android).</li><li>You want to create an output interface in various languages.</li></ul>

Table DB-1:
(Cont.)

Choose this format ...	When ...

WebHelp Plus	▪ You need to support Windows XP or Windows Server® 2003.
	▪ You want all of the WebHelp features plus:
	  - Quicker user searches
	  - The ability to perform searches for non-XHTML files, such as PDFs or Excel files, that may or may not be part of your project
	  - The ability to merge Flare output so it appears as a single Help system

WebHelp AIR	▪ You want all of the WebHelp features plus:
	  - You want a single file for your output.
	  - Your users will store and open your output locally (not from a server or website).
	To create online documents in WebHelp AIR:
	▪ You and users must install Abobe® AIR™ (go to http://get.adobe.com/air/ for a free download).
	▪ You must install Java Runtime Environment (go to http://java.sun.com/javase/downloads/index.jsp for a free download).

DotNet Help	▪ You need to support Microsoft .NET® applications. ▪ You want users to be able to choose to view the output in English, French, German or Japanese (via MadCap Help Viewer). ▪ You want users to be able to search by using wildcards.
HTML Help	▪ You need to support 32-bit Microsoft Windows® applications. ▪ Users are not connected to a network. ▪ You want a single file for your output.

HOW ONLINE OUTPUT LOOKS (SKINS)

The appearance of online output is controlled by a **skin**. A skin is a file that stores settings that determine how your online output looks (size, position), including its features (Table of Contents, index, glossary, search) and buttons.

Flare comes packaged with a default skin, which is automatically added to each new project you create. The default skin is located in the Skins folder of the Project Organizer.

> **Note** — Flare includes three WebHelp Mobile skins. You'll need to add a mobile skin to your project to build WebHelp Mobile output. To build HTML5 output, you'll need an HTML5 skin.

Figure DB-2:
Skins folder
of the
Project
Organizer

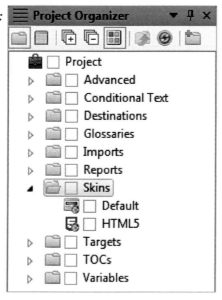

A Flare project can have multiple skins. For example, you might have different skins for different types of online output.

You can change the appearance of online output by editing the skin. See "Adding and editing skins" on page 252.

ABOUT DITA DOCUMENTS

Flare allows you to both import DITA documents and to export
DITA from a Flare project. DITA output is code output—XML tags
encode text and external file links. You can create print or online
output from your DITA output by using any application that can
publish DITA content.

WHAT IS DITA?

DITA—Darwin Information Typing Architecture—is an XML-based
technical documentation standard developed by the Organization
for the Advancement of Structured Information Standards (OASIS)
to support content sharing and reuse by using standard types of
topics (such as concept, task, and reference topics).

DITA documents include multiple files (one per topic) and a
DITAMAP file (like a table of contents) that contains links to topics.
For more information about the DITA standard see:
http://xml.coverpages.org/dita.html.

See Appendix G to learn how to import or export DITA content.

ABOUT EPUB DOCUMENTS

EPUB documents are meant to be viewed electronically on ebook
readers, tablets, or with ebook applications. You can create EPUB
documents including MOBI documents from a Flare project. See
Appendix H for more information.

ABOUT RIGHT-TO-LEFT LANGUAGES

Flare supports right-to-left (RTL) languages such as Arabic, Hebrew,
and Farsi. Here is a brief overview of this feature. For additional
details, see Flare's Help system.

SELECTING THE LANGUAGE

You can select a RTL language in Flare wherever you normally would select a language.

Table DB-2:
Methods for
selecting
a language

To select a language for ...	Do this ...
An entire project	Select the language when you create a new project with the Start New Project Wizard or on the Language tab of the Project Properties dialog.
A specific target	Use the Language tab in the Target Editor for that target.
A specific topic	Open that topic's Properties dialog (right-click the topic and select **Properties**) and select the language from the Language tab.
Content within a topic or snippet	With the topic open, select the desired text, select **Home** tab → **Language**, then select the desired language from the Select Language dialog.

EDITING RTL LANGUAGE CONTENT IN THE XML EDITOR

By default, the XML Editor shows content in right-to-left order if a RTL language was selected for the entire project, or for topics in which a RTL language was selected. Besides viewing RTL content, you can edit that RTL content directly in the XML Editor.

SUPPORTED OUTPUTS

RTL languages are supported in skins and in all Flare outputs except for DotNet Help and FrameMaker.

> **Note** — To display online output in a particular language, you must enter the translated text for each part of the skin (such as an accordion title) in a language skin. See Flare's Help system for more information.

WHAT'S NEXT?

Before you tackle your first Flare project, take a look at the next chapter, "A Quick Tour." It will help you become more familiar with the Flare user interface before you begin using the product.

Then proceed to Step 1: Get Started, where you'll start planning and creating your first Flare project.

A Quick Tour

In this chapter …
- About the Flare workspace
- Left pane
- Middle pane
- Right pane
- Toolbars
- Status bar

Overview

Flare is a powerful tool for developing topic-based documents. However, its flexible user interface can be a challenge for new users.

This chapter describes the basic elements of the Flare user interface. It includes examples that will help you know what to expect when you start using Flare for yourself. When you become more comfortable using Flare, you'll probably want to adjust the user interface as you prefer.

The Flare workspace

When you first open Flare, you'll see the Flare **workspace** as shown in (Figure QT-1). Notice that the Flare workspace contains a left, middle, and right pane, each of which is discussed next.

Also notice the Start Page in the middle pane of the workspace. The Start Page provides a quick way to get started with Flare, to get help, or to catch up on news from MadCap Software. You can start a new project by selecting one of Flare's many project templates or you can open Flare's New Project Wizard to begin a project from scratch. Open an existing project by browsing for it or by selecting it from the list of recently opened projects. Click the Tutorials tab to watch video tutorials, or click the Help Resources tab (Figure QT-2) for links to additional help resources, such as the MadCap Software Forums.

About active panes and windows

In the Flare workspace, toolbars and menu options will change, depending on which part of the workspace is **active**. This concept applies to tabs in the middle pane as well.

To make a pane or tab active, simply click in the desired part of the workspace. Unavailable options are dimmed.

Figure QT-1:
Flare
Workspace

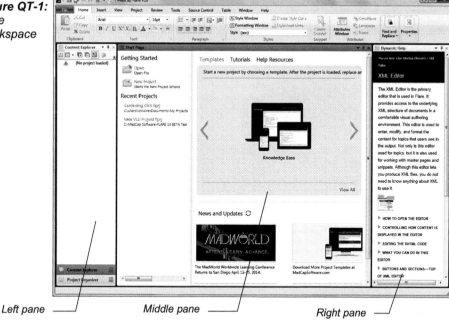

Left pane ——————— Middle pane ——————— Right pane ———

Figure QT-2:
Help
Resources
available
from the
Start Page

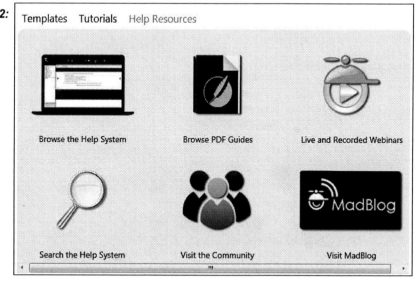

LEFT PANE

The left pane of the Flare workspace helps you organize and move among the parts of your Flare project.

ACCORDION BARS

In the left pane, you'll notice **accordion bars** as shown in Figure QT-3. (Accordion bars apply to the right pane also.)

Accordion bars indicate which window is active in the pane. You can easily switch from one window to another by clicking its accordion bar, which brings the window to the front and makes it active. The File Preview Bar shows the name of the file or folder selected in the Project Organizer or Content Explorer.

Figure QT-3:
Left pane

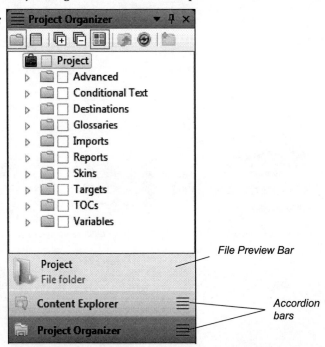

When you begin using Flare, the **Project Organizer** and **Content Explorer** open in the left pane, both of which you'll use often.

PROJECT ORGANIZER

The Project Organizer is used to view project files and open them in
the middle pane. Figure QT-4 shows how the Project Organizer
looks for a new project.

Click to expand all folders.

Figure QT-4:
Project
Organizer
with a few
folders
expanded

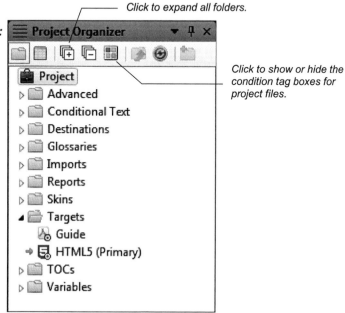

Click to show or hide the
condition tag boxes for
project files.

You can also create sub-folders for the various project folders (like
the Targets folder).

You don't need to understand all of the folders and files in the
Project Organizer right now, but you will use them frequently as you
create your projects.

> **Note** — Double-clicking a file in the Project Organizer opens it in the
> middle pane.

CONTENT EXPLORER

You'll use the Content Explorer to open and move among topics in your Flare project. **Topics** can contain text, images, audio files, movie files, and other items.

Figure QT-5 shows how the Content Explorer looks after you create a few topics. Notice that it contains several folders in addition to topic files (HTM files) and resource files.

Figure QT-5:
Expanded
Content
Explorer

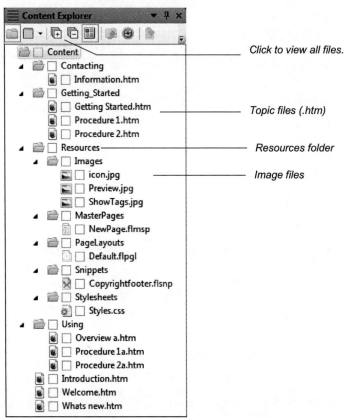

You can also create sub-folders under the "Content" folder and its sub-folders.

As shown in Figure QT-5, every new Flare project contains a **Resources** folder that holds parts of your project that are not topics, such as images, master pages and page layouts. You'll learn more about these items later.

MIDDLE PANE

When you first launch Flare, the middle pane shows the Start Page (Figure QT-1), a handy place to open a project, get help, or view news from MadCap Software.

Most of the time, the middle pane shows one of Flare's numerous editors. Figure QT-6 shows the middle pane with three editors open: the XML Editor (active), the TOC Editor and the Target Editor.

In some editors, it's common to have several items of the same type open. For example, you can have several topics open at the same time, each in their own instance of the XML Editor.

> *Tip* — As you work with Flare, you're bound to lose track of what's open in the middle pane. When this happens, first save all open documents by clicking **Save All** on the Quick Access toolbar, and then click **Window → Close All Documents** (or click the down arrow and select **Close All Documents Except This One** — meaning the active document. You can also close a single document by clicking **x** on its tab.

Topic in the XML Editor   Tabs show file names.

Figure QT-6:
Open editors
in the middle
pane

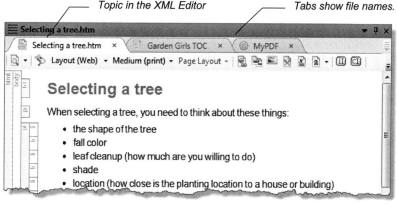

> *Tip* — When you have multiple files open, reorder them by dragging their tabs.

In some editors, you may also see tabs along left edge as shown in Figure QT-7. In such instances, the highlighted tab is the open one.

Figure QT-7:
*Tabs along
the left
edge of an
editor*

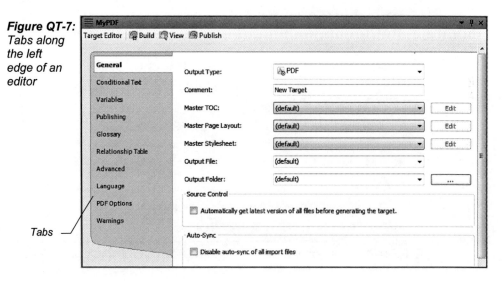

Tabs

Now let's look at a few commonly used editors.

XML EDITOR

The XML Editor, shown in Figure QT-8, is used to create and edit topics. You'll use this editor to:

- Enter, edit, and format text

- Insert images, symbols, links, and cross-references

- Create and format tables and lists

Despite this editor's name, you don't need to be an XML expert in order to use it.

Top toolbar   Content area

Figure QT-8:
XML Editor

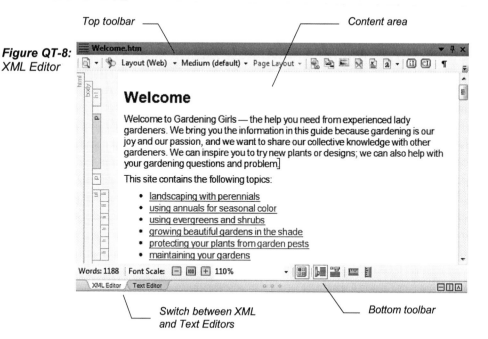

Switch between XML   Bottom toolbar
and Text Editors

With the XML Editor, you can view content in two modes:

- **Web Layout mode** — To see how a topic would look as online output (Help systems and knowledge bases).

- **Print Layout mode** — To see how a topic would look as print output (such as Word or PDF files).

Regardless of the mode, the XML Editor has four main parts:

- **Top toolbar** — To switch viewing modes and add things such as links, cross-references and images.

- **Content area** — To enter, edit, and format content.

- **Bottom toolbar** — To magnify text and view XML Editor components, such as rulers and structure bars.

- **Tabs at the bottom** — To switch between the XML Editor and the Text Editor.

The XML Editor is more fully described in Step 2: Learn the XML Editor, and Appendix C: XML Editor Reference.

TOC EDITOR

The Table of Contents (TOC) Editor is used to create a Table of Contents, which is used to organize and open topics.

Double-clicking a TOC in the Project Organizer opens that TOC in the TOC Editor (Figure QT-10). You can name your TOC files as you please.

Figure QT-9:
TOC file in the Project Organizer

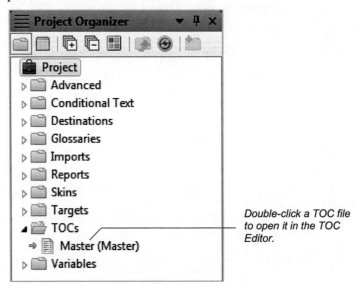

Double-click a TOC file to open it in the TOC Editor.

Like other editors, the TOC Editor opens in the middle pane with its own toolbar. Figure QT-10 shows how a fully expanded TOC in the TOC Editor looks.

You'll learn more about using the TOC Editor in Step 4: Create Navigation Aids.

Click to expand all TOC folders.

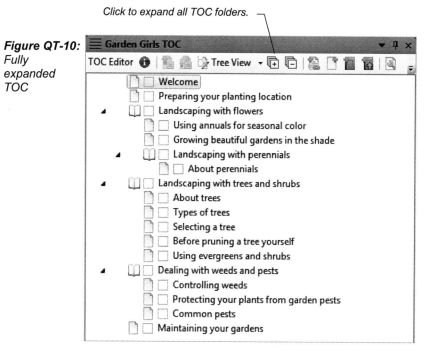

Figure QT-10:
Fully
expanded
TOC

RIGHT PANE

The right pane houses a variety of windows, such as the Spell Check window and Flare's Dynamic Help. As in the left pane, each window has an accordion bar, and some also have their own toolbars.

You'll learn more about the contents of the right pane in other chapters.

RIBBONS AND TOOLBARS

As you've already learned, many editors and windows in Flare have their own toolbars, which apply only to their individual windows.

Flare also contains global toolbar buttons, which are shown in a familiar ribbon layout. The File tab opens a pull-down menu with common project tasks such as creating and opening projects and saving your work. Other tabs open their respective ribbons, such as the Home ribbon, shown next.

Figure QT-11: *Home ribbon*

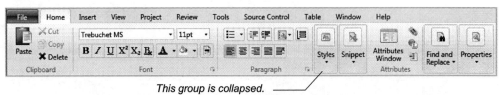

This group is collapsed.

> **Tip** — Certain buttons on the ribbon may be unavailable, depending on which window is active.

RIBBON GROUPS

Each ribbon is divided into groups of related buttons, like Clipboard, Font, and Paragraph, as shown in Figure QT-11. When you reduce the size the Flare application window, some groups collapse to show only the group name and not its buttons. (In Figure QT-11, the "Styles" and "Snippet" groups are collapsed.) Likewise, when you increase the size of the Flare window, collapsed groups expand to reveal their buttons, as shown here.

Figure QT-12: *Styles group expanded*

MINIMIZING THE RIBBONS

The nice thing about a ribbon layout is that you can easily minimize the ribbons, giving you more room to view your topics and content in the middle pane. When you minimize the ribbons, only the tab name is shown. Clicking the tab name displays the ribbon again, until you click elsewhere in the interface. To minimize the ribbon, right-click anywhere on a ribbon and select **Minimize the Ribbon**.

CHANGING TO TOOLBARS

If you wish, you can change the ribbon interface to the more classic toolbars used in prior versions of Flare. (Select **File** tab → **Options** → **Interface** → **Tool strip**.)

RIBBON BUTTON MENUS

Some ribbon buttons, like the "New" button have pull-down menus.

Figure QT-13:
Ribbon buttons
that have
pull-down
menus

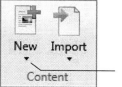

Click to open a pull-down menu.

Click a button's down arrow to open its pull-down menu. (In some cases, clicking the face of the button also opens the menu; in other cases, it opens a dialog.)

useful

QUICK ACCESS TOOLBAR

The Quick Access toolbar, conveniently located above the ribbon, provides toolbar buttons for features you'll use most often, like saving your work and undoing an action.

Figure QT-14:
Quick Access
toolbar

You can add any ribbon button to the Quick Access toolbar by right-clicking the button you want to add, and selecting **Add to Quick Access Toolbar**.

STATUS BAR

The Status bar (at the bottom of the Flare workspace) shows the progress of MadCap Analyzer as it scans your project.

Flare automatically scans your project with its internal analyzer whenever you open it. (A more robust external analyzer—MadCap Analyzer™—can be purchased separately.)

This book describes how to use the internal analyzer (see Appendix E: Track and Troubleshoot). To learn about the external analyzer, search on "About Analyzer" in the Flare Help system.

WHAT'S NEXT?

Let's get started!

Move on to Step 1: Get Started, where you'll plan your project and learn about a few common features.

Step 1:
Get Started

STEP 5: Create Output
5A: Print Output
5B: Online Output

STEP 4:
Create
Nav Aids

STEP 3:
Develop
Content

STEP 2:
Learn the
XML Editor

STEP 1:
Get Started

In this chapter ...
> Plan your Flare project
> Use our Flare roadmap
> Create a Flare project
> Open a Flare project
> Add a topic
> Preview a topic
> Open a topic
> Check spelling
> Add a target
> Save your work
> Create and manage templates

OVERVIEW

I've found that a bit of planning is the key to satisfaction and success with Flare, including planning for maximum content reuse. If you take the time to plan out your project, the learning curve will be shorter and you'll be happier with the outcome—plus you can focus on only the Flare features you need.

To help you get started, Appendix A contains a series of planning worksheets, which are intended to be used together.

In this chapter, you'll learn what you need to think about, which decisions to make up front, and where to go from here.

PLANNING AND MANAGING YOUR FLARE PROJECT

To plan and manage your Flare project, copy Parts 1 – 6 in Appendix A: Planning Worksheets, and answer these questions.

DO YOU HAVE EXISTING SOURCE CONTENT?

If no, you'll type your content directly into Flare.

If yes, you'll also need to answer these questions using Part 1 of Appendix A:

- What form is your source content in (Word, FrameMaker, HTML, DITA, print, other)?

- Do you need to keep the source content and the Flare content in synch when the content changes? Do both need to be updated?

- Will you maintain the content by using the source application (Word, FrameMaker, etc.) or by using Flare? In other words, do you want changes to flow from content in the source application to Flare or do you want to make changes only in Flare?

WHAT KIND OF OUTPUT DO YOU WANT TO CREATE?

You can create output that will be used online or printed. You can also create EPUB output and export DITA code. Use Part 2 of Appendix A to complete this information.

Print output can be any of the following:

- Microsoft Word document
- Adobe FrameMaker document
- Adobe PDF file
- Microsoft XPS file
- XHTML

Online output can be any of the following:

- HTML5
- DotNet Help
- Microsoft HTML Help
- WebHelp
- WebHelp Plus
- WebHelp AIR
- WebHelp Mobile
- Eclipse Help

See the Document Basics chapter for more information about the types of output you can create with Flare.

WHAT ARE THE SIMILARITIES AND DIFFERENCES BETWEEN OUTPUTS?

Plan for content reuse by identifying content that is common to multiple outputs, content that is unique, and content that is likely to change. Define variables, and condition tags upfront. Determine if you need to use the global project linking feature and store common content in a global project.

HOW WILL CONTENT BE MANAGED AND SHARED?

If you are part of a team of writers, it's especially important to plan for content management and sharing. Flare provides these features for managing and sharing content:

- **Built-in support for source control applications** like Apache Subversion, Microsoft® Visual Source Safe, and Microsoft Team Foundation Server. You can control changes to your project files by checking them out and in—directly from your Flare project.

- **Can be integrated with other source control applications** that support the Microsoft SCC API.

- **Integration with Microsoft SharePoint®**. You can connect to a SharePoint server, check Flare topics in and out, link SharePoint files with your Flare project so you can edit them in Flare or in SharePoint, synchronize Flare and SharePoint files, and publish your Flare output to a SharePoint server.

- **External resources**. (The ability to store and maintain content outside of your Flare project) For more information about external resources, see "About External Resources" in Flare's Help system.

- **Global project linking**. (The ability to create a global project that contains common content, which can be linked to and imported into any number of "child" projects). For more information about global project linking, see "Using global project linking" on page 365.

Best Practices — Establish and follow conventions for naming projects, folders in the Content Explorer, topic files, and project files, such as snippets, TOCs, targets, etc. Decide if you want to follow a standard practice for structuring content in the Content Explorer. Lastly, decide how to document project design and decisions. These practices are particularly important if you're working on a team or if others will assume responsibility for maintaining the projects you create.

WHAT REPORTS DO YOU NEED?

Flare's Report Editor provides reporting options that use information about your project, captured by MadCap Analyzer, to help you manage project development and troubleshoot problems. You can generate reports by categories of information and print the reports right from Flare. For example, you can report on files with condition tags, files with tracked changes and annotations, and topics not linked to anything, plus much more. For more information, see "Creating project reports" on page 340.

HOW WILL YOU TRACK CONTENT DEVELOPMENT?

You can track project file development by author, status, or by file tags you define with Flare's file tagging feature. Using File status tags in combination with Flare's reporting feature allows you to create and print reports that show the status of topic development. See "Assigning file tags" on page 337 for more information.

HOW WILL CONTENT BE REVIEWED?

How content gets reviewed depends on the software your reviewers have and their preferred way of working. Use Part 3 of Appendix A to identify how content will be reviewed.

WHAT'S NEXT?

Ready to move on?

Let's take a look at a "roadmap" to help you navigate from here, so you can ignore the features that don't pertain to your project.

ROADMAP FOR USING FLARE

When you begin using Flare, you may find the user interface and the huge range of options a bit overwhelming. The roadmap on the next few pages will help you focus on those features you need to use for your project.

Again, follow along in Appendix A and complete the worksheets to get started.

HOW TO USE THIS ROADMAP

Start with "Basic tasks," which you'll need to complete for every Flare project.

Next, look at "What's your input?" Input is your source content. On the left, find the column that represents the type of input you're working with. The right column shows the tasks for each input type.

Lastly, look at "What's your output?" Output is what you want to create from your Flare project. On the left, find the column that represents the type of output you want to create (online, print, DITA code, or EPUB). Review the decisions you need to make and complete the tasks in the right column.

BASIC TASKS

For every Flare project, do these tasks …

- Create a new Flare *project*—the structure that contains your content and the project's supporting files (page 47).
- Create a Flare TOC and add items to it. (Step 4: Create Navigation Aids)
- Add content to your project. (Step 3: Develop Content)
- Create navigation aids. (Step 4: Create Navigation Aids)
- Apply styles from a stylesheet to control the appearance of topic content. (page 146).
- Build and distribute your output.

WHAT'S YOUR INPUT?

Input type	Decide …	Do these tasks …
No existing electronic source content	Which topics will you include? Which images will you include?	- Create an outline for the Table of Contents (not a Flare task). It doesn't have to be perfect since you can easily change the Flare TOC at any time. - Create content with Flare's XML Editor. Type text, create lists and tables, insert images, and add other optional elements (such as snippets and variables) to topics. (Step 2: Learn the XML Editor, Step 3: Develop Content, Step 4: Create Navigation Aids, and Appendix F: Single-Sourcing)

42

Input type	Decide …	Do these tasks …
Word or FrameMaker files	Which application will you use to maintain the content—Flare or the source application?	■ Prepare your Word or FrameMaker document for importing (page 276). ■ Set up the import details (how to handle styles, where to split content into topics, whether to link source files to Flare, whether to use Easy Sync for automatic importing of changed source files, etc.; page 276). ■ Import the content (pages 283 for Word and 292 for FrameMaker).
HTML files	Do you want to keep source content styles or use a Flare stylesheet?	■ Import the content (page 302).
DITA files	Which application will you use to maintain the content—Flare or the source application?	■ Set up the import details: how to handle styles, whether to link source files to Flare, whether to use Easy Sync for automatic importing of changed source files, etc. (page 372). ■ Import the content (page 375). For more information, see Appendix G and search for "DITA" in the Flare Help system.
MadCap Contributor		■ Receive topics via email from a MadCap Contributor author. ■ Incorporate topics into your project. *Note* — You can also receive stylesheets and page layout files from MadCap Contributor.

WHAT'S YOUR OUTPUT?

Output type	Decide …	Do these tasks …
Online output	Which type of online output do you need (WebHelp, HTML5, HTML Help, WebHelp Mobile, Eclipse, etc.)?	■ Create online navigation aids (TOC, index entries, links). See Step 4: Create Navigation Aids, on page 163.
	How will you structure topics in the TOC?	■ *(If you want headers, footers, or mini-tocs)* Create a master page and set up headers and footers. See procedure beginning on page 251.
	How will your final output look (fonts, colors, spacing)?	■ *(If you want to change the appearance of the skin)* Edit the default skin (or one of your own). See page 252.
	Will you use the default skin or a custom skin? (Custom skins are not covered in this book.)	■ Set up the target with the output file name, TOC name, condition tags to include or exclude, and master page (if using one). See page 233.
		■ Build the online output. See Step 5B: Create Online Output, on page 256.
		■ Test the online output. See page 258.
		■ Deliver the online output.
		These tasks are described in Step 4: Create Navigation Aids, and Step 5B: Create Online Output.

Output type	Decide …	Do these tasks …
Print output	Which type of print output do you want to create? (PDF, Word, FrameMaker, XPS, XHTML)	■ Add optional elements (images, cross-references, snippets, variables).
	What will the print output contain (Table of Contents, index, glossary)?	■ *(Depending on your decisions)* Create topics for front and back matter elements, such as a print TOC and print index. See page 213.
	Do you need a simple layout or a more complex layout with different headers, footers, or page-number formats for front matter, chapters, and back matter?	■ Create a topic outline (a Flare TOC) that indicates the topics to be included in the print output. See page 216.
	What should headers and footers contain?	■ *(Depending on your decisions)* Set up and customize page layouts (headers and footers). See procedure beginning on page 219.
		■ *(If you set up page layouts)* Set chapter breaks by linking page layouts to topics in the topic outline (Flare TOC). See procedure beginning on page 230.
		■ Set up the target with the output file name, outline TOC name, page layout names, and condition tags or exclude. See page 233.
		■ Build the print output. See page 235.
		These tasks are described in Step 3: Develop Content, Step 4: Create Navigation Aids, and Step 5A: Create Print Output.

Output type	Decide …	Do these tasks …
DITA code	Which topics will you include?	■ Create a TOC. See page 164.
	How will you structure topics in the TOC?	■ Set up the target. See Appendix G.
		■ Build, test, and deliver the exported DITA files. See Appendix G.
		For more information, search for "DITA" in the Flare Help system.
EPUB	Which topics will you include?	■ Add optional elements (images, cross-references, snippets, variables).
	How will you structure topics in the TOC?	■ (Depending on your decisions) Create topics for front and back matter elements, such as a print TOC and print index. See page 213.
	What will the output contain (Table of Contents, index, glossary)?	■ Create a topic outline (a Flare TOC) that indicates the topics to be included in the output. See page 216.
	Which format do you need: .epub or .mobi?	■ Set up the target. See Appendix H.
		■ Build, test, and deliver the EPUB file. See Appendix H.
		These tasks are described in Step 3: Develop Content, Step 4: Create Navigation Aids, and Appendix H: Create EPUB Output.

COMMON TASKS

There are certain tasks that you'll do over and over again in Flare. These common tasks are grouped here. They consist of:

- Creating a new Flare project
- Opening an existing Flare project
- Adding a topic
- Previewing a topic
- Checking spelling
- Adding a target
- Saving your work

Always consult the roadmap (starts on page 41) if you're uncertain where to begin.

CREATING A FLARE PROJECT

Regardless of what you're creating and where the content comes from, you always need to create a Flare **project** to hold your content. Let's get to it!

A project is like a container that holds related information (topics, TOCs, image files, dictionary, stylesheet) in a single unit.

Flare simplifies the process of creating a project by providing a wizard that walks you through the choices you need to make. The wizard creates the project framework, to which you'll add topics, a TOC, images, page layouts, etc.

Before using the Start New Project Wizard next, use Part 6 of Appendix A to decide:

- Where you will store your project if not in the default folder
- If a source control application will be used (optional)

Using the Start New Project Wizard

Use this procedure to create a new project.

When you select **New Project** on the Start Page, Flare opens the Start New Project Wizard.

The **Start New Project Wizard** asks you to make choices about your project. Click **Next** to move from one screen to the next. As you move through the screens, you can accept the default settings for all remaining choices by clicking **Finish** instead of **Next**. This closes the wizard and skips additional choices.

> *An exception* — If you create the project and import the content simultaneously, you don't have to use the wizard. However, for simplicity, this book doesn't cover that feature. To learn more about this option, open the Flare Help system and search on "Creating a project by importing."

To keep things simple, the following procedure takes you through the steps for creating a new project that is *not* bound to a source control application. If you want your Flare project to be bound to a source control application, see "Binding your project to a source control application" on page 50.

▶ To create a project:

1.   Select **File** tab → **New Project**. The Start New Project Wizard opens.

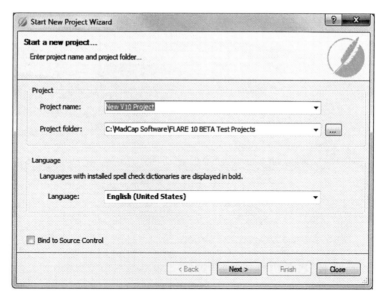

2. Type a unique project name.

3. (*Optional*) To save your project in a folder other than the default folder, click and select a different folder.

4. (*Optional*) To use a source control application with your Flare project, see "Binding your project to a source control application," next.

5. Select the language for the project and to use when spell-checking your topics.

6. Select **Empty** from the Source section.

> **Note** — As you gain experience, consider using one of your own templates ("My Templates") for new projects instead of using factory templates. To learn how to create a project template, see "Creating a project template" on page 71.
>
> Flare contains several sample templates that contain starter topics and files. This is an alternative to starting from scratch. The template "Web Print Mobile" is a good choice if you want to single-source content to multiple types of output.

7. From the list of Available Targets, select the type of output you want to create.

8. Click **Finish**.

The project is created and the Content Explorer (left pane) lists your first topic, "Topic.htm."

> **Best Practice** — Store a backup copy of your entire project on a server or secondary storage device, and back up often! A quick way to back up your project is to select **Project** tab → **Zip Project**.

Binding your project to a source control application

Binding your project to a source control application is optional. Source control applications can help you manage your Flare content by allowing you to coordinate and control changes to it. This is especially helpful when:

- Multiple authors need access to content.

- Authors need to store backup versions of files as they change.

Binding (linking) your Flare project to a source control application lets you take advantage of your source control application's version control and change control features.

When you create a Flare project, you can indicate which source control application you are using and where to store Flare project files within it. The source control application manages versions of project files as they change and prevents multiple users from accessing the same file simultaneously.

Flare provides *programmatic support* for Microsoft Visual Source Safe (VSS), Microsoft Team Foundation Server (TFS), Apache™ Subversion®, and Perforce. This means that tasks such as checking in and checking out files, and adding files to source control *can* be done from within Flare.

Because Flare files are stored in XML format, Flare is *compatible* with all source control applications on the market. This means that you can add your project files to any source control application to use that application's source control features. However, for applications other than those mentioned above, source control tasks such as checking in or checking out files, *cannot* be done automatically from within Flare.

Note — To use a source control application other than VSS, TFS, Subversion or Perforce directly from Flare, see "Using an API to Integrate Source Control" in the Flare Help system. You can also search on "source control" in the Flare Help system for detailed information about using Flare with a source control application.

The source control application must already be installed on your computer before you can bind a new project to it.

▶ **To create a project that is integrated with source control:**

1. Complete Steps 1 – 3 of the procedure for creating a new project (page 48).

2. Click **Bind to Source Control**, then **Next**.

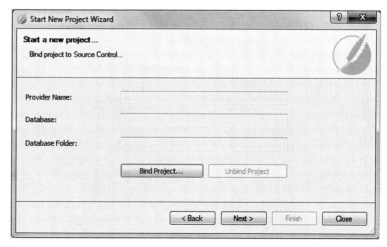

3. Click **Bind Project**.

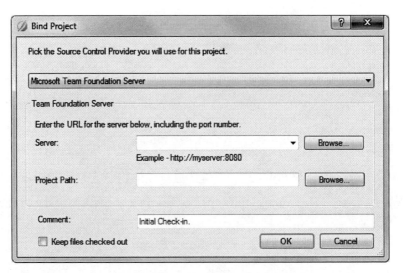

4. Select the Source Control Provider from the list and enter the applicable information for the provider you are using. (You might need to enter a user name and password.)

If you selected …	Use this option …
Microsoft Visual SourceSafe	a. Click **Browse** (to the right of "Database") and select the INI file for the VSS database.
	b. Click **Browse** (to the right of "Database Folder") and select the VSS database folder in which to store your Flare project files.
Microsoft Team Foundation Server	a. In the Server field, type the URL for the server, or click **Browse** to find and select it.
	b. Click **Browse** (to the right of "Project Path") to select the Team Foundation project to bind your Flare project to.
Subversion	a. In the Server field, type the URL for the server.
	b. Click **Browse** (to the right of "Project Path") to select the Subversion project to bind your Flare project to.
Perforce	a. In the Server field, type the URL for the server.
	b. Click **Browse** to connect to the Perforce server.
	c. Enter the streaming protocol.

If you selected ...	Use this option ...
Third Party Plug-in	a. Select your source control program from the Provider list.
	b. Click **Browse** to select the project to bind your Flare project to.

5.   Click **OK** after making your selections.

6.   Continue with Step 5 of the procedure for creating a new project. (page 48).

OPENING A FLARE PROJECT

You can open multiple instances of Flare, but each instance can only have one open project. If you open an existing project, the current project closes automatically. If you have unsaved changes, you'll be prompted to save them.

▶ To open an existing Flare project:

1.   Select **File** tab → **Open**.

2.   Navigate to the folder that holds the project you want to open (Documents\My Projects\<project name>, by default).

3.   Double-click the project file (For example, MyProjectName.flprj).

> *Tip* — The Start Page shows projects you've recently opened. You can open a project listed on the Start Page by clicking its project name; or, you can select **File** tab and select it from the Recent Projects list.

ADDING A TOPIC

Throughout this book, you'll see the words **topic**, **content**, and **project** used often. Let's take a moment to review what these terms mean:

■   A **topic** is the "box" in which content is stored. Each topic is a file (with an .htm extension) that conforms to the XML specification.

- **Content** is various types of information contained in a topic, such as text, tables, lists, and images.

- A **project** is simply a collection of topics and related files, which are stored in project folders.

To create a new project, you'll create Flare topics and add content to them. Your content can be new or imported (see Appendix B: Import Content, for more about importing content).

Methods used to add a topic

You can add topics from the TOC, from the Content Explorer, or by using the Project tab. Which method should you use? Read on …

Table 1-1: Methods used to add a topic

To …	Do this …
Add a topic to your project *and* to a TOC simultaneously (saves time)	Add the topic from the TOC Editor toolbar, as explained in Step 2 of the next procedure. This method automatically links the topic to the TOC entry it creates. (A TOC entry must link to a topic in order to open that topic in the output.)
Quickly add a topic without linking it to a TOC	Add a topic using the Content Explorer toolbar, Project tab, or by right-clicking the desired folder and selecting **New → Topic**. (You can easily add the topic to a TOC later.)

> **Note** — If you decide to add a TOC later, you can do so easily. See "Creating a Table of Contents" on page 164.

▶ To add a topic:

1. Make sure that the Flare project to which you want to add topics is open.

2. If you need to add a TOC item, take these steps. Otherwise, skip to Step 3, next.

   a. Select the Project Organizer.

   b. Expand the TOCs folder.

   c. Double-click the TOC you want to open. The TOC Editor opens in the middle pane.

d. On the TOC Editor's toolbar, click **Create a new topic and link to it** 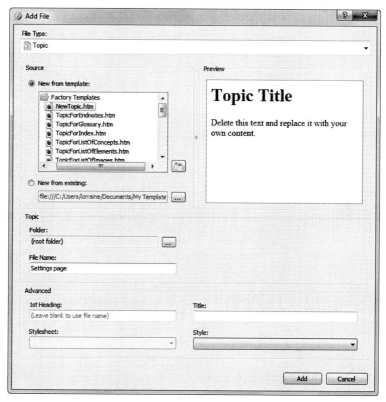.

e. Skip to Step 4 below.

3. If you don't need to add a TOC item (or prefer to add it to a TOC later), select **Project** tab → **New**.

4. Select **Topic** for the file type, then fill in the fields on the Add
    File dialog.

Option	Description
New from template	(Recommended) **Factory Templates** provided with Flare. (A preview of the selected template is shown on the right.)
New from existing	Used to choose one of your own project or topic templates. (A preview of the selected template is shown on the right.) To learn more about creating your own templates, see "Working with templates" on page 68.
Folder	The sub-folder to store the topic in (defaults to the folder currently selected in the Content Explorer). (*Optional*) Click ⸽...⸽ and select a different folder.
File Name	The file name for the topic. **Best Practice** — Avoid spaces between words. This causes problems on UNIX servers. Use underscores instead.
1st Heading	The text of the first heading.
Title	The topic title. Leave this field blank if you want the first heading in your topic to be used as a topic title (recommended). **Note** — A topic's title is shown in the TOC when you link to or insert that topic.
Style	The style for the first heading in your topic. Leave blank to use Flare's h1 style (recommended).
Stylesheet	This field is unavailable if you've specified a stylesheet for the project or primary target; otherwise, you can select a stylesheet to attach to the topic.

5. Click **Add**.

The new topic opens in the XML Editor and is added to the list of
topics in the Content Explorer. If you added the topic from a TOC,
the new topic is also added to the TOC.

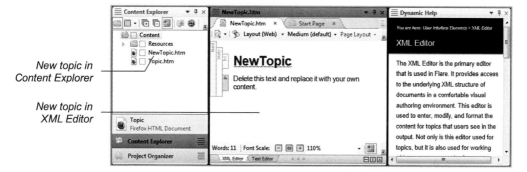

New topic in Content Explorer

New topic in XML Editor

Now you can add content to your topic in the form of text, lists, tables, audio files, movies, and images.

PREVIEWING A TOPIC

Previewing a topic lets you:

- See what the topic will look like when it is built.

- Test the topic's links before you build the output.

You can preview the topic that is active in the XML Editor. You have a choice of previewing the topic in the format associated with the primary target, or selecting a different target for previewing. Conditions included and excluded for the target are used to display the preview.

> **Note** — Preview is not available for Word or FrameMaker targets.

▶ To preview the active topic:

1. On the XML Editor's top toolbar, click the icon on the **Preview as primary target** button to use the primary target to format the preview.

    To preview the topic using a different target, click the arrow on the right side of the button and select the target from the list.

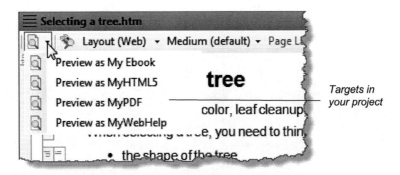

Targets in your project

Here's a topic previewed as WebHelp:

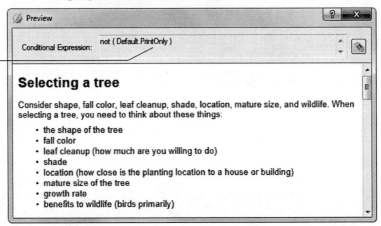

This target excludes content tagged with the "PrintOnly" tag.

If the selected target is set up to exclude certain condition tags, then content tagged with those condition tags is not shown.

2. If you want to include or exclude different condition tags and preview the topic again, click **Modify Conditional Expression** (top right part of the Preview dialog).

A list of condition tags opens.

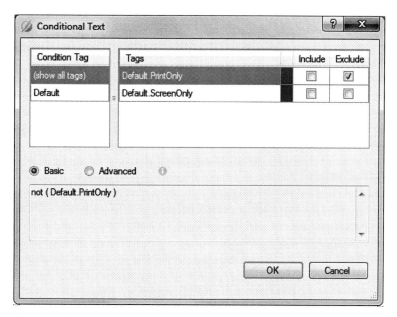

3. Change the excluded or included conditions as desired and click **OK**. The Preview window is re-displayed.

4. Close the Preview window.

> **Tip** — You can also filter out content tagged with specific condition tags right in the XML Editor window. Simply click **Select the conditional expression to apply to the document** in the XML Editor's top toolbar, select the conditions to exclude (filter out), and click **OK**. All content tagged with the excluded tags is hidden from view.

OPENING A TOPIC

You can have several topics open at once, each in its own XML Editor page. Each topic has a tab. The title bar indicates which topic is active and visible in the XML Editor window.

> **Note** — When only one file is open in the middle pane, no filename tabs are shown. When more than one file is open, Flare shows a tab for each open file.

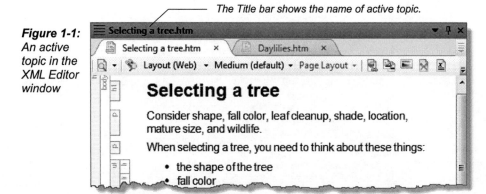

The Title bar shows the name of active topic.

Figure 1-1:
An active
topic in the
XML Editor
window

▶ To open a topic:

1. Make sure that the Flare project is open and that the Content
    Explorer is in view.

2. Do one of the following:

    ▪ Double-click the topic in the Content Explorer. (If you've
      created sub-folders in the Content Explorer, you might have
      to expand a sub-folder to find the topic.)

    ▪ If the project's TOC is open and in view in the middle pane,
      right-click the topic in the TOC and select **Open Link** from
      the menu.

    > **Note** — You can also open a topic by double-clicking it in the TOC, if
    > **Toggle the double-click behavior: open topic or display properties**
    > 🖱 on the TOC Editor toolbar is set to open topics, not topic properties.

    The topic opens in its own XML Editor page in the middle pane.

CHECKING SPELLING

You have these options for spell-checking your project's topics:

▪ Flare can check spelling automatically as you type, or

▪ You can check spelling manually.

Checking spelling as you type

Flare can check spelling as you type in the topic (or snippet) currently in view. With this option turned on, Flare highlights possible spelling errors with a red zigzag underline.

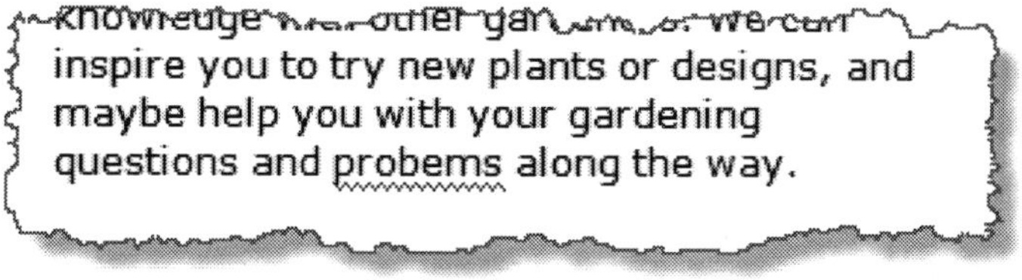

Figure 1-2:
A spelling error

You can turn this option on or off for individual topics. You might have two topics open and have Spell Check While Typing turned on for one topic and off for the other. If your spelling errors aren't being highlighted in the active topic, you probably have this option turned off for that topic.

▶ **To turn on spell-checking while typing:**

- Select **Tools** tab → **Spell Check While Typing**.

▶ **To resolve a potential spelling error:**

1. Right-click the word that Flare highlighted. A menu appears listing possible spellings of the word.

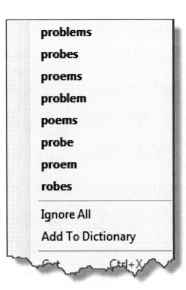

2. Do one of the following:

To ...	Do this ...
Replace the misspelled word with a suggested word	Select the correct word from the list.
Keep the highlighted word spelled as it is and ignore other instances of this word in this topic file	Select **Ignore All**. This option does not affect other topics. Flare will still flag this word as a possible spelling error in other topics if spell-checking is turned on for those topics.
Keep the highlighted word spelled as it is and add the highlighted word to the dictionary	Select **Add To Dictionary**. If you add the word to the dictionary, Flare will not flag this spelling as questionable in other topics or snippets.

Checking spelling manually

You can have the spell-checker analyze one or more topics for possible spelling errors in:

- The active topic (the one that is currently visible)

- All open topics

- All topics in the same folder as the active topic

- All topics (even if not open) in the project

▶ To check spelling in one or more topics:

1. Select **Tools** tab → **Spell Check Window**. The Spell Check window opens in the right pane, and the first misspelled word in the active topic is highlighted.

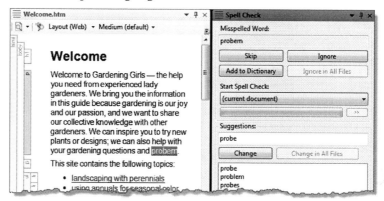

2. To check spelling in more than one topic, select these options from the Start Spell Check field:

To check spelling in ...	Do this ...
The active document only	Select **current document**.
All topics in the open project	Select **whole project**. Flare opens topics that have questionable spellings one at a time in the order in which they are listed in the Content Explorer.
All open topics	Select **all open documents**.
All topics in the same folder as the active topic	Select **documents in same folder**. Flare opens topics with questionable spellings one at a time in the same order in which they are listed in the folder.

3. Do one of the following:

To ...	Do this ...
Change the spelling to a suggested word	Select a suggested word and select **Change**.
Keep the word as it is and move to the next misspelled word	Select Skip.
Keep the word as it is, move to the next misspelled word, and ignore other occurrences of this word in this *topic*	Select **Ignore**.
Keep the word as it is, move to the next misspelled word, and ignore all other occurrences of this word in this *project*	Select **Ignore in All Files**.
Keep the word as it is, add the word to the dictionary, and move to the next misspelled word	Select **Add to Dictionary**.

4. When the spell-check is complete, click **OK**.

5. (*Optional*) Close the Spell Check window.

6. Click **Save All** to save all spelling corrections and terms you added to the dictionary.

7. (*Optional*) Close the topics that Flare opened due to questionable spellings.

Adding terms to the dictionary

Use this procedure to add new terms to an existing dictionary. (If the dictionary doesn't exist, you can create it by adding a word to it when you check spelling.)

▶ **To add terms to a dictionary:**

1. If the dictionary already exists in the Project Organizer, expand the **Advanced** folder, then double-click the dictionary. The Dictionary Editor opens in the middle pane, showing current entries.

2. Click **New item** ![icon] in the Dictionary Editor's toolbar. A new blank line appears.

3. Type the term to be added in the Word column. You can also type a Comment if desired.

4. Click **Save All** ![icon] to save the dictionary file.

ADDING A TARGET

You can add a target to the Targets folder (the default), or to a subfolder of the Targets folder (if you've already created one).

> **Best Practice** — Create Target subfolders to help keep similar targets organized.

Use the following procedure to add a target to your project.

▶ To add a target to your project:

1. In the Project Organizer, right-click **Targets** and select **Add Target** from the menu.

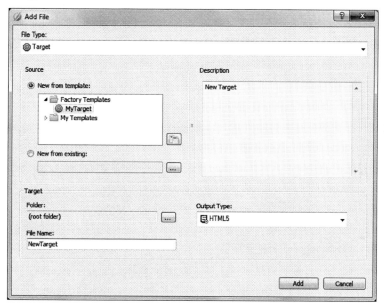

2. (*Optional*) To save the target to a subfolder of the Targets folder, click ⬚ and select the desired subfolder.

3. In the File Name field, type a name for the new target.

4. Select the Output Type from the list.

5. Click **Add**. The new target is listed in the Targets folder and opens in the Target Editor.

6. Set up the target for the type of output you want to create.

    ▪ **To set up a target for print output**, see "Task 8: Set up the print target" on page 233.

    ▪ **To set up a target for online output**, see "Setting up an online target" on page 253.

SAVING YOUR WORK

It's a good idea to save your work periodically instead of waiting until you're ready to exit Flare. There are two ways to save your work:

▪ **Save only the item currently in view.** You might be viewing a topic, a TOC, a list of styles in a stylesheet, a variable list, a list of condition tags, or any other content related to your project.

▪ **Save your entire project**.

As shown in Figure 1-3, Flare lets you know if you have any unsaved work by placing an asterisk (*) to the right of the file name on the tab (or title bar) for any item (topic, TOC, index, stylesheet, import file, etc.) that has changed.

Figure 1-3:
Unsaved
topic

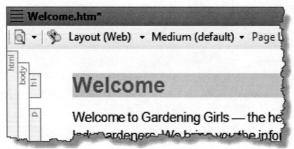

> **Note** — The active topic is the one currently visible in the middle pane of the XML Editor.

As shown in Figure 1-4, there are no unsaved changes in the active topic ("Selecting a tree"), but there *are* unsaved changes in another open topic ("Welcome").

Figure 1-4:
Unsaved changes in an inactive topic

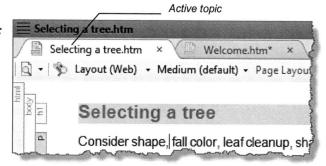

> **Best Practice** — Use **Save All** [icon] routinely to save the changes in all open topics.

▶ **To save the active file:**

Do one of the following:

- Click **Save File** [icon].

- Select **File** tab → **Save**.

- Type **CTRL + S**.

Flare saves the active file (the file shown in the middle pane).

▶ **To save your entire project:**

Do one of the following:

- Click **Save All** [icon].

- Select **File** tab → **Save** → **Save All**.

- Type **CTRL + SHIFT + S**.

Flare saves all project files.

> **Tip** — As you work with Flare, you're bound to lose track of what's open in the middle pane. When this happens, first save all open documents by clicking **Save All** 🖫 on the Quick Access toolbar, and then click **Window** tab → **Close All Documents** (or click the down arrow and select **Close All Documents Except This One** — meaning the active document. You can also close a single document by clicking **x** on its tab.

WORKING WITH TEMPLATES

You can save a lot of time by creating templates. Templates allow you to create topics that are consistent in appearance, without creating and reformatting elements you use frequently. You can also create templates for project files, such as TOCS, targets, and page layouts. You can even create a template of an entire project.

When you add a new topic from your own topic template, you'll replace any placeholder text with new content just as you would do with any MadCap-supplied template.

> **Important** — If you create a template from a file that contains links to other files, those links remain in place. Copy the linked files into your project and store them in the same location relative to the files they link to.

RECOMMENDATIONS

- Create more than one topic template to use with different types of topics. For example, you might have one template for overviews, another for step-by-step procedures, and a third for frequently asked questions.

- Include an empty formatted table in your topic templates. (You can delete it from topics later if you don't need it.) See "Inserting a table" on page 118 for details.

BEFORE CREATING YOUR FIRST TEMPLATE

Use the Template Manager to assign a folder, either on your local computer or on a network drive, for storing your templates.

> **Tip**—Selecting a network folder to hold your templates allows you to share template files with other Flare users.

When you use the Template Manager to assign a folder, Flare creates sub-folders for each different template type—content (topics), TOCs, page layouts, skins, and projects, for example. When you create templates, Flare automatically places your template files in the appropriate sub-folders.

To assign a template folder, see "Using the Template Manager" on page 72.

CREATING A TEMPLATE FOR A FLARE TOPIC OR PROJECT FILE

This procedure describes how to create a template for any Flare file—TOCs, topics, skins, targets—except for a Flare project. To create a template for a project, see "Creating a project template" on page 71.

▶ **To create a template for a Flare topic or project file:**

1. Open the Flare file you want to use as a template.

2. *For topic templates*, add items you'll use often, such as paragraphs, headings, tables, and lists, and format them as you want future elements to look. Add any boilerplate text required (see Step 2: Learn the XML Editor).

   For other types of templates, set up the file as desired. For example, for a page layout template, set up headers and footers.

3. Select **File** tab → **Save** → **Save As Template**.

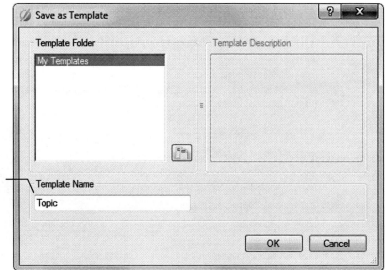

The template name defaults to the file name of the topic you are saving as a template.

4. Under Template Folder, select the folder in which to save the template.

5. Type a Template Name and click **OK**.

6. A confirmation box opens, showing the template name and path. Click **OK**.

    When you later add a new topic or other project file, the new template will be listed in the folder you selected in Step 4 above.

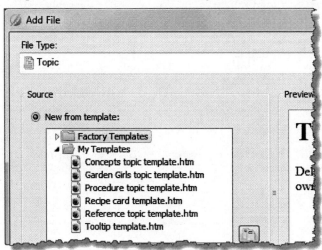

CREATING A PROJECT TEMPLATE

This procedure describes how to create a template for a Flare project. When you create a project template, you can choose which files to include in the template.

▶ **To create a project template:**

1. Open the Flare project you want to use as a template.

2. Select **Project** tab → **Save Project As Template**. The Project Template Wizard opens.

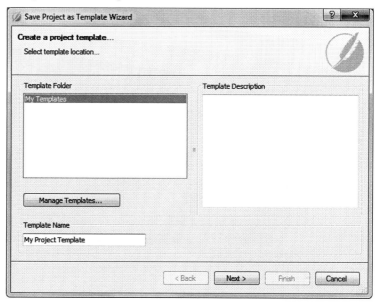

3. Under Template Folder, select the folder where your template will be saved.

4. In the Template Name field, type a name for the template.

5. Click **Next**. The wizard displays folders and files from the (Content Explorer's) Content folder that can be included in the template. By default all content files are checked (included).

> **Tip** — Fully expand folders to view their contents.

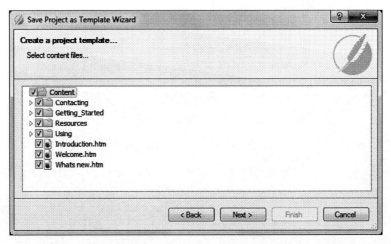

6. Clear the checkboxes of the content files you want excluded from the template and click **Next**. The wizard displays folders and files from the (Project Organizer's) Project folder that can be included in the template.

7. Clear the checkboxes of the project files you want excluded from the template and click **Finish**. The project's files are copied and a confirmation box opens showing the template name and path.

8. Click **OK**.

    When you later add a new project, the new template will be listed on the "Select a project template" dialog of the Start a New Project Wizard.

USING THE TEMPLATE MANAGER

The Template Manager makes it easy to work with templates. You can perform tasks such as:

- Adding template files

- Creating template folders

- Opening templates for editing

- Deleting template folders and files

- Editing template descriptions

▶ To use the Template Manager:

1. Select **Tools** tab → **Manage Templates**.

> **Note** — You can also open the Template Manager by clicking 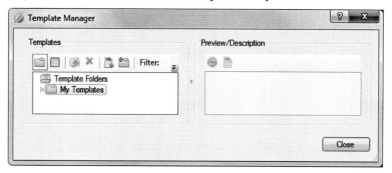 (on the Save as Template dialog) or **Manage Templates** (on the Save Project as Template Wizard) when you create templates.

2. Expand the folders to view the templates they contain.

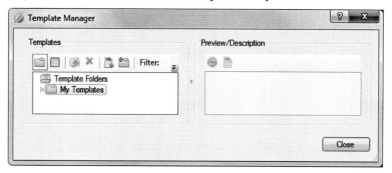

3. Use these options as desired:

To ...	Do this ...
Browse for and add a new template folder to the list	Click **New Template Folder** .
Create a new folder that you can add as a template folder	Click . In the Select Folder dialog, click **Make New Folder**.
See a preview of the template	Click the template.
Open the selected template for editing	Double-click the template.
Edit the template description (does not apply to topic templates)	Click the template and click **Edit Template Description** . In the Edit Template Description dialog, change the description and click **OK**.
Rename the selected template	Select the template and press **F2**.
Copy, paste, or cut the selected template	Use standard editing commands (**CTRL + C**, **CTRL + V**, and **CTRL + X**).

To ...	Do this ...
Delete the selected template	Click **Delete** ✖.
Browse for and add an existing template from the Windows Explorer Open dialog	Click **Add Template File** 🗐.

4.   When finished, close the Template Manager.

WHAT'S NEXT?

If you've created a project, added a topic to it, and you're not sure what to do next:

- Look at the roadmap beginning on page 41.

- Find the rows that match your scenario.

- Follow the list of tasks in each part of the roadmap.

You might even place a bookmark (the old-fashioned kind) at page 41, because you'll want to come back to the roadmap as you work through your first Flare project. Good luck to you, and enjoy!

RECOMMENDATION

At this point, complete the next chapter, Step 2: Learn the XML Editor. It will give you a solid background in using the XML Editor to add text to a topic as you try out additional features in the remainder of this book.

Step 2:
Learn the
XML Editor

STEP 5: Create Output
5A: Print Output
5B: Online Output

STEP 4:
Create
Nav Aids

STEP 3:
Develop
Content

STEP 2:
Learn the
XML Editor

STEP 1:
Get Started

In this chapter ...
> Simplify your workspace
> Enter text
> View XML code
> View cursors and text blocks
> Manipulate text
> Format text
> View layout modes
> Create a new topic
> Save a project
> Auto Suggestion
> Rulers

OVERVIEW

This chapter contains a tutorial and supplemental information about using the Flare XML Editor. With the tutorial, you'll learn how to:

- Add topics and enter text into them

- View a topic's XML code

- Change the appearance of text by applying styles and local formatting

- Save your work

You'll also learn about certain elements in the XML Editor that you'll see commonly, such as tags, structure bars, and various types of cursors.

WHAT IS XML?

XML (Extensible Markup Language) is a World Wide Web Consortium (W3C) specification that defines markup languages used to support document sharing.

Content is marked with **tags** that describe the content according to XML rules. In essence, this lets you separate the content from its formatting, making content easy to reuse in other applications or on different computers.

You can even edit XML files in a different XML editor without losing data or formatting. Hence, you are not locked into using the Flare XML Editor if you prefer to use a different one.

TUTORIAL SETUP

Before you begin this tutorial, make sure you have completed these tasks in Step 1: Get Started, using the default values that appear:

- Create a project (page 47)

- Add your first topic (page 53)

Be sure to **set aside 45 minutes** to complete this tutorial chapter. It's better to complete all of the tasks in succession.

TASK 1: SIMPLIFYING YOUR WORKSPACE

As you learned in Step 1: Get Started, when you create or open a topic, the XML Editor opens in the middle pane. To give you more room for working with content in the middle pane, consider closing the elements you won't be using routinely.

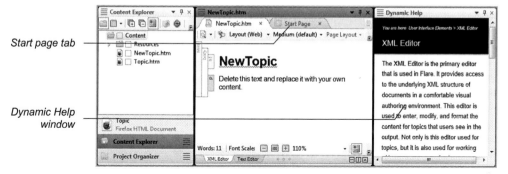

Start page tab

Dynamic Help window

1. Close the Dynamic Help window. (This maximizes the space available for the XML Editor.)

2. Close the Start Page (click the **x** on its tab).

The workspace should now look like this:

TASK 2: ENTERING TEXT

To get started, you'll type a heading and few paragraphs of text, which you'll use to learn more about the XML Editor in the rest of this chapter.

1. Highlight **NewTopic** in the XML Editor and type **Welcome**.

    Notice that what you typed replaces the existing placeholder text. You'll also see that the cursor changes shape, which you'll learn about later.

    Once your project has much more content, including snippets and variables, you'll probably see the Auto Suggestion popup.

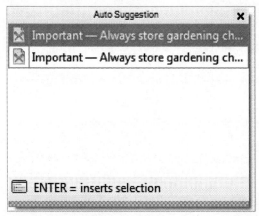

    Auto Suggestion offers suggestions for completing words and phrases from snippets, variables and frequent terms and phrases that you've set up in advance. If you just keep typing, the Auto

Suggestion popup will disappear. For more information, see "Using Auto Suggestion on page 99.

3. Highlight **Delete this text and replace it with your own content** and type:

    Welcome to Gardening Girls, the help you need from experienced lady gardeners. We created this web site because gardening is our joy and passion, and we want to share our knowledge with other gardeners.

    As you can see, entering text in the XML Editor is very much like using a word processor, but there are important differences, as you'll learn in a bit. Let's type more text.

4. Press **ENTER** to begin a new paragraph, just as you would with a word processor. Don't worry about the spacing between paragraphs. You'll fix that later.

5. Now enter the following paragraphs:

    What we offer

    This site contains information about the following topics:

    Landscaping with perennials

    Using annuals for seasonal color

    Growing beautiful gardens in the shade

    When you're finished, the XML Editor should look like this:

Tag bars

Click these tabs to switch between editors.

Notice the XML Editor and Text Editor tabs at the bottom of the XML Editor window and the tag bars to the left of your content. Tag bars tell you important information about how your document is structured. You'll learn more about this next.

That's enough typing for now. Let's see what your topic and its tags look like "under the hood" (the XML code).

TASK 3: VIEWING THE CODE

To view a topic's code, you'll use Flare's Text Editor. (You can also edit the tags and the content with the Text Editor, but that's not a task for new Flare users.)

1. Click the **Text Editor** tab at the bottom of the XML Editor.

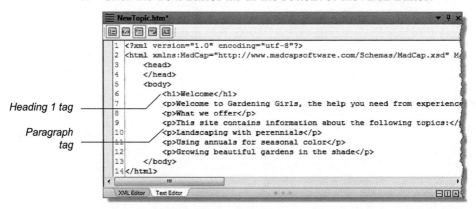

Notice what just happened. The topic's XML code is now open in the middle pane.

2. Click the **XML Editor** tab at the bottom of the XML Editor to view the WYSIWYG topic content again.

3. Switch to the **Text Editor** again (click its tab).

You can also split the window and view the topic in both the XML and Text Editors at the same time. To find out how, search Flare's help for "internal text editor" and read about "Split View."

> **Note** — The Text Editor shows you all of a topic's XML code, but the XML Editor only shows you what's between the "<body>" and "</body>" tags.

In the Text Editor, Flare shows you the tags it automatically assigned to the text you entered ("body," "h1" and "p"). Flare also decided where your tags should start and end, based on when you pressed ENTER. Notice that the end of a tag is preceded by a slash (as in </h1> and </p>).

Starting tag   *Ending tag*

<p>Using annuals for seasonal color</p>

So why does this matter? Because although you probably won't work with tags in your XML code when you're new to Flare, eventually you probably will. It's good to know what lies underneath the text you see in the XML Editor.

Now let's switch back to the XML Editor.

4.   Click the **XML Editor** tab.

Although tags sound complicated if you're not familiar with them, the good news is that Flare manages XML rules for you so you can't create an XML document that is not "well-formed."

With more complex topics, you'll see several additional tags. Here are some of the more common Flare tags, shown in the tag bar you'll see to the left of your content.

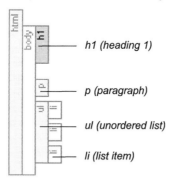

h1 (heading 1)

p (paragraph)

ul (unordered list)

li (list item)

Let's save your work now.

5.   Click **Save File** 💾 in the Quick Access toolbar.

TASK 4: VIEWING CURSORS AND TEXT BLOCKS

Most people use the word **paragraph** to describe a unit of text in a document. Flare uses the term **block** to describe any major unit of content that is within a starting and ending tag.

This is done to avoid confusing the concept of paragraphs with paragraph tags (<p>). This book uses the term **text block** to refer to units of text.

Figure 2-1:
Text blocks

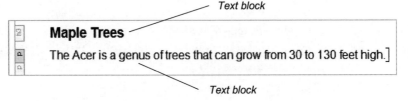

Note — When using the XML Editor, you cannot type more than one consecutive space unless they are non-breaking spaces.

Flare also gives you clues about how tags are related to your content by changing the shape of the cursor. Let's see how this works.

1. Click after the word "Welcome." Notice how the cursor changes to a right bracket (]).

A right bracket indicates that whatever you type will have the characteristics of the text to the left of the cursor. The tag bar is also highlighted (in this case, h1).

2. Type a space, then type **Gardeners!** See how the text takes on the characteristics of the text in first text block?

3. Now click before the "W" in "What we offer." The cursor changes to a left bracket ([), indicating that what you type will have the same formatting as the text to the right. Notice that the tag bar now shows p as the current tag.

Asterisk indicates unsaved changes in this topic

Current tag

4. Click anywhere in the first paragraph to see how the cursor changes again.

This is the traditional "insert" cursor you're probably used to from word processing.

There are lots of cursors in Flare as described in "Cursor types" on page 308. For now, just make sure you understand how the bracketed cursors work.

TASK 5: MANIPULATING TEXT

The XML Editor works very much like a word processor when it comes to manipulating text.

1. Move your cursor to a new location and click it once, then again and again until you've clicked it a few times in succession. See how Flare progressively selects more and more text as you continue to click?

This is a great shortcut when you want to select words and text blocks for editing. Try it out a few times, and notice how the tag bars change to indicate what is highlighted.

You can copy (**CTRL + C**) and paste (**CTRL + V**) text in Flare just as you would in most word processors. (You can copy and paste within a topic, from one topic to another, or from an external source—such as a Microsoft Word document.)

> **Note** — A complete list of common editing functions, plus navigation commands such as **PAGE UP** and **HOME**, are listed in "Shortcuts when working with text" on page 309 and "Navigational shortcuts" on page 312 for your reference.

You can also right-click to view a menu that contains options like copy, paste, and delete.

> **Note** — Right-click a tag bar for options that affect the entire text block. Right-click selected text for options that affect only the selected text.

Let's see how this works by deleting a text block. When you delete an entire text block, its tags will also be deleted.

2. First, click in the word **shade**.

3. Now hover your cursor over the block's tag bar (p). Right-click the tag bar and select **Delete**.

The entire text block is deleted, including the starting and ending tags.

Now let's see how to copy selected text.

4. Double-click to select the word **perennials**.

5. Right-click the word **perennials** (not the tag bar) and select **Copy** from the resulting menu.

6. Click before the word **for** and press **CTRL + V** to paste in the text.

7. Correct the wording by typing a space after perennials and by typing the word **and** between annuals and perennials.

TASK 6: FORMATTING TEXT

When using Flare, it's important to understand the difference between local formatting and formatting with styles.

-   **Local "inline" formatting** — Formats are defined in line with the content (within a tag). With this method, formatting affects only the content contained within the beginning and ending tags in which the inline formatting resides.

-   **Styles** — Formats are defined with style rules that you set up ahead of time in a **stylesheet**, which is simply a collection of styles. When you change a style, it changes in every place where the style was applied.

Whether you choose to use local formatting or styles to control the look of your content depends on several factors, as discussed in "Local formatting vs. styles: which to use" on page 143.

> **Best Practice** — Use styles instead of local formatting. Local formatting increases the size of the XML code, which means your browser may take longer to display the content. Plus, styles make maintenance easier. Change the style in the stylesheet, and the formatting is changed everywhere that style is applied.

In this tutorial you'll practice both applying styles and adding local formatting. You'll start by applying a local format to text.

1. Click the **Home** tab. This is where local formatting is often done.

   The Font and Paragraph groups each have a dialog box launcher button, which opens the applicable Properties dialog.

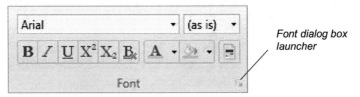

Font dialog box launcher

2. In the XML Editor, highlight **joy** then click the **Font** dialog box launcher. The Font Properties dialog opens.

3. On the **Font** tab, in the Style list, select **Bold**, and then click **OK**.

4. Click the **Text Editor** tab (bottom of the window). The XHTML code for this topic opens in the middle pane.

Bold applied with local formatting

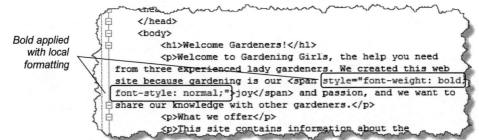

```
      </head>
      <body>
           <h1>Welcome Gardeners!</h1>
           <p>Welcome to Gardening Girls, the help you need
from three experienced lady gardeners. We created this web
site because gardening is our <span style="font-weight: bold;
font-style: normal;">joy</span> and passion, and we want to
share our knowledge with other gardeners.</p>
           <p>What we offer</p>
           <p>This site contains information about the
```

5. Now click the **XML Editor** tab.

6. Highlight **passion** and open the Style list in the **Styles** section of the **Home** ribbon. (Depending on the size of your Flare window,

you might need to click the down arrow under "Styles" to see the Style list.)

Click to open the style list.

Only the styles that apply to selected text are shown.

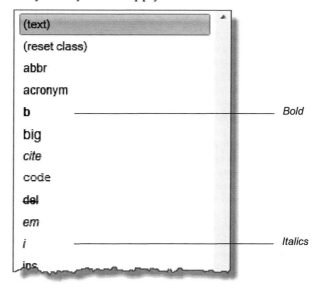

Bold

Italics

7. Select **b** (bold). The bold style is applied to the selected text. Click **Save All** and look at the code again.

Bold applied with a style

```
    </head>
    <body>
        <h1>Welcome Gardeners!</h1>
        <p>Welcome to Gardening Girls, the help you need
from three experienced lady gardeners. We created this web
site because gardening is our <span style="font-weight: bold;
font-style: normal;">joy</span> and <b>passion</b>, and we
want to share our knowledge with other gardeners.</p>
        <p>What we offer</p>
        <p>This site contains information about the
```

Notice that the "b" tag accomplishes the same thing as the local style, but with much less code.

> ***Note*** — You can also use the **Bold** **B** button on the Home ribbon to apply the "b" style.

8. Now close the Text Editor and click anywhere in the text you formatted.

Span bars

Notice that a new type of structure bar, called span bars, has appeared along the top of the content area. **Span bars** indicate how formatting is applied where the cursor is located.

> ***Note*** — If you don't see span bars, click **Toggle show spans** in the bottom toolbar.

Next you'll see how to apply local formatting and styles to a text block.

You can attach a different stylesheet if you create one, but since you don't have any, you'll use Flare's default stylesheet. (Unless you specify otherwise, Flare attaches its default stylesheet, called **Styles.css**, to your topic.)

9. Click in any text block in the XML Editor, and then click the **Paragraph** dialog box launcher. The Paragraph Properties dialog opens.

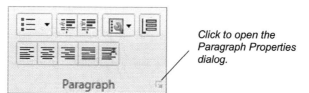

Click to open the Paragraph Properties dialog.

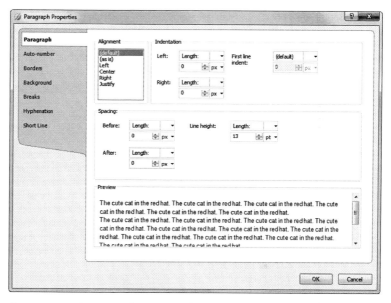

Any properties you change on this dialog apply local formatting to the text block your cursor is in.

Okay, enough about local formatting! To learn about when to use local formatting and when to use styles, see "Local formatting vs. styles: which to use" on page 143.

Let's look now at how you'll apply styles to text blocks.

10. Click in the text block "What we offer" and open the Style list in the **Styles** section of the **Home** ribbon, as you did in Step 6. (You might have to click the down arrow under "Styles" on the Home ribbon.)

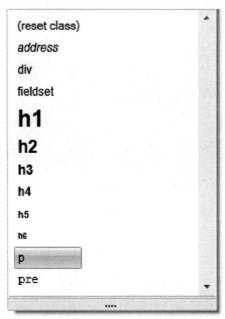

Notice that the style box now shows "p" instead of "text."

Notice also that the list of styles for text blocks is different than the list of styles for selected text. Flare shows you only those styles that apply *either* to selected text *or* to a text block (or to a table cell if your cursor is inside a table).

11. Select **h2** (heading level 2). Voila! The h2 style is applied to the entire text block as shown next.

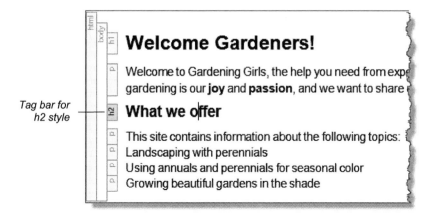

Tag bar for
h2 style

Notice that Flare shows a tag bar for the h2 style you just applied. You can always look at the tag bar to see which style is applied to a text block.

Next, you'll take a look at various layout modes in Flare.

Task 7: Viewing Layout Modes

As you will learn in Step 5A: Create Print Output, and Step 5B: Create Online Output, you can create content specifically designed to be used online or in print. To help you see how your content will look, the XML Editor can display your content in two modes:

- **Web Layout mode** — To see how your content will look as online output (websites, Help systems, etc.). Headers and footers *are not* shown in this mode.

- **Print Layout mode** — To see how your content will look as print output (Word, PDF, FrameMaker files, etc.). Headers and footers *are* shown in this mode.

If Print Layout mode is selected, you can select a page layout in which to view your topic. You'll select the page layout from the Page Layout list in the XML Editor's top toolbar.

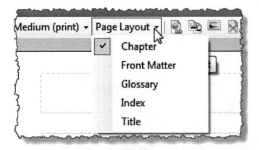

When you're writing content for each type of output, it's helpful to see the components that make up that output—right in the editor you're working in. That's where Flare's layout modes can help. Let's see how this works.

1. Click [Layout (Web) ▼] in the XML Editor's toolbar. Notice that the button indicates the current mode (Web Layout).

    A message appears stating that the medium will change (to "default" for Web layout mode, and "print" for Print Layout mode). You'll learn a bit about mediums in a moment.

2. Click **OK**. The XML Editor re-displays your topic in Print Layout mode.

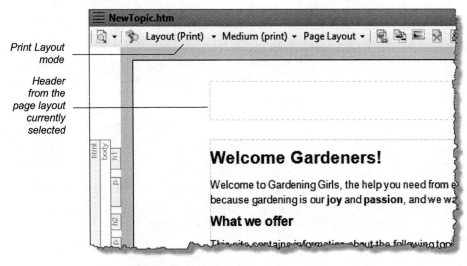

3. Click [Layout (Print) ▼] to switch back to Web Layout mode.

WHAT ARE MEDIUMS?

Mediums let you customize styles for a particular output. For example, you might want the "p" style for online output to use a sans serif font (like Verdana), which is easy to read onscreen. But for print output, you might want the "p" style to use a serif font (like Times New Roman), which is easier to read in printed documents.

If you want to use a medium, you must set up the medium's styles in the Stylesheet Editor and then select the applicable medium when you set up a target. The medium you select will be used for that target's output.

> **Note** — When users print an online help topic, the *print* medium is automatically used to format the topic for printing.

For now, you only need to remember that Flare automatically changes the medium when you change the layout mode.

TASK 8: ADDING ANOTHER TOPIC

As you use Flare, you'll normally have more than one topic open at once, each with its own tab in the XML Editor. But only one topic—the **active topic**—is visible at a time. To switch to a different open topic (and make it active), just click its tab.

Now you'll create a new topic (without creating its corresponding TOC entry) to learn more about topic tabs.

1. Select **Project** tab → **New**. The Add File dialog opens.

2. Fill in the fields as described in the procedure for adding a topic on page 54.

3. Click **Add**. The new topic opens in its own tab (and is listed in the Content Explorer in the left pane).

Topic tabs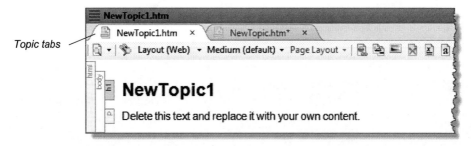

4. To switch between topics and make a topic active, click its tab.
    Try switching between topics a couple times to see how this
    works.

> **Best Practice** — Limit the number of open topics to three or four. Most
> people find it difficult to keep track of several topics at once.

TASK 9: SAVING A PROJECT

Enough practice for now. It's time to save your work.

Flare allows you to save the active topic or your entire project. You'll
save your project.

1. Click **Save All** 📙 in the Quick Access toolbar. Notice that the
    topic tabs no longer show asterisks, meaning that all changed
    content has been saved.

2. Close Flare if you're not ready to move on to Step 3: Develop
    Content, in this book.

> **Best Practice** — Use **Save All** 📙 rather than **Save File** 💾. That way,
> you'll be sure to save all your work before exiting.

LEARN MORE

This section provides more detail about some of the features you
used during this tutorial. Appendix C: XML Editor Reference has
shortcuts and charts for quick reference when working with the
XML Editor.

USING *XML* EDITOR TOOLBARS

The XML Editor has two local toolbars:

You'll use the **Top toolbar** to switch view modes and add links, cross-references, and images, plus other tasks.

Figure 2-2: *Top toolbar*

You'll use the **Bottom toolbar** to change the magnification of the text in Web Layout mode, to page through a document in Print Layout mode, and to view structure bars.

Figure 2-3: *Bottom toolbar in Web Layout mode*

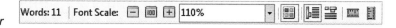

Figure 2-4 *Bottom toolbar in Page Layout mode*

See Appendix C: XML Editor Reference, for complete list of toolbar buttons.

USING STRUCTURE BARS

Structure bars—visual cues that show the structure of a topic's tags—provide a quick and convenient way to access XML Editor features (such as inserting rows and columns in tables). Flare contains these structure bars:

- **Tag bars** — Appear to the left of the content area and show tags for each block in your topic. (The highlighted bar shows which block your cursor is in.)

html
body
h1
p
ul
li
h1 (heading 1)
p (paragraph)
ul (unordered list)
li (list item)

Figure 2-5: *Tag bars*

- **Span bars** — Appear at the top of the content area and show span tags—formatting such as bold, italics, and conditional text applied directly to characters.

i (italics)
MadCap conditional text tag
b
i
MadCap:conditionalText
b (bold)

Figure 2-6: *Span bars*

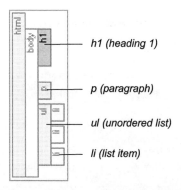

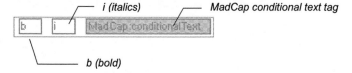

Structure bars show table structure

When you click inside a table, structure bars show the structure of your table.

- Tag bars show the structure of the table's rows. Table element tags ("tr" for table row and "td" for table data) appear with the topic's structure bars.

table
tbody
tr
td
The tag for the cell your cursor is positioned in.

Figure 2-7: *Tag bars when your cursor is in a table cell*

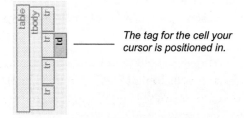

> ***Note*** — The Flare Help topic "About Structure Bars" has excellent illustrations of various tag bars.

- Span Bars show the structure of a table's columns. There is one bar, labeled with the column's width (or "auto" if the columns automatically adjust to the contents or window size), for each column in the table in which your cursor is positioned.

Figure 2-8:
Span bars when your cursor is in a table cell

Toggling tag and span bars on and off

To view more of a topic, you may want to toggle tag and span bars off in the XML Editor tab for that topic. If you use them frequently, you may want to keep them visible.

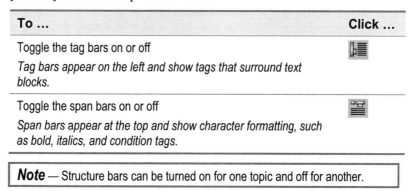

To ...	Click ...
Toggle the tag bars on or off *Tag bars appear on the left and show tags that surround text blocks.*	
Toggle the span bars on or off *Span bars appear at the top and show character formatting, such as bold, italics, and condition tags.*	

Note — Structure bars can be turned on for one topic and off for another.

Structure bar menus

Besides providing visual cues, structure bars provide menus for working with the text in your topics. Right-clicking a structure bar causes its menu to appear. Left-clicking selects the block or table.

Options available on a menu vary depending on the topic element you click. Here are two examples of menus. The first is for a text block formatted with the <p> tag; the second is for a table cell, which is formatted with a <tr> tag.

Figure 2-9:
Menus for a <p> tag and a <tr> tag

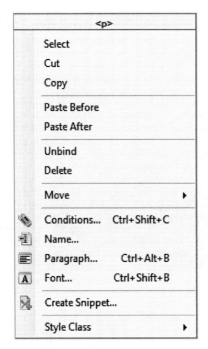

VIEWING MARKERS

Markers are used to flag certain elements (such as index entries, bookmarks, and variables) that you've inserted into a topic or snippet. You can view or hide them by clicking the down arrow on the **Show tags** ⊕ ▾ button (XML Editor's top toolbar) and selecting **Show Markers** from the list.

Figure 2-10:
Bookmark marker in view

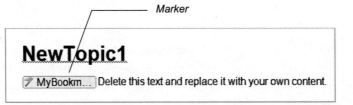

Marker

You'll learn more about markers later, in the topic about creating indexes in Step 4: Create Navigation Aids. See "Creating index entries" on page 188.

You can also view your topic after filtering out (hiding) content that's tagged with a condition tag. You'll see how to do this in Appendix F: Single Sourcing.

USING AUTO SUGGESTION

Auto Suggestion is an XML Editor feature that automatically offers suggestions for completing words and phrases. As you type, Auto Suggestion displays a popup that shows snippets and variables that begin with the words you are typing. If you see the word or phrase you want inserted, you can quickly select it, saving typing time. You can also add your own frequent terms and phrases to custom Auto Suggestion files, which can appear in the popup also.

Typing "Imp" caused the following suggestions to appear.

Figure 2-11: Auto Suggestion popup

Lists snippets and variables that begin with the words you are typing.

Once the Auto Suggestion popup appears, here's what you can do.

▶ To select a suggestion:

- Double-click the row or click the row once and press **ENTER**.

▶ To ignore the suggestions and dismiss the popup:

- Keep typing the word or close Auto Suggestion.

If you find yourself dismissing the popup often, try changing the Auto Suggestion settings. If you decide that Auto Suggestion is not helpful for your project, you can disable it.

▶ To create a custom Auto Suggestion list:

1. In the Project Organizer, right-click the **Advanced** folder and select **Add Auto Suggestion List File**.

2. In the File Name field, type a name for the new file and click **Add**. The file opens in the middle pane.

3. Add the desired words to the list, and save the list.

▶ To add words to the Auto Suggestion list as you type:

1. Highlight the desired words, right-click and select **Create Auto Suggestion**.

2. Complete the applicable steps shown in the following chart, depending on the type of message that appears:

If ...	Do this ...
The message states: *"Added '<term>' to <filename>"*	The project has only one auto suggestion file, and the highlighted word was automatically added to that file.
The message states: *"There are no auto suggestion files in the project. Do you want to add one?"*	▪ Respond (**Yes** or **No**) to the message. ▪ If you clicked "Yes" the Add File dialog opens. Type a file name and click **Add**.
A dialog lists the names of existing auto suggestion files.	▪ Select the file you want to add the highlighted word to, and click **Create**.

CHANGING AND DISABLING AUTO SUGGESTION

By changing Auto Suggestion settings, you can change the results that appear in the Auto Suggestion popup. You can:

▪ enable or disable suggestions from specific files

- limit the number of suggestions shown in the popup (up to 25)

- specify the minimum number of characters to be typed before the popup opens (from 3 to 12)

You can also disable Auto Suggestion.

▶ To change or disable Auto Suggestion:

1. Select **File** tab → **Options** (lower right corner of the File tab).

2. On the Options dialog, click the **Auto Suggestion** tab.

3. To disable Auto Suggestion, clear the **Enable Auto Suggestion** checkbox. Change other options as desired.

RULERS

Rulers in the XML Editor work the same as in most word processing programs. Flare provides two buttons in the XML Editors' bottom toolbar for viewing rulers.

Figure 2-12:
Horizontal and vertical rulers

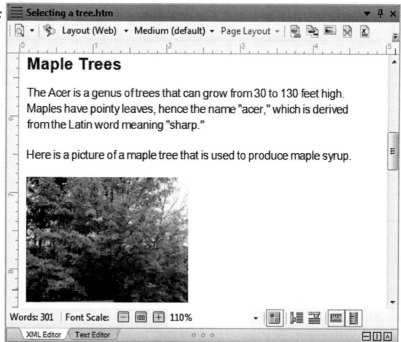

> *Note* — A ruler can be in view for one open topic, but not in view for another.

▶ To show or hide the horizontal ruler:

- Click **Toggle Show the horizontal ruler** .

▶ To show or hide the vertical ruler:

- Click **Toggle Show the vertical ruler** .

▶ To change a ruler's units of measure:

1. Click the ruler.

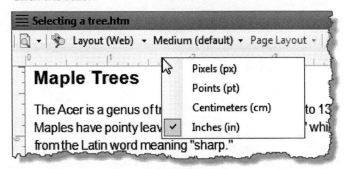

2. Select the units of measure you want (pixels, points, centimeters, inches).

WHAT'S NEXT?

Ready to learn more about Flare?

The next chapter, Step 3: Develop Content, describes how to develop content after you have entered or imported it. Specifically, you'll explore how to work with lists, tables, images, styles, special symbols and characters, image thumbnails, QR codes, and text redaction.

Step 3: Develop Content

STEP 5: Create Output
5A: Print Output
5B: Online Output

STEP 4:
Create
Nav Aids

STEP 3:
Develop
Content

STEP 2:
Learn the
XML Editor

STEP 1:
Get Started

In this chapter ...
➤ Copy text into a topic
➤ Delete a topic
➤ Check for links to files
➤ Work with lists
➤ Work with tables
➤ Work with images
➤ Show image thumbnails
➤ Insert QR codes
➤ Add symbols and
  special characters
➤ Format your content
➤ Customize styles
➤ Mark text for redaction

OVERVIEW

Throughout this book, you'll see **content** and **topic** used often. Let's take a moment to review what these terms mean:

- A **topic** is a standalone unit of content. Each topic is a file (with an .htm extension) that conforms to the XML specification.

- **Content** is various types of information contained in a topic, such as text, tables, lists, images, links, and multimedia.

A Flare **project** is simply a collection of topics and related files, which are stored in **project folders**.

In this chapter, you'll learn how to:

- Copy and paste content into a topic (without importing it)

- Delete a topic

- See what a file links to

- Add lists, tables, images, and special characters to topics

- Format your content

- Customize styles

- Mark sensitive text to be concealed (text redaction)

Your content can be new or imported (see Appendix B: Import Content, for more about importing content). This chapter does *not* describe how to create navigational aids (links, TOCs, indexes) that point to topics. That's covered in Step 4: Create Navigation Aids.

Let's begin by learning how to copy text into a topic.

> **Note** — To learn how to create new topics, see "Adding a topic" on page 53.

COPYING AND PASTING CONTENT INTO A TOPIC

There may be times when you have small pieces of text you want to insert into topics. Copying and pasting is the fastest and easiest way to do it. This method works well for small blocks of text that will not become standalone topics. You can even paste images into Flare.

▶ **To copy and paste text into a topic:**

1. Open the Flare topic you want to paste the text into.

2. Select the source text and press **CTRL + C** to copy it (from Word, FrameMaker, another Flare topic, or any other word processing application).

3. Place your cursor where you want to insert the text and press **CTRL + V**. The content is pasted immediately. If you're pasting content from an external application, a paste icon 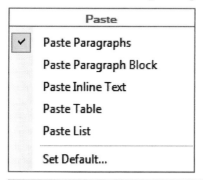 appears. The text is automatically pasted in the default format (as a paragraph, unless you change the default).

    To change the format, click the paste icon and select a different paste option. To set the default for pasting content, select **Set Default**. Then select the paste option that you want as a default.

Paste
✔ Paste Paragraphs
Paste Paragraph Block
Paste Inline Text
Paste Table
Paste List
Set Default...

> *Tip* — The paste icon remains visible until you perform another action (such as typing text or selecting a menu option) within the same topic.

▶ To copy and paste an image into a topic:

1. Open the Flare topic you want to paste the image into.

2. Select the image to be copied and press **CTRL + C**.

3. Place your cursor where you want to insert the image and press **CTRL + V**.

4. Navigate to the folder in your Flare project in which to store the image (typically in the Content Explorer's Resources/Images folder), type a name for the image file, and click **Save**.

    The image is stored in your project and pasted into the topic.

DELETING A TOPIC

You can delete a topic from your project, but use caution when doing so, as other topics or project files might link to that topic. When you delete a topic, its index markers are also deleted.

> **Best Practice** — Before deleting a topic, save a backup copy of your project. Then check for and remove links to that topic. See "Checking for links to a topic" on page 108.

Use the following procedure to delete a topic from your project.

▶ To delete a topic:

1. Make sure that the Flare project is open and the Content Explorer is in view.

2. Right-click the topic and select **Delete** from the menu.

3. Click **OK** to confirm the deletion.

    If the topic has links to other files, such as links to other topics or a TOC, the Link Update dialog opens.

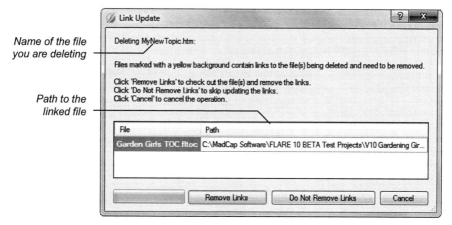

Name of the file you are deleting

Path to the linked file

4. Do one of the following:

To ...	Do this ...
Delete the topic and remove all links to it	Click **Remove Links**. ***Note*** — *Removing* the link to a TOC creates an unlinked TOC item. *Removing* the link to another topic leaves the unlinked text of the link in the other topic.
Delete the topic without removing links to it	Click **Do Not Remove Links**. ***Note*** — *Leaving* the link to a TOC or other topic creates a broken link in the TOC or topic.
Cancel without deleting this topic	Click **Cancel**.

If you selected **Remove Links** or **Do Not Remove Links**, the topic is deleted from your project.

5. Click **Save All** to save your work.

CHECKING FOR LINKS TO A TOPIC

The Link Viewer window lets you see what a topic or file is linked to. You can check links to and from any project file, such as topics, TOCs, targets, snippets, skins, even variable sets. For example, you might want to see if a topic is included in a TOC before you delete that topic.

Use the following procedure to check for links to and from a topic or project file.

▶ To check for links:

1. From the Content Explorer or Project Organizer, open the topic or project file you want to check links for.

> **Tip** — To open the Link Viewer window without first opening the topic, right-click the topic or project file and select **View Links** from the menu.

2. Select **View** tab → **Link Viewer**. The Link Viewer window opens in the right pane (by default).

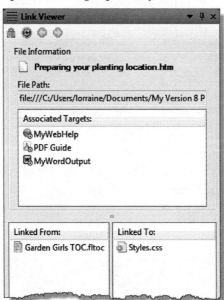

Broken links are identified in the Link Viewer window by this icon 🔗.

3. (*Optional*) Complete the following tasks as needed.

To ...	Do this ...
Open a linked file	Double-click the file name in the Link Viewer.
View links for a different topic or file	Do one of the following: • Activate the file (click its tab or open it in the middle pane). • Right-click the file in the Content Explorer or Project Organizer and select View Links.
Refresh the Link Viewer window (Helpful if you changed links.)	Click **Refresh** in the Link Viewer toolbar.
Toggle between locking and unlocking the Link Viewer window (Locking lets you activate other topics and files without changing the display.)	Click **Lock the Link Viewer** in the Link Viewer toolbar.
View the previous set of links you've already viewed	Click **Show links for previous file** in the Link Viewer toolbar.
View the next set of links you've already viewed	Click **Show links for next file** in the Link Viewer toolbar.

4. Close the Link Viewer window.

WORKING WITH LISTS

As with most word processing programs, Flare lets you add various types of lists to your content, including:

- Single-level lists
- Multi-level lists
- Numbered lists, sequenced by numbers or letters
- Bulleted lists

You can also add items to lists, rearrange, sort, and merge them.

CREATING A LIST

Before you create a list, you should know your options.

DECISION TIME!

✓   Do you want to create a bulleted list or a numbered list?

✓   If you want a bulleted list, what type of bullets do you want (black circle, empty circle, or square)?

✓   If you want a numbered list, what type of numbers do you want (Arabic, lower-case alphabetic, upper-case alphabetic, lower-case roman numerals, or upper-case roman numerals)?

Note — In the XML world, bulleted lists are also called **unordered lists** because the order of the items *is insignificant*. Numbered lists, such as step-by-step procedures, are called **ordered lists** because the order of list items *is* important.

Creating a single-level list

Use this procedure to create single-level bulleted or numbered lists.

▶ To create a single-level list:

1.   In the desired topic, place your cursor where you want the list to start.

2.   Select the **Home** tab.

3.   If you want the default bullet list, click the face of the **Bullet List** button; otherwise, click the button's arrow and select the type of list you want to create.

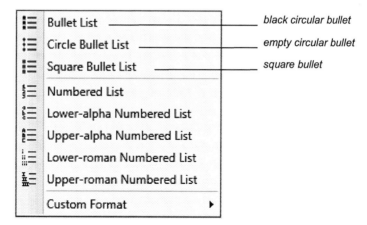

4. Type the text of the list item.

5. At the end of the line for the first list item, press **ENTER** (only once). A second list item is created.

> **Tip** — If you press **ENTER** more than once, Flare thinks that you're done creating the list. Instead of giving you more list items, it gives you paragraphs in which to type text. If this happens, simply place your cursor at the end of the last list item you typed, and press **ENTER**. Your list will continue where you left off.

6. Continue adding items, if you'd like, pressing **ENTER** after each.

> **Note** — You can also create a list by typing the text first, selecting it, and then selecting the type of list to apply to the text.

Creating a multi-level list

You've just seen how to create a simple one-level numbered or bulleted list. But not all lists are simple. For example, if you're writing step-by-step instructions, you might need to break out one step into a series of smaller tasks—each one a step.

Example of a multi-level list

1. First numbered item
    a. First second-level item
    b. Second second-level item
2. Second numbered item
3. Third numbered item

Use the following procedure to create a multi-level list with Flare's indenting feature.

> **Note** — To learn how to create a multi-level list by using styles, search on "creating multi-level lists" in the Flare Help system. You can also create a custom format for lists up to 10 levels deep (an advanced feature). See Flare's Help system for details.

▶ To create a multi-level list:

1. Create a single-level list that contains all of the items.

2. Indent the desired items by clicking **Indent Items** on the **Home** ribbon.

3. Apply the desired list type to the indented items. (Click the arrow on the **Bullet List** button and select the list type.)

INSERTING PARAGRAPHS BETWEEN LIST ITEMS

When creating a list, you might want to include paragraphs between list items. Here's a quick keyboard shortcut. Simply click your cursor within the list item you want a paragraph after and press CTRL plus the semicolon key (**CTRL + ;**). To insert another paragraph after it, move to the end of the list item and press **ENTER**. Type or insert your paragraph content. When you're ready to make another list item, press **SHIFT + TAB** or click.

CHANGING LISTS

Flare includes many options for changing lists, such as:

- Rearranging items
- Sorting items
- Assigning a different number to an item
- Merging two or more lists into one

The **List Actions** button 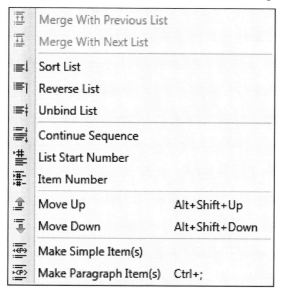 shows what you can do with lists.
Next, you'll read about some of the more frequently used list actions.

Figure 3-1:
List actions
menu

Merge With Previous List	
Merge With Next List	
Sort List	
Reverse List	
Unbind List	
Continue Sequence	
List Start Number	
Item Number	
Move Up	Alt+Shift+Up
Move Down	Alt+Shift+Down
Make Simple Item(s)	
Make Paragraph Item(s)	Ctrl+;

Rearranging lists

You can easily rearrange the items in a list by moving them up or
down.

▶ To rearrange a list:

1. Place your cursor within the list item to be moved.

2. On the **Home** tab, click **List Actions**.

3. Select **Move Up** or **Move Down**.

4. Continue moving items until the list is arranged to your liking.

> *Tip* — You can also move an item by dragging and dropping its tag bar.

Sorting a list

List items can be sorted in ascending order based on the text
contained in each list item.

For example, suppose you have the following list items:

1. AAA
2. SSS
3. MM
4. MMMMM
5. BB
6. FFF

A sorted list would look like this.

1. AAA
2. BB
3. FFF
4. MM
5. MMMMM
6. SSS

Notice that the sequence numbers don't stay with the text. In this case, the list started with number 1 and it still does, even after being sorted.

▶ To sort a list:

1. Place your cursor anywhere in the list.

2. On the **Home** tab, click **List Actions** .

3. Select **Sort List**.

   The list items are sorted in ascending alphabetical order.

   > **Note** — To switch the order from ascending to descending or vice versa, select **Reverse List** from the List Actions menu.

Re-numbering a list

Flare lets you set a starting number to any item in an ordered list. Items that follow that item will automatically be re-numbered (unless you have set their starting number.)

You can also reset the number of an item. This assigns the next number in the sequence (based on the previous list item). The List Actions button contains three options for setting and resetting sequence numbers in ordered lists: **Continue Sequence**, **List Start Number**, and **Item Number**. (See Figure 3-1.)

You'll learn about these options next.

▶ To assign a number to the first item in a list:

1. Place your cursor on any item in the list.

2. On the **Home** tab, click **List Actions** , then select **List Start Number**.

3. On the Set List Item Value dialog, use the up and down arrows to select a starting number.

    The first item in the list is set to the starting number you selected, and the remaining list items are re-sequenced in ascending one-unit increments. For example, if you set the first item to 20, the remaining items will be numbered starting at 21.

▶ To assign a sequence number to any item in a list:

1. Place your cursor on the list item whose number you want to set.

2. On the **Home** tab, click **List Actions** , then select **Item Number**.

3. On the Set List Item Value dialog, use the up and down arrows to select a starting number.

    The item is set to the starting number you selected and the items that follow it are re-sequenced in ascending order.

Merging lists

If your topic has lists that need to be combined, you can easily merge them. But before merging them, the lists must be consecutive (in other words, you cannot combine lists that have non-list elements between them). Make sure you delete any non-list items before trying to merge two lists or move the second list so it immediately follows the first.

> *Tip* — To merge three lists, just merge the first two into one, and then merge that list with the next one.

Can I merge different types of lists?

Yes, you can merge two lists that are of different types. For example, you can merge a numbered list with a bulleted list. When Flare combines the lists, it applies the list type from the first list to the second list.

Suppose the first list looks like this:

1. first numbered item
2. second numbered item
3. third numbered item

And the second list looks like this:

- first bullet item
- second bullet item
- third bullet item

After you combine them, the list will look like this:

1. first numbered item
2. second numbered item
3. third numbered item
4. first bullet item
5. second bullet item
6. third bullet item

What happens to the sequence numbers when I merge lists?

As you can see from the example, if the first list is an ordered list, Flare automatically applies the next number in sequence to the first item in the second list. So the result is a seamless, perfectly sequenced group of list items.

▶ To merge two lists:

1. In the topic that contains the two lists, verify that there are no non-list elements between the two lists.

   > **Note** — You might need to remove the text that's between the lists or copy the second list and paste it immediately after the first list. (To delete text, see "Deleting text" on page 310.)

2. Place your cursor on any item in either list.

3. On the **Home** tab, click **List Actions** .

4. Select **Merge With Next List** or **Merge With Previous List** (depending on which list—the first or second—your cursor is located in).

WORKING WITH TABLES

Tables allow you to organize information in a graphical format that is easier for most people to read than blocks of text. Tables consist of cells (the intersection of rows and columns), which can contain text, images, variables, or snippets.

INSERTING A TABLE

Here are two different methods for inserting a table in the active topic. The first lets you insert a table with headers and footers and specify the table's characteristics (borders, caption, alignment, etc.); the second allows you to quickly insert a simple table with default characteristics and no headers or footers.

> **Tip** — Regardless of which method you choose, you can easily change a table's characteristics later by selecting **Table** tab → **Table Properties**.

▶ To insert a table and select its characteristics:

1. Place your cursor where you want to insert the table.

2. Select **Table** tab → **Insert Table** [image]. The Insert Table dialog opens. (See page 158.)

3. Fill in the fields on each tab of the Insert Table dialog. For descriptions of the fields, see Table 3-2 and Table 3-3, starting on page 159.

▶ To insert a simple table:

1. Place your cursor where you want to insert the table.

2. Select **Table** tab→ Insert Table button down arrow.

3. Hover your mouse over the grid until the desired number of rows and columns are highlighted, then click to insert the table.

You now have a table that is ready for content. To type text in the table's cells, simply position your cursor in a cell and type. You can also add images and links. To format the table, see page 143.

> **Tip** — To create a paragraph after a table, position your cursor in the last cell of the table and press the Down Arrow key. The cursor becomes a horizontal line positioned underneath the table. When you start typing you'll get a new paragraph.

SHOWING GRID LINES

Table gridlines help you to see where table cells are. You can easily turn gridlines on or off as needed. Grid lines appear in the XML

Editor only; they do not show up in your output. (If you want borders around cells, see "Formatting tables" on page 143.)

▶ To show (or hide) grid lines:

- Select **Table** tab→ select (or clear) **Show Gridlines**.

USING STRUCTURE BARS TO MANIPULATE TABLES

With Flare's XML Editor you can show or hide the tag and span bars that show the structure of your table (and your topic).

Tag bars and span bars make it easy to select, insert, delete, resize, and move rows and columns in your tables. (You can also use Flare's **Table** ribbon to do some of these things.)

Structure bar menus have choices that are meaningful based on your cursor location. For more information about structure bars and their menus, see "Using structure bars" on page 95.

> **Note** — The following tasks require tag and span bars to be visible. If you don't see them, click **Toggle show blocks** 🔲 and **Toggle show spans** 🔲 in the XML Editor's bottom toolbar.

Selecting rows and columns

▶ To select a row or column:

- Place your cursor in the row or column you want to select and click the applicable "tr" tag bar or "col" span bar.

▶ To select the entire table:

- Right-click the "table" tag bar and select **Select → Table**.

> **Note** — You can also use the Table ribbon (**Select All Cells** down arrow) for these tasks.

Inserting rows and columns

▶ To insert a row:

- Right-click the "tr" tag bar for the row after which (or before which) you want to insert a row and select **Insert New (Above)** or **Insert New (Below)**.

  A blank row is inserted either above or below the row whose bar you clicked.

> ***Tips—***
>
> You can also place your cursor where you want to add the row and select **Table** tab → **Rows Above** or **Rows Below**.
>
> To insert a row at the end of the table, place your cursor the last cell and press **TAB**.

▶ To insert a column:

1. Click inside the table and right-click the "col" span bar for the column after which (or before which) you want to insert a column.

2. Select **Insert New (Left)** or **Insert New (Right)**.

   A blank column is inserted to the left or right of the column whose span bar you clicked.

> ***Note*** — You can also place your cursor where you want to add a column and select **Table** tab → **Columns to the Left** or **Columns to the Right**.

Deleting rows and columns

▶ To delete a row or column:

- *For rows*, right-click the "tr" tag bar for the row you want to delete and select **Delete**.

  For columns, click inside the table, then right-click the "col" span bar for the column you want to delete and select **Delete**.

> **Note** — You can also place your cursor in the row or column you want to delete, select the **Table** tab, then click the **Delete Table** button's arrow, and select **Columns** or **Rows**.
>
> Selecting a row or column and pressing the **Delete** key clears the content only; it does not delete the row or column.

Resizing rows and columns

▶ To resize a row:

1. Hover your cursor between the "tr" tag bar of the row you want to resize and the row below it until you see a vertical double-arrow.

2. Drag the arrow to change the row's height.

   Flare shows the height of the row in pixels, which changes dynamically as you drag the row.

> **Note** — You can also right-click the row's "tr" tag bar and use the resize arrows in the menu to set the size. (Click the blue arrow when done.) `23  ▲▼ px ▾ ↵`

▶ To resize a column:

1. (Click inside the table to see the span bars.) In the span bars, hover your cursor over the line between the column you want to resize and the column to its right until you see a horizontal double-arrow.

2. Drag the arrow to change the column's width.

   Flare shows the width of the column in pixels, which changes dynamically as you drag the column. When you stop dragging, the span bar shows the new width in pixels.

> **Note** — You can also resize a column by right-clicking the column's span bar and clicking the resize arrows in the menu. (Click the blue arrow when done.) `1.00  ▲▼ em ▾ ↵`

Moving rows and columns

▶ **To move a row:**

- Drag the row's "tr" tag bar and drop it when the arrow points to the place you want to move it to.

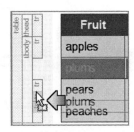

▶ **To move a column:**

1. Click anywhere inside the table and hover your cursor over the span bar for the column to be moved. The cursor turns into a hand.

2. Drag the column's "col" span bar and drop it when the arrow points to the place you want to move it to.

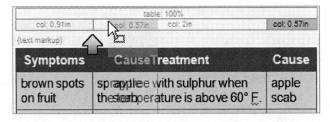

CONVERTING TABLES TO TEXT AND TEXT TO TABLES

Sometimes you might need to create a table from existing text blocks or the other way around. Flare lets you do both.

▶ **To convert a table to text:**

- Click inside the table, and then select **Table** tab → **Convert to Text**.

  By default, text from each table cell becomes a separate paragraph. However, by clicking the paste icon , you can select a different conversion method. You can convert table text into a single paragraph, separated by commas or by the text string you enter. You can also set a default method for future conversions.

▶ To convert text to a table:

1. Select the text, and then select **Table** tab → **Insert Table**. The Insert Table dialog opens.

2. Select the number of columns and (table body) rows, the number of header rows, and the format of the text to be converted, such as paragraphs or text separated by commas (Text to Table section).

CUTTING AND PASTING TABLE ROWS, COLUMNS, AND CELLS

You can cut and paste rows from a table in order to split up a table.

▶ To cut and paste table content:

1. Select the rows, columns, or cells to be removed.

2. Right-click and select **Cut** (or press **CTRL + X**)

3. Right-click the new location and select **Paste** (or click the location and press **CTRL + V**).

   If you're cutting rows or columns, a paste icon appears on the right side of the table.

4. Click the icon to select options for cutting the table content. You can cut both the content and the row or column, or you can remove only the text inside the table rows or columns. You can also set a default method for cutting content.

MERGING TABLES

If you have two consecutive tables (in a topic or snippet) that you'd like to combine, you can merge them by using the paste icon.

Note — You can only merge tables that have the same number of columns.

▶ To merge two tables:

1. Remove all content (paragraphs, etc.) between the tables.

2.　If you want to select options for merging the tables, click the paste icon 🖻 that appears on the right side of the table.

The option "Merge Table Up" causes the bottom table to use the stylesheet (or formatting) of the top table. "Merge Table Down" causes the top table to use the stylesheet (or formatting) of the bottom table. "Don't Merge Tables" shows the tables one after the other, but does not merge their styles/formatting. You can also set a default method for merging tables.

SORTING TABLE CONTENTS

You can easily sort an entire table or specific rows.

▶ To sort the contents of a table:

1.　Do one of the following:

To ...	Do this ...
Sort the entire table	Click in any cell of the column you want to sort by.
Sort specific rows on the first column's contents	Select the rows to be sorted.
Sort specific rows on a different column's content	Select only the cells in the column you want to sort on for as many rows as you want to sort.

2.　Select **Table** tab → **Ascending** down arrow → **Ascending** or **Descending**.

WORKING WITH IMAGES

Flare lets you add images, such as photographs, screen captures, and illustrations, to your topics.

The image can be a vector or raster file in any of these formats: BMP, EMF, EPS, EXPS, GIF, HDP, JPG, JPEG, PNG, PS, SVG, SWF, TIF, TIFF, WDP, WMF, XAML, and XPS.

Vector images (like SVG, PS, and EPS) are converted to raster-based PNG files if the images are used in WebHelp or DotNet Help.

IMAGE THUMBNAILS

Images in your topics can be shown as thumbnails (miniature, low-resolution images) in your online output or in the XML Editor window. This gives you more room for viewing text in the XML Editor. In output, this lets users see more of a topic's text. See "Showing images as thumbnails" on page 131.

WHERE ARE IMAGES STORED?

By default, Flare stores images in the Resources\Images folder of the Content Explorer. If the image you want to add is not already in this folder, Flare puts it there when you add the image to your topic.

> ***Tip*** — You can copy images to the Resources\Images folder from Windows Explorer before you're ready to add them to topics.

You can add an image from the Resources\Images folder to any topic in your project. When you add an image to a topic, Flare inserts a link to that image; it does not embed the image in the topic. This keeps project sizes smaller, since the image is stored only once.

FLARE MANAGES IMAGE FILE CHANGES

When you add an image to a topic, Flare keeps a link to that image. If you later change its name in the Resources\Images folder, you can easily update the image file name in all links to that image. Therefore, your link between the file and the image in your topic will not be broken!

And here's another feature that's pretty cool. If you edit the image using an external application and replace it (keeping the file name the same), the image in your topic is automatically updated.

An example

Let's say that you copied a photograph called "MyPhoto.jpg" to the Resources\Images folder, inserted it into a topic, and then noticed that the photo has red-eye. To fix it, you can just open the photo in your photo editing software, remove the red-eye, and re-save the photo to the Resources\Images folder. When you view the photo in your topic you'll see that the red-eye is gone!

> **Tip** — To replace an image that has callouts created with MadCap Capture, use MadCap Capture's Replace feature.

ADDING AN IMAGE

Follow these instructions to add an image to a topic and to the open project.

▶ **To add an image to a topic:**

1. Place your cursor where you want to insert the image.

2. Click **Insert an image** in the XML Editor toolbar.

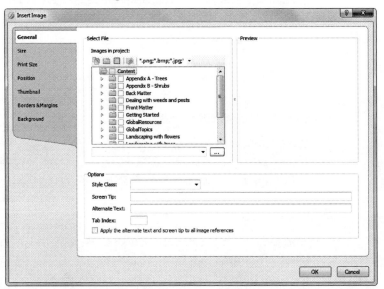

3. In the General tab, select an image to insert by doing one of the following:

    ▪   Select one of the images listed (by default in the Resources\Images folder).

- Click [···] to navigate to it.

A preview of the image appears at the right of the dialog.

4. (*Optional*) Select a style class to apply to the image. If no style class is selected, the style defaults to "img."

5. (*Optional*) Type a screen tip (text that appears when you hover your cursor over the image in the output).

6. (*Optional*) Type alternate text if you need to produce output that is compliant with Section 508 of the United States Rehabilitation Act. Alternate text is helpful when visually impaired individuals use screen readers. To apply the alternate text everywhere the image is used, select **Apply the alternate text and screen tip to all image references**.

7. Click **OK**.

If the image is not already in your project, a dialog confirms that the image will be copied to your project.

8. Click **OK** to copy the image to your project.

The picture is added to your topic and to your project's Resources\Images folder (if not already there).

9. Save your topic.

ADDING SCREEN CAPTURES WITH MADCAP CAPTURE

With Flare and MadCap Capture™ (a free companion product to Flare) you can add and edit screen captures directly from Flare. Capture stores graphic elements in layers, so you can capture a screen shot and add graphic elements (like callouts) to it. To edit an image with Capture, simply right-click the image and select **Edit With MadCap Capture**. To find out more, see your MadCap Capture Help system.

RESIZING AN IMAGE

After you add images to your topics, you have a few ways to resize them. You can resize an image locally or you can control an image's size with styles.

So which method should you use? Here's what you might consider:

Do this ...	When ...
Resize images locally	You have only a few images in a project and image sizing doesn't need to be consistent, or you have one or two images that need to be sized differently from the others.
Resize images with styles	You have many images and need consistent image sizing throughout your project or you need different image sizes for print vs. online output.

Resizing and image quality

Flare supports images in vector or raster format. The type of format determines if image quality is affected when images are resized or cropped.

- **Vector images** — Can easily be resized without any loss of quality. (Vector images are composed of points connected by lines and curves that form objects that are defined mathematically.)

- **Raster (bitmap) images** — Can be resized, but when you enlarge them, the image might become blurry because the dots move farther apart. (Raster images are composed of a collection of dots, called pixels, arranged in a grid pattern called a bitmap.) You can however, crop a raster image with no loss of quality.

Digital cameras and scanners generally create files in raster formats, such as JPG, BMP, TIF, TIFF, GIF, and PNG files. Some illustration applications (such as CorelDRAW®) create files in vector format; others (such as Adobe Photoshop®) create files in raster format.

> *Tip* — If possible, create images in their final sizes to avoid any issues with resizing.

Resizing images locally

Here are two ways to resize images locally.

▶ To resize an image locally by using a mouse:

1. Hover your cursor over the image to be resized. A button 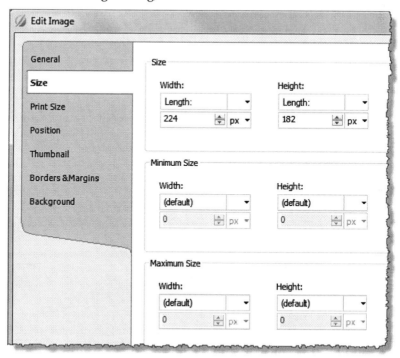 appears in the image's lower right corner.

2. Drag the button diagonally *toward* the center of the image (to reduce image size) or diagonally *away from* the center of the image (to enlarge the image).

▶ To resize an image locally by using properties:

1. In the XML Editor, right-click the image to be resized and select **Edit Image**.

2. On the Edit Image dialog, click the **Size** tab.

4. Set image sizes as follows:

To ...	Do this ...
Set an exact image size	In the Size section, set the Width or Height and unit of measure. To maintain an image's aspect ratio (keep it in proportion), either set the image to the desired Width (select **Length** to do this) and select **Automatic** for the Height, or vice versa. 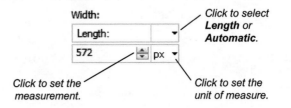
Set a minimum image size	In the Minimum Size section, set the minimum Length and unit of measure. To maintain an image's aspect ratio (keep it in proportion), set either the Width or the Height, but not both. **Note** — If the original image is *smaller* than the measurement you set, Flare enlarges the image. If the original image is *larger*, Flare doesn't change the image size.
Set a maximum image size	In the Maximum Size section, set the maximum Length and unit of measure. To maintain an image's aspect ratio (keep it in proportion), set either the Width or the Height, but not both. **Note** — If the original image is *larger* than the measurement you set, Flare reduces the image size. If the original image is *smaller*, Flare doesn't change the image size.

Important — If you set Size tab options only, those settings will be used for both online and print output. If you set options on the Print Size tab also, then its options will be used for print output and Size tab options will be used for online output.

5. If you want the image to be one size for online output and a different size for print output, click the **Print Size** tab to set the

image size for print output only. (The **Size** tab settings will then be used for online output only.)

Use the chart above to set the options for the **Print Size** tab.

When you click OK, the image is resized according to the size(s) you entered.

Resizing images with styles

Use the "img" style or a class of the img style to control the size of images in your topics.

▶ **To resize an image with styles:**

1. Open your stylesheet in Simplified View.

2. Double-click the **img** style or the style class applied to the image you want to resize.

> **Note** — The Size tab of the Properties dialog used by the Stylesheet Editor in Simplified view is identical to the Size tab of the Properties dialog you use when formatting an image locally.

3. On the Size tab, set image sizes as described in Step 3 of the procedure for formatting an image locally by using properties (the previous procedure).

For more information about formatting with styles, see "Applying styles from a stylesheet" on page 146.

SHOWING IMAGES AS THUMBNAILS

Flare lets you show images as thumbnails (miniature, low-resolution images) in your online output or in a topic as you edit it.

WHY SHOW IMAGES AS THUMBNAILS?

Viewing images as thumbnails gives you more room for viewing text as you edit a topic in the XML Editor. In output, it lets users of your content see more of the topic's text while still giving them the option of viewing the full-size image. You can easily see the full-size image by clicking or moving the mouse over the thumbnail, depending on how you format the thumbnail image.

SHOWING IMAGES AS THUMBNAILS WHILE EDITING A TOPIC

In the XML Editor, you can easily toggle between viewing images in the active topic as thumbnails and viewing them in full size. You can set this option on a topic-by-topic basis. If you choose to view image thumbnails in the active topic, the images are reduced to a maximum size of 48 pixels high by default. (You can change the maximum size.)

> **Note** — Viewing images as thumbnails in the active topic does not affect how those images appear in the output. However, if images are formatted as thumbnails for output, those images will appear as thumbnails in the XML Editor. To view images as thumbnails in output, see "Showing images as thumbnails in online output" on page 133.

Example

Here's an example of a topic with a full-size image.

Figure 3-2: *A full-size image in a topic*

Here's an example that shows a Limelight Hydrangea when its blooms are first open. These snowball-like blooms open to a creamy white, but change to a mix of light pink and light green. Gardeners often cut the blooms just after they start to turn pink and bring them inside for dried flower arrangements.

The image takes up a good deal of space in the topic. Here's the same topic with image thumbnails turned on.

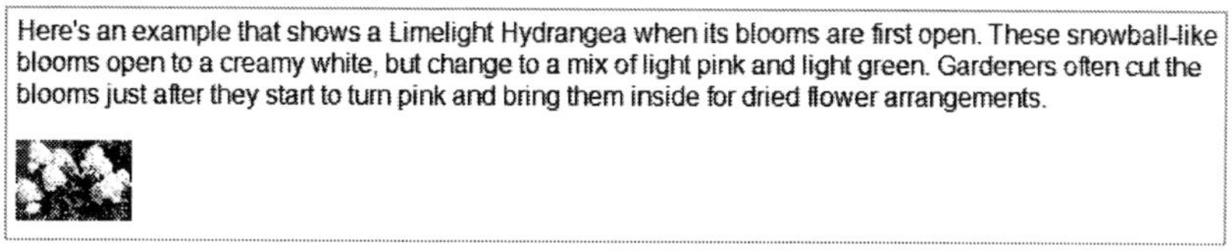

Figure 3-3:
A thumbnail image in a topic

> Here's an example that shows a Limelight Hydrangea when its blooms are first open. These snowball-like blooms open to a creamy white, but change to a mix of light pink and light green. Gardeners often cut the blooms just after they start to turn pink and bring them inside for dried flower arrangements.
>
>

▶ To toggle between thumbnails and full-size images:

- Click the arrow on the **Show tags** button in the XML Editor's top toolbar, and select **Show All Images As Thumbnails**.

All images in the topic are either shown as thumbnails or full size (depending on how you viewed them previously).

SHOWING IMAGES AS THUMBNAILS IN ONLINE OUTPUT

To minimize the space taken up by images in your online output, you can show images as thumbnails. Users will then see more of a topic's text. When they want to view the image, they either click the thumbnail or move the mouse over it (depending on how you set up the thumbnail). The image is shown full-size.

An example

Figure 3-4 shows an example that shows how your image might look if you don't use thumbnails in your output.

Figure 3-4:
Online output showing a full-size image (no thumbnail image)

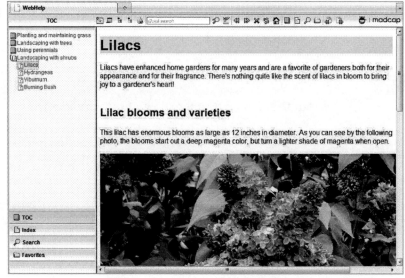

Figure 3-5 shows the same topic with images shown as thumbnails. In this example, the thumbnails are set up to show the full-size image when you click the thumbnail.

Figure 3-5:
Online output showing an image thumbnail

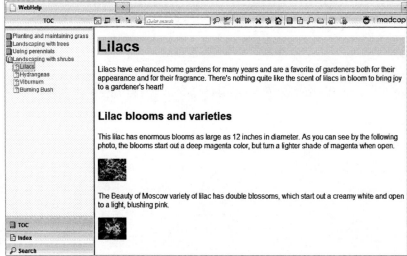

When you click the thumbnail, the full-size image is shown.

Figure 3-6:
Full-size image appears when the thumbnail is clicked.

How to show thumbnails in online output

You'll show thumbnails in online output by formatting the image, either locally or with a style from a stylesheet.

DECISION TIME!

✓ Do you want to apply thumbnails to only one or two images? If so, apply local formatting to images.

✓ Do you want many images in your project to appear as thumbnails in output? If so, apply styles to images.

Applying local formatting to images

When you want to format only a few images as thumbnails, local formatting is a fine choice. To format all images in your project as thumbnails, it's best to use a style. See "Applying styles to images" on page 137.

▶ To format an image as a thumbnail with local formatting:

1. Open the topic containing the image.

2. Right-click the image and select **Edit Image** from the menu.

3. Click the **Thumbnail** tab.

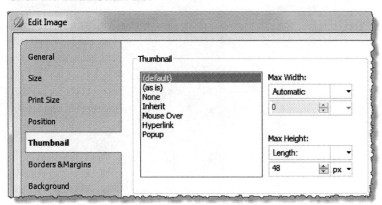

4. Select one of the following options:

Select this option ...	If you want the user to see the full-size image ...
Mouse Over	In a popup window when the mouse is over the thumbnail.
Hyperlink	In a new window after clicking the thumbnail.
Popup	In a popup window after clicking the thumbnail.

5. To set a maximum thumbnail image size, set either the Max Width or the Max Height (but not both). Select **Length**, a unit of measure, and a value for the unit of measure.

6. Click **OK**. The image is shown as a thumbnail in the XML Editor window (even if the **Show All Images As Thumbnails** option is not selected).

7. Click **Save All** to save your work.

After building your online output, you'll see the image appear as a thumbnail as in Figure 3-5. View the full-size image by clicking it or by moving the mouse over it (depending on the choice you made in Step 4 above).

Applying styles to images

If you want to format more than one or two images as thumbnails, then styles are a better choice than local formatting.

> **Tip** — Create a class of the img style to use only for thumbnails and use the img style for other images that you don't want displayed as thumbnails. (See "Adding a style class" on page 154.)

▶ To format images as thumbnails with styles:

1. Open the topic containing the image.

2. Right-click the image and select **Style Class → Edit Style Class** from the menu. The stylesheet opens in the Stylesheet Editor.

3. If you see "Simplified View" to the right of "Stylesheet Editor" click it to switch to Simplified View, otherwise the editor is already in Simplified View.

    The style applied to the image is highlighted at the top of the styles list.

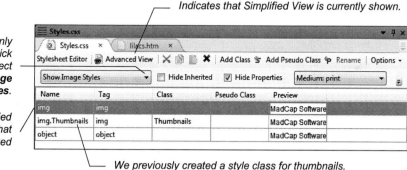

Indicates that Simplified View is currently shown.

To show only image styles, click here and select **Show Image Styles**.

The style applied to the image that was right-clicked

We previously created a style class for thumbnails.

4. Double-click the highlighted style (or the thumbnail class if you created one).

5. Click the **Thumbnail** tab.

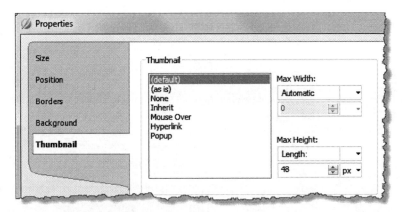

6.   Select one of the following options:

Select this option ...	If you want the user to see the full-size image ...
Mouse Over	In a popup window when the mouse is over the thumbnail.
Hyperlink	In a new window after clicking the thumbnail.
Popup	In a popup window after clicking the thumbnail.

7.   To set a maximum thumbnail image size, set either the Max Width or the Max Height (but not both). Select **Length**, a unit of measure, and a value for the unit of measure.

8.   Click **OK** then click **Save All** ![save icon] to save your work.

9.   Close the Stylesheet Editor.

     The image is shown as a thumbnail in the XML Editor window (even if the **Show All Images As Thumbnails** option is not selected).

     After building your online output, you'll see the image as a thumbnail as in Figure 3-5. View the full-size image by clicking it or by moving the mouse over it (depending on the choice you made in Step 6 previously).

Other options

Selecting **None** causes the full-size to be displayed rather than a thumbnail. **Inherit** causes the image to use the thumbnail settings that are applied to the tag in your topic in which the image is nested.

PROBLEMS WITH THUMBNAIL SETTINGS

When viewing output, if you see a distorted image when you click or when you mouse over the thumbnail, your original image might be larger than the Maximum Width or Maximum Height you set for the "img" tag. Here are two ways to fix this:

- Select Hyperlink instead of selecting Mouse Over or Popup.

- Reduce the size of your original image so it does not exceed the maximum size set for the img style.

INSERTING QR CODES

QR codes can be scanned by web cameras and mobile devices to access URLs, text, email addresses, and other types of information. You can create QR codes in the XML Editor and insert them directly into your topics, snippets, master pages, or page layout content frame.

▶ To insert a QR code:

1. Place your cursor where you want to insert the QR code and Select **Insert** tab → **QR Code**. The Insert QR Code dialog opens.

2. On the General tab under Settings, select the content type. The remaining settings vary depending on the content type you select. Enter the content for the QR code, such as the email address (to the right of "mailto:").

3. (*Optional*) Fill in remaining fields on this and other tabs as desired.

4. When you're done filling in fields, click **OK**. The QR code is inserted in the Flare topic.

ADDING SYMBOLS AND SPECIAL CHARACTERS

▶ **To add symbols and special characters:**

1. Place your cursor where you want to insert the special character.

2. Do one of the following:

To insert ...	Do this ...
a character from the Character dialog	Click the face of the Character [a] button, select the desired character, click **Insert**, and click **Close**.
The current quick character	Press F11 or click the Character button's down arrow and select **Insert Quick Character** from the list.
One of your favorite characters	Click the Character button's down arrow and select the desired favorite character from the list.
A non-breaking space or non-breaking hyphen	Click the Character button's down arrow and select **Non-breaking Space** or **Non-breaking Hyphen** from the list.
A recently used character	Click the Character button's down arrow and select the desired character from the recently used list.

SETTING THE DEFAULT QUICK CHARACTER

▶ **To set the default quick character:**

1. Click the face of the **Character** [a] button.

2. On the Character dialog, select the desired character or symbol and click the **Make quick character** button.

FORMATTING YOUR CONTENT

Formatting makes your content look better. For example, you can make your content pop by giving it a background color or changing the color of your text. Even a few changes make a big difference!

Typically, you'll want to use different font sizes for different types of headings. And for your body text, you'll likely want a font that is smaller than the font you use for headings. Actually, I can't think of a good reason *not* to format your content.

When you create topics from a Flare template, Flare's **Styles.css** stylesheet is automatically attached (more about stylesheets coming up.) Your topics will have some styles applied, as shown in Figure 3-7.

Figure 3-7: Topic with default styles

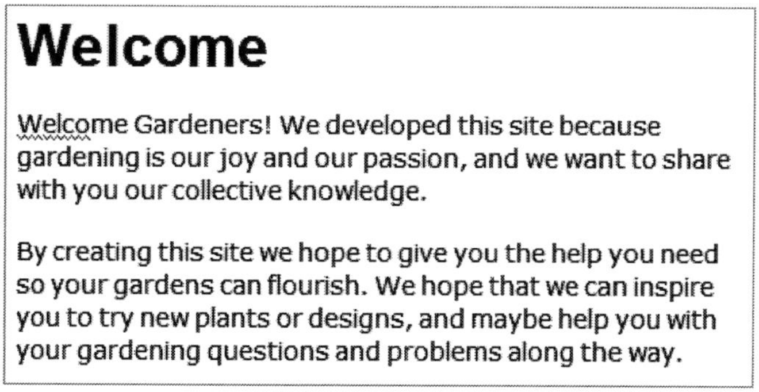

Welcome

Welcome Gardeners! We developed this site because gardening is our joy and our passion, and we want to share with you our collective knowledge.

By creating this site we hope to give you the help you need so your gardens can flourish. We hope that we can inspire you to try new plants or designs, and maybe help you with your gardening questions and problems along the way.

By changing the formatting, you can add eye-catching touches such as those shown in Figure 3-8.

Figure 3-8: Topic with color, italics, bold added

Welcome

Welcome Gardeners! We developed this site because gardening is our *joy* and our *passion*, and we want to share with you our collective knowledge.

By creating this site we hope to give you the help you need so your gardens can flourish. We hope that we can inspire you to try new plants or designs, and maybe help you with your gardening questions and problems along the way.

WAYS TO FORMAT CONTENT

As mentioned earlier in this book, there are two ways to apply formats to your content:

- With local formatting
- With styles from a stylesheet

This section covers both of these methods.

WHAT'S THE DIFFERENCE?

Both styles and local formatting can be applied to selected text, text blocks, and tables. The difference between them is how the formatting is applied, how it's maintained, and the amount code each add to your topic files.

Local formatting

Local (inline) formatting is applied by clicking certain toolbar buttons or by setting properties for the selected text, text block, or table. To change the format later, you must find the text that you applied it to. If you applied the same format in many places (in one or more topics), changing the format could be a daunting task.

Formatting with styles

A style's formatting is applied by selecting a style from a stylesheet (a collection of styles). A style is a named set of characteristics (formats) that are contained in a file called a cascading stylesheet (CSS). It's called "cascading" because the styles flow down from higher-level "parent" elements (such as body tags) to lower-level "child" element (such as paragraph tags). Child elements inherit the formatting of their parent elements.

By applying styles to text throughout your project, you can give your project a consistent look that is easy to change. If you need to change the formatting, you change it in one place—in the stylesheet—and the change is propagated everywhere the style is applied.

You can apply a stylesheet to a project to target or to a topic. When applied to a project, the styles are available for all project content.

When applied to a target, the styles are available for all target content.

> **Note** — If you use one master stylesheet for a project and another for a target, the stylesheet applied to the target takes precedence. The stylesheet applied to a topic takes precedence over the one applied to a target.

LOCAL FORMATTING VS. STYLES: WHICH TO USE

Both local formatting and styles are useful in different circumstances. Here's some information to help you decide which to use when.

Table 3-1: When to use local formatting vs. styles

Use this option ...	When ...
Local formatting	■ You want to apply the format to only one or two areas of text in one topic. (Applying lots of local formats increases the size of the underlying XML code, which means the browser might take longer to display the output.) ■ You don't need to use the same formatting in other topics or projects. ■ The formatting is not likely to change.
Style from a CSS	■ You want your topics to have a consistent appearance. ■ You want to use the same formatting in many places in the same or different topics. ■ You want to use the same formatting in different projects. ■ The formatting is likely to change.

FORMATTING TABLES

Besides local formatting and topic stylesheets, Flare gives you an additional option for formatting tables: table stylesheets. Table stylesheets allow you to define formatting patterns, such as shading on alternating rows or columns. Table stylesheets are an advanced topic not covered in this book.

So which option are you going to choose?

RECOMMENDATION

For your "throwaway" Flare project, start with local formatting. Then use the styles that Flare provides. When you're ready, try changing the properties of those styles as desired.

The default topic stylesheet (Styles.css) contains styles (table, th, td, and tr) for formatting table content.

> **Note** — For more detailed information about styles, see the *MadCap Flare Styles Guide*, available by selecting **Help** tab → **PDF Guides.** Click the link for the **Styles Guide**.

APPLYING LOCAL FORMATTING

You can apply formatting within a text block or to an entire block of text by using the Text Format toolbar or by changing the properties of the text you select or text block your cursor is in.

> **Tip** — To quickly remove inline formatting (including formatting applied with the Bold, Italic, and Underline buttons), select the text or text block and click
>
> **Unformat** ![Unformat icon] on the Home tab.

▶ To apply local formatting to selected text:

1. Select the text to apply the format to.

2. On the **Home** tab, select the desired toolbar button (Font Family, Font Size, Color, Background Color).

   > **Note** — Although the Bold, Italic, and Underline toolbar buttons add inline styles; they do not add local formatting because they are actually styles in your stylesheet.

▶ To apply local formatting to a text block (paragraph):

1. Place your cursor anywhere in the text block you want to format.

2. On the **Home** tab, click the **Paragraph** dialog box launcher button (lower right corner of the Paragraph section).

3. Change the properties as desired on the various tabs of the Paragraph Properties dialog.

Applying local formatting to tables

If you select "default" for the table style when you insert a table in a topic, your table will be formatted like this:

Figure 3-9:
Default
table style

Table header

Table rows

Most likely, you'll want to format the table for maximum readability (as well as for aesthetics). For example, you might add color to the background or to the text of your table's cells; or maybe you'd like the table header to be distinct from the table rows. You can apply formatting (color, borders, spacing) to tables by using buttons on the Text Format toolbar or by changing the properties of a table's text.

Here's an example of how you can dress up the table shown in Figure 3-9.

Figure 3-10:
Table after
formatting
with
color

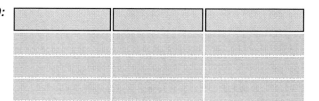

Use this procedure to format tables with local formatting.

▶ To apply local formatting to a table:

- Set the formatting for the text in a table's cells as described in this table:

To ...	Do this ...
Format all text in one cell	Click inside the cell you want to format, select the **Home** tab, and select applicable Font buttons (Font Family, Font Size, Color. etc.) or click the **Font** dialog box launcher button to open the Font Properties dialog.

To ...	Do this ...
Apply a background color to text	Select the text to apply the color to, select **Home** tab → **Background Color** button [icon] down arrow, and select a color from the chart.
Format selected text in one or more cells	Select the text to format, select **Home** tab, and select applicable Font buttons (Font Family, Font Size, Color. etc.) or click the Font dialog box launcher to open the Font Properties dialog.
Set the following for one or more cells: • Alignment of text • First line indentation • Line height • Borders and padding (spacing around cell text) • Hyphenation • Background properties	To format one cell, click inside the cell to be formatted. To format contiguous cells, select the cells. On the **Home** tab, select the Paragraph dialog box launcher (lower right corner of the Paragraph section). Then select characteristics from the Cell Properties dialog.

APPLYING STYLES FROM A STYLESHEET

Flare projects use two types of stylesheets:

- **Topic stylesheets** — to format content in your topics.

- **Table stylesheets** —for advanced formatting options such as shading on alternating rows and columns. (Table stylesheets are not covered in this book.)

Flare comes packaged with one topic stylesheet (**Styles)** and four table stylesheets (**Basic, Columns, Inner, Rows**). A Flare project can have multiple stylesheets of each type.

This book describes how to apply styles from a topic stylesheet to text in a topic (including text in tables). When you add a table, the *topic* styles "th" (table header) and "td" (table data) are automatically applied to your header and non-header rows. Changing those topic styles changes the look of your table text.

Figure 3-11:
Topic and Table Stylesheets in the Content Explorer

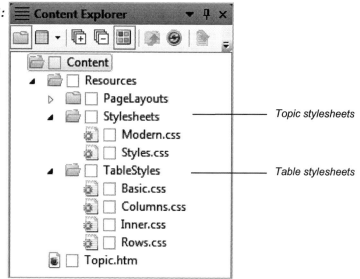

When you create a new Flare project, Flare automatically makes **Styles** the default topic stylesheet for the project. When you create a topic for that project, Flare automatically uses the project's default stylesheet for that topic, so its styles are automatically available for your use.

> **Important** — Flare does *not* automatically attach table stylesheets to projects. If you want to add a table stylesheet to your project, you can do that when you create a table.

Where do styles come from?

Flare stylesheets use the standard styles (like p and h1 – h6) and properties developed by the World Wide Web Consortium, plus special styles and properties defined by MadCap to support Flare features. MadCap styles begin with "MadCap" (for example, MadCap|xref) and MadCap properties begin with "mc" (such as mc-heading-format).

These styles are automatically included in every Flare stylesheet. You cannot delete standard or MadCap styles; however, you can disable them so they don't appear in the Stylesheet Editor's styles list. I don't recommend that new users disable styles.

> **Important** — Use caution if you disable styles as they will not be available for use in Flare (unless re-enabled).

Applying styles to text

There are different ways to apply a style to text in a topic. You can use the Style list on the Home ribbon, the Style window, the Floating Style Picker, or tag structure bars. This book will show you how to use the Home ribbon to apply styles.

For text blocks, the tag bar is labeled with the tag, which is named for the style that is applied to the text block ("h2" as shown here).

Tag bar ——

The style list also shows the style currently applied to the text block your cursor is in or the text currently selected.

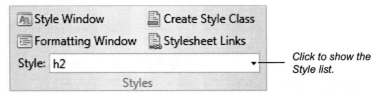

Click to show the Style list.

▶ To apply a style to selected text:

1. Select the text to apply the format to.

2. On the **Home** tab, from the **Styles** group, open the **Style** list and select the text style to apply.

▶ To apply a style to a text block:

1. Click anywhere in the text block where you want to apply a style.

2. On the **Home** tab, from the **Styles** group, open the **Style** list and select the text style to apply.

   The style you selected is applied to the text block and the text block's tag is changed to reflect the new style.

CUSTOMIZING STYLES

In this section, you'll learn how to customize styles in a topic stylesheet by using Flare's Stylesheet Editor. First, you'll see what's in a cascading stylesheet.

CASCADING STYLESHEETS

Stylesheet (CSS files) contain style rules that define how your content is formatted. Here's an example of a style rule for the "p" style:

```
p
{
    font-size: 10pt;
    font-family: Arial;
    line-height: 13pt;
    margin-top: 6pt;
    margin-bottom: 6pt;
}
```

Property — font-size: 10pt; — Value

margin-top: 6pt; — Declaration block

A style rule consists of a selector ("p" in this example) and one or more declaration blocks. A declaration block contains a property (such as "margin-bottom"), and a value ("6pt"), plus appropriate syntax (colons and semi-colon).

Style classes

If you want a custom version of a style, you'll use a style "class." A style class inherits its formatting from its parent. However, a style property assigned to a class overrides the same property if assigned to the parent.

Here's an example of a class of the p style:

```
p.note
{
        font-size: 9pt;
        margin-top: 3pt;
        margin-bottom: 3pt;
        padding: 3px;
        color: #004a6f;
        border-style: solid;
        border-width: 1px;
        border-color: #0080c0;
}
```

The class name is separated from its parent class with a period. The selector is "p.note" in this example. Notice that the style rule for p.note does not contain the property font-family. It inherited that style from its parent, the p style.

> **Note** — A Pseudo class is a special type of class used to format hypertext links in different states (active, hover, visited, etc.) or to format an initial cap or drop cap.

Here's what these two styles look like in our topic:

My Topic

This text block is formatted with the "p" style.

Note: This text block is formatted with the "p.note" style class.

WAYS TO CHANGE STYLES

There are two ways to change style rules in a stylesheet:

- Use Flare's Stylesheet Editor, which writes the style rules to the CSS file for you

- Use Flare's Text Editor to directly edit the style rules in a CSS file

This section discusses how to use the Stylesheet Editor. If you wish to edit style rules with Flare's Internal Text Editor, you'll need a good CSS reference. (Consider *Styling Web Pages with CSS*, by Tom Negrino and Dori Smith for an introduction to CSS, *CSS The Definitive Guide*, by Eric A. Meyer as a comprehensive reference, and *CSS to the point*, by Scott DeLoach as a quick reference.)

> **Note** — If you open a CSS file with the Text Editor, you won't see all of the styles listed in the Stylesheet Editor. You'll see only those styles whose values override default values. To override a style not shown in Text Editor, simply type the style rule with values for one or more properties.

CHANGING STYLES WITH THE STYLESHEET EDITOR

The Stylesheet Editor has two views: Simplified and Advanced. You'll switch between them by clicking [Simplified View] or [Advanced View]. In Simplified View, you'll use dialogs to change style formatting. In Advanced view, you'll assign values to CSS style properties.

> **Note** — Both Simplified View and Advanced View list every style. However Simplified View does not show every property of every style. It lists only the most common properties. In Advanced View you can see and change all properties.

The following procedure covers both views.

▶ To change a style with the Stylesheet Editor:

1. In the Content Explorer, expand the Resources and Stylesheets folders and double-click Styles.css (or the stylesheet you wish to change). The stylesheet opens in the Stylesheet Editor.

> **Important** — In the Stylesheet Editor, be sure to select the medium whose styles you want to change (such as "default" for online output and "print" for print output). If you don't see your style changes applied in your topic, you might have changed the styles in a different medium than the one you intended to change.

If you're in Simplified View, the 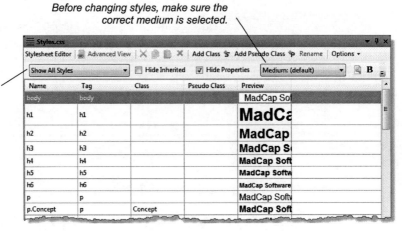 button is visible and you'll see this:

Before changing styles, make sure the correct medium is selected.

You can filter the list of styles with this button.

a. Double-click the style you want to change. A Properties dialog opens; showing tabs and options applicable only to the style you selected. Here is the Font tab of the Properties dialog for the p style:

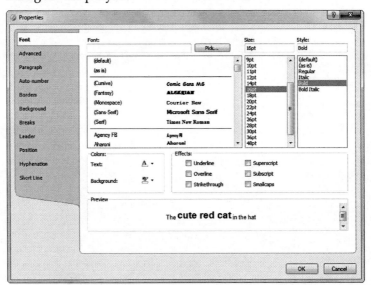

b. Change options on the Properties dialog as desired.

If you're in Advanced View, the 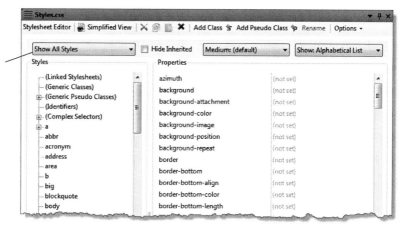 Simplified View button is visible. If "Show: Alphabetical List" was selected last, you'll see this:

You can filter the list of styles with this button.

If "Show: Property Groups" was selected last, you'll see this:

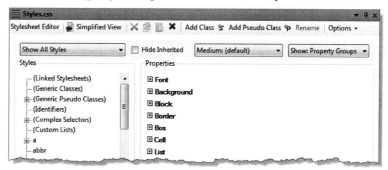

a.   In the left pane, expand the style you want to change. The left pane now lists that style's classes. The right pane shows the properties for that style.

b.   Select the style you want to change (the parent or one of its classes).

c.   In the right pane, click the field to the right of the property to set a value.

Here's what the Editor shows for the note example on page 149:

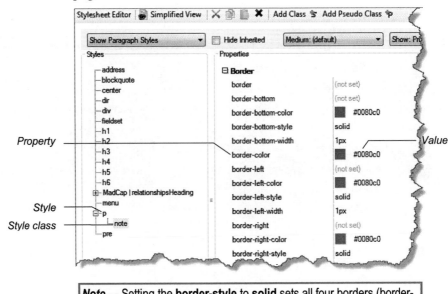

Note — Setting the **border-style** to **solid** sets all four borders (border-bottom-style, border-left-style, etc.) to solid. (The same is true for "border-color" and "border-width.")

2. Click **Save All** to save your work.

3. Close the Stylesheet Editor.

ADDING A STYLE CLASS

Adding a style class allows you to create a custom version of a style.

▶ To add a style class:

1. Open the applicable stylesheet in the Stylesheet Editor (in either Simplified or Advanced View).

2. Select the style you want to add the class to, and select Add Class.

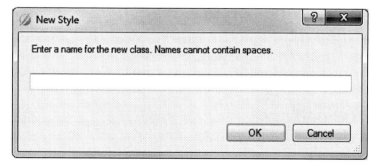

3. Type a name for the new class and click **OK**.

4. Set the formatting as desired for the new class.

5. Click **Save All** to save your work.

6. Close the Stylesheet Editor.

MARKING TEXT FOR REDACTION

Flare's text redaction feature is handy when you need to conceal confidential or sensitive information in printed output. For example, you might want to black-out names, social security numbers, account numbers, or financial data.

> **Note** — This feature applies only to PDF and XPS print output.

To redact text in print output, simply mark the text you want to redact and select a redaction method for your print output targets.

You choose when to conceal and when to reveal text

Marking text as redacted is especially useful when you want to *selectively* reveal sensitive information. Simply mark the sensitive information as redacted text, then create multiple targets and set the redaction method in each target to conceal or reveal the redacted text. The concealed text is replaced by black rectangles that show where information was contained.

What you can redact

You can redact any type of content: text (characters and entire paragraphs), images, and tables.

Formatting

You can format text for redaction using either local formatting or styles. You can create a character style to apply to selected text or a paragraph style to apply to a text block. As in other cases, if you need to redact only a small quantity of text, local formatting is fine; if you have a lot of text to redact, consider creating a style for text redaction.

▶ **To mark text for redaction with local formatting:**

1. Select the text to apply redaction to.

2. Select **Home** tab → **Redact** .

   The text you selected is highlighted in gray as shown here. It will be redacted when you build your output.

   > We expect the Pinewood project to generate approximately $350,000 in revenue the first year and $525,000 the second year. Initially, use cost accounting code 4325 for all expenses related to the Pinewood project.

   Text marked for redaction ——————————

3. Click **Save All** to save your work.

   Now that the text is marked, you'll select a method for displaying the redacted text in your output. You do this in the target you use to create the output.

   > **Note** — The target's output type must be PDF or XPS.

▶ To select the redaction method:

1. In the Project Organizer, expand **Targets** and double-click the desired PDF or XPS target. The Flare Target Editor opens.

2. Click the **Advanced** tab.

3. In the Redacted text section, select the redaction method to use for this target: **Blackout**, **Highlight**, or **Display as normal text** (no highlighting).

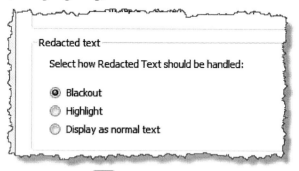

4. Click **Save All** 💾 to save your work.

When you build your output, your selection determines how the redacted text appears, as shown in these examples.

Figure 3-12: Redacted text — Blackout method

> We expect the Pinewood project to generate approximately $▮▮▮ in revenue the first year and $▮▮▮ the second year. Initially, use cost accounting code ▮ for all expenses related to the Pinewood project.

Figure 3-13: Redacted text — Highlight method

> We expect the Pinewood project to generate approximately $350,000 in revenue the first year and $525,000 the second year. Initially, use cost accounting code 4325 for all expenses related to the Pinewood project.

With the blackout option, the text is actually removed and replaced by black rectangles before Flare builds the output. Although the marked text is removed from the output, it still exists in your topic.

LEARN MORE

This section contains more information about the features you used in this chapter. Refer to it as needed.

THE INSERT TABLE DIALOG

The Insert Table dialog contains options for adding a table to a topic and for setting up the table's characteristics (number of columns, number of rows, table caption, etc.) It contains two tabs: **General** and **Borders**.

The General tab

The General tab contains options for setting the size of the table, its caption, its style, and how columns are sized.

Figure 3-14:
Insert Table dialog, General tab

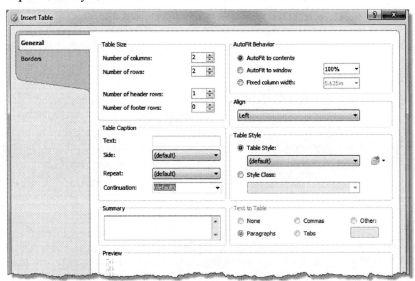

	In this section ...	Do the following ...
Table 3-2: Options on the Insert Table dialog, General tab	Table Size	Select the size of the table: • **Number of columns** — Select or type the number of columns. • **Number of rows** — Select or type the number of rows. • **Number of header rows** — Select or type the number of header rows. • **Number of footer rows** — Select or type the number of footer rows. (Helpful for entering footnotes about a table's contents.)
	AutoFit Behavior	Select the method for adjusting column width: • **AutoFit to contents** automatically adjusts the column width to fit the size of the text it contains and wraps the contents to fit the window size. *Note* — For best results, use the **AutoFit to contents** option. • **AutoFit to window** automatically adjusts the column width to fit the window size. • In the drop-down box to the right, if you enter a *percentage*, the table will fill up to that percentage of the window width (even if it means padding the end of a cell with blanks). If you select *automatic*, Flare will not pad the cells with blanks in order to fit the window width. If you set a *length*, the table will not resize wider than the number you set, regardless of the window width. • **Fixed column width** sets all columns to a fixed width, but automatically adjusts the column widths equally to fit the window if resized. To set the column width, open the list to the right of this field, click its down arrow and set the "length." *Note* — In the two drop-down boxes to the right, **default** returns to the default, which is "not set."
	Align	Select the table alignment: Left (default), Center, or Right.

Table 3-2:
(Cont.)

In this section ...	Do the following ...
Table Caption	If you want to add a table caption, type it in the **Text** field and select the position of the caption from the Side list (**Above table** or **Below table**). If the table continues on the next page, select **Repeat** to repeat the table caption. (The default is no repeat.) In the **Continuation** field, type the text (such as a space plus "(Continued)") you want to be appended to the caption text when it appears on subsequent pages.
Summary	To make your output more accessible to people with disabilities, type a summary for the table.
Table Style	▪ If you want to use a table stylesheet for this table, select **Table Style** and then select the table stylesheet from the list. ▪ To use table styles from a topic stylesheet, click **Style Class**. ▪ To create a new table stylesheet, click the icon part of this button . (This adds the style to the project and to the table you are creating.)
Text to Table	To convert text to a table, select the format (typically **Paragraphs**) of the text to be converted, and select the number of rows, columns and header rows.
Preview	Select to preview the table's style and the choices you made on this tab (such as table size and caption).

The Borders tab

The Borders tab contains options for applying and formatting borders around the cells of your table.

Figure 3-15:
Insert Table
dialog,
Borders tab

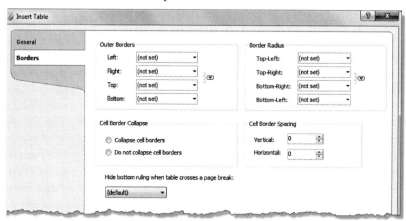

Table 3-3:
Options on
the Insert
Table dialog,
Borders tab

In this section ...	Do the following ...
Outer Borders	Set the borders for the Left, Right, Top, and Bottom of the table individually,
	- or -
	Set the same borders for the entire table by clicking the down arrow shown to the right of the border fields. In either case, this popup appears:

*Click here and select **Length** to set a line thickness.*   *Click to set the line color.*

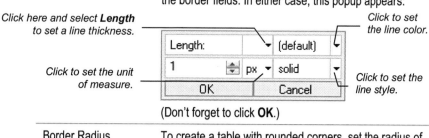

Click to set the unit of measure.   *Click to set the line style.*

(Don't forget to click **OK**.)

Border Radius	To create a table with rounded corners, set the radius of the Top-Left, Top-Right, Bottom-Right, and Bottom-Left corners of the table individually or for the entire table.

Set the top or bottom radius.   *Set the left or right radius.*

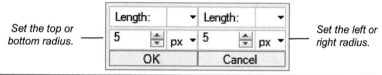

Table 3-3: *(Cont.)*	In this section ...	Do the following ...
	Cell Border Collapse	Select how you want inner borders to appear:
		▪ **Collapse cell borders** – Click this option to join the border lines between cells like this:
		▪ **Do not collapse cell borders** – Click this option to detach cell borders like this:
	Cell Border Spacing	Increase or decrease the Vertical and Horizontal space (in pixels) between your table cells. Applies only to borders that are not collapsed and tables that do not have outer borders.
	Hide bottom ruling when table crosses a page break	Select **True** to hide the bottom border when splitting a table between pages, or **False** to show the bottom border.

WHAT'S NEXT?

Now that you've formatted your content and added elements such as tables and images, it's time to think about how users will move around in your output. Proceed to Step 4: Create Navigation Aids, to learn about the navigation aids—TOCs, links, bookmarks, cross-references, and indexes—that you can add to your project.

Step 4:
Create
Navigation Aids

STEP 5: Create Output
5A: Print Output
5B: Online Output

STEP 4:
Create
Nav Aids

STEP 3:
Develop
Content

STEP 2:
Learn the
XML Editor

STEP 1:
Get Started

In this chapter ...

➤ Create a TOC
➤ Create links
➤ Create bookmarks
➤ Test links
➤ Add cross-references
➤ Create index entries
➤ Format a print index

OVERVIEW

This chapter discusses navigation aids that apply to both online and print output. To learn more about navigation aids that apply to online output only, see Step 5B: Create Online Output.

You can create these types of navigation aids with Flare:

- Table of Contents

- Links

- Cross-references

- Indexes

CREATING A TABLE OF CONTENTS

Flare's Table of Contents (TOC) feature is used for different purposes, depending on whether you're creating print or online output:

- **For online output,** users see the Flare TOC in the output. Users can use the TOC to browse for information and open topics.

- **For print output,** users *do not* see the Flare TOC in the output. Users see only the Table of Contents that Flare built from the headings in topics. With print output, the Flare TOC is used as a topic outline when you build output.

- **For DITA output,** the Flare TOC is used to create the DITAMAP file.

With either output, you decide which topics to include.

A TOC gives your topics structure and can be used to organize content and to work in that structure. With Flare, you can create a TOC in two ways:

- By creating your topics and TOC simultaneously

- By creating your topics, creating your TOC, and linking TOC entries to your topics

Regardless of the method you choose, creating your project's TOC is your first step in building output.

Flare TOC files have an .fltoc file extension.

MULTIPLE TOCs

Flare allows you to create multiple TOCs. Why would you do this?

Suppose you need two TOCs for output that will contain different topics, such as "full" and "light" versions. Or perhaps you plan to build both print and online output, and you want your print output to include an index and a TOC.

Flare always labels one as the Master TOC.

MASTER TOC

When you create a new project, Flare creates a default TOC, which automatically becomes the Master TOC and is named "Master." You'll see it listed like this in the Project Organizer:

Figure 4-1:
Master
TOC

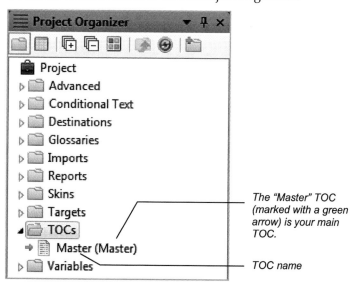

The "Master" TOC (marked with a green arrow) is your main TOC.

TOC name

Designating a TOC as "master" allows you to take advantage of the **Master TOC** button on the Project ribbon, and is useful for merging multiple TOCs into one. See "Linking TOCs" on page 166.

> *Note* — When you import a project, Flare creates a TOC that is named the same as the import file. This TOC is automatically designated as the Master TOC.

▶ **To designate a TOC as the master:**

1. In the Project Organizer, expand the TOCs folder and right-click the TOC file you want to make into the master.

2. Select **Make Master TOC**.

> *Best Practice* — Record the name of the Master TOC on the Target Settings form provided in Appendix A.

WHAT CAN A *TOC* ITEM LINK TO?

A TOC item can link to any of the following:

- a topic in the current project

- an external file (a file outside of the project where the TOC resides)—even a PDF file!

- another TOC

- a website

- a browse sequence

- a target in another Flare project

- an external Help system

- a CHM file (only if you're building HTML Help output)

- a MadCap Mimic™ movie

LINKING *TOCs*

It's typical to link TOC items to topics in the same project, but you can also link a TOC item to another TOC in order to merge the TOCs. For instance:

- If you share common content with other authors, you could create a TOC just for that content. Then you could share the TOC and its topics with the other authors.

- If multiple authors create topics that need to be merged for output, each author could create a TOC for their part of the output. A master TOC would link the TOCs to pull them together. (The TOCs would be merged when you build the output, and the result would be one seamless TOC.)

▶ **To see what a TOC item links to:**

- Hover your cursor over the TOC item. You will see what the item links to in the Content Explorer.

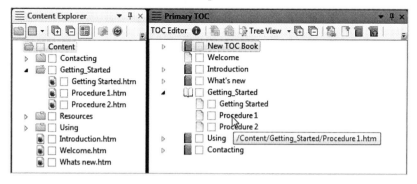

CREATING A TOC

You can create a TOC before you begin creating topics or at any time thereafter. You might find it faster to create a TOC and add TOC items and topics to your project simultaneously. However, if you prefer, you can add topics to your TOC later by simply dragging and dropping the topics from the Content Explorer.

▶ **To create a TOC:**

1. In the Project Organizer, right-click the **TOCs** folder and select **Add Table of Contents** from the menu.

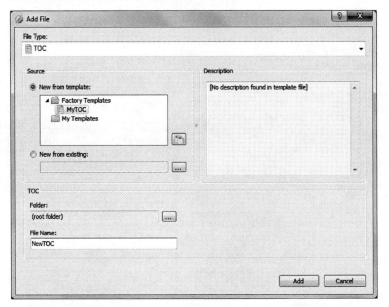

2. In the File Name field, type a name for the new TOC.

3. Click **Add**. The new TOC is listed in the TOCs folder and opens in the TOC Editor.

▶ **To open a TOC:**

- In the Project Organizer, expand the TOCs folder and double-click the desired TOC. The TOC Editor opens in the middle pane and shows the contents of the TOC.

▶ **To add topics to a TOC:**

- Drag and drop topics from the Content Explorer into the open TOC.

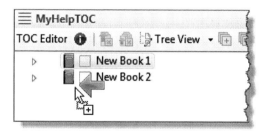

The text that appears in the TOC defaults to the topic title, which by default is the topic's first heading.

> **Note** — A topic title is one of the properties available for a TOC item. You can enter or change it in the Properties dialog.

OPENING A TOPIC OR THE PROPERTIES DIALOG

When you double-click a TOC item in a TOC, it will either open the topic in the XML Editor or open the Properties dialog for the topic. You control which action will occur with this button on the TOC Editor toolbar:

Toggle the double-click behavior: open topic or display properties

This button acts as a toggle between the two modes.

> **Note** — If you typically use one mode more than the other, you might set this button for the preferable mode and leave it set that way.

CREATING NEW BOOKS IN A TOC

TOC books provide a way to group topics into sections, similar to chapters in a book. Use them to organize your topics into a meaningful hierarchical structure. TOC books can link to the same things that TOC items can, or they can link to nothing at all.

▶ To create a new TOC book:

- Click **New book** in the TOC Editor toolbar.

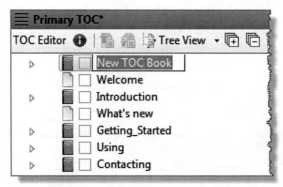

When you create a new TOC book, Flare automatically creates a new topic (called "New Entry") within it.

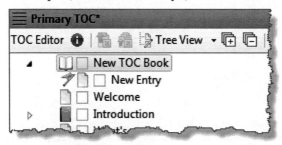

CREATING NEW *TOC* ITEMS

▶ To create a new TOC item:

1. Select the TOC folder or TOC item you want to add the item to.

2. Click **New item** in the TOC Editor toolbar.

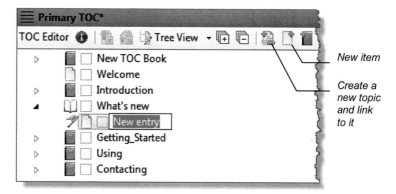

New item

Create a new topic and link to it

Notice that the new TOC item isn't linked to anything yet. You can link a TOC item to a topic at any time by right-clicking and selecting **Link to Topic**. Also, adding a TOC item to an existing TOC item changes the existing item into a TOC book.

Note — To create a TOC item and topic simultaneously and link the two, click **Create a new topic and link to it** instead of the **New item** button.

RENAMING A *TOC*

▶ **To rename a TOC:**

1. In the Project Organizer, expand the TOCs folder.

2. Right-click the desired TOC and select **Rename** from the menu.

3. Type the new name and press **ENTER**.

REARRANGING ITEMS AND BOOKS IN A *TOC*

Use the following buttons on the TOC Editor toolbar to move TOC books and items left, right, up, or down in the TOC. Moving books and items to the left and right changes their hierarchy in the TOC.

CREATING LINKS

Flare lets you add various types of links to your topics.

TYPES OF LINKS

A link allows users to quickly jump to additional or related information. You can create links to:

- topics or files inside or outside your project

- information in the same topic

Links can be created for online, print, and DITA output.

> **Note** — In Table 4-1, links in **boldface** are described in this book. Other types of links are described in Flare's Help system.

Table 4-1: Types of links

This link ...	Does this ...
Cross-reference	Jumps from text in one topic to another topic or bookmark within a topic. Cross-references can be used in online or print output, but they are especially useful for print output. Unlike text hyperlinks, cross-references can include commands for inserting elements like page numbers and topic titles. Cross-reference link text is updated by Flare when you build output. See ""Adding cross-references" on page 180 for more information.
Text hyperlink	Jumps to a specified location. See ""Creating text hyperlinks," next, for more information.
Text popup	Opens a popup that contains text you specify.
Topic popup	Opens a popup that contains another topic.
Bookmark	Jumps to a bookmark (a marker you create to identify a specific location in a topic). You can link to bookmarks in the same topic with a text hyperlink or in any topic with a cross-reference. See "Creating text hyperlinks," next, and "Creating bookmarks and linking to them" on page 177 for more information.
External link	Links to a file outside your project.
Image hyperlink	Opens a link associated with an image.

Table 4-1: (Cont.)	This link ...	Does this ...
	Movie link	Opens a link that plays a movie created with MadCap Mimic, Adobe Flash, Windows Media, or Apple QuickTime.
	Audio link	Opens a link that plays an audio file created with MadCap Echo, Adobe Flash, Windows Media, or Apple QuickTime.
	Toggler	Hides and shows a piece of content. When a user clicks a "toggler hotspot," tagged content is shown or hidden (toggled).
	Drop-down text	Hides and shows a piece of content as a list. When a user clicks this type of link, content is displayed below the link.
	Expanding text	Hides and shows a portion of a paragraph. When a user clicks this type of link, the condensed paragraph is expanded for viewing.
	Concept link ("See Also" or "A-link")	Opens a group of topics related to the current topic.
	Related Topics link	Opens a topic related to the current topic. See "Creating related topics links" on page 176 for more information.
	Relationship Table	Organizes related topics by category (such as related tasks, related concepts, and related reference topics) by placing links in your online output or cross-references in your print output. Although often used with DITA, you don't need to create DITA output to use a relationship table. For more information, search for "relationship tables" in Flare's Help.
	Keyword link ("K-link")	Opens topics related to the current topic by using index keywords shared by both.
	Shortcut control	Launches an application program or window with a relationship to the current topic.

CREATING TEXT HYPERLINKS

A text hyperlink is a commonly used type of link that enables a user to jump to another location, such as a:

- file in the current project

- place in the current topic (heading, bookmark, or top of topic)

- place in a different topic (heading, bookmark, or top of topic)

- topic or file outside your project

- topic in a CHM file (only if you're building HTML Help output)

- website

> **Note** — You can also set up an email address as a text hyperlink. When a user clicks the link, his or her email application opens with an email address in the "To" field.

▶ To insert text hyperlinks:

1. Open the topic in which to insert the link.

2. In the topic, select the text you want to use as the link (the hotspot).

3. Select **Insert** tab → **Hyperlink** or click **Insert a hyperlink** 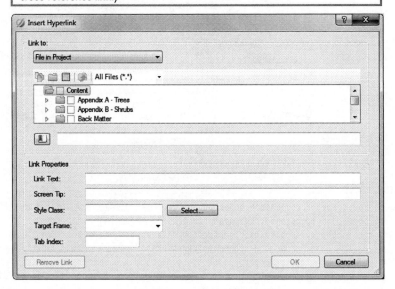 in the XML Editor toolbar.

> **Tip** — You can also insert a hyperlink by dragging and dropping the topic from the Content Explorer into the topic. (If web layout mode is displayed, this creates a text hyperlink; if print layout mode is displayed, this creates a cross-reference link.)

4. Select an option in the **Link to** drop-down use the following chart as a guide.

Use this option ...	To ...
File in Project	Link to a file or bookmark in the project. After selecting this option, click the file you want to link to, which can be a topic, an image, or other file types, or click **Bookmark** and select a location in the document. *Note* — To change the Content Explorer view and the types of files shown, use the options in the Link to section of the dialog.
Place in this Document	Link to the top of the topic or a heading or bookmark within it. After selecting this option, use the hierarchy displayed to select the place in the topic to link to.
External File	Link to a topic or file (such as a PDF file) outside the project. After selecting this option, click ⌐...⌐ then find and open the file you want to link to. The topic's path name appears on the Insert Hyperlink dialog. *Important* — To be sure that your output will link properly to the file, place a copy of the file in your project's Content folder before linking to it. Files located elsewhere (such as in the project folder) are not copied to the output folder.
Website	Link to an external file, such as a website URL. After selecting this option, enter the complete URL (including the http://) in the Website field.
Email	Link to an email address. After selecting this option, enter the email address and subject in the appropriate fields or select a recent email address. For information about when this could be used, see Flare's Help system.
HTML Help File	Link to a topic in a CHM file. (*Applies only when creating HTML output.*)

5. Use the following chart to choose optional link properties (listed in the Link Properties section of this dialog).

Use this option ...	To ...
Link text	Change the text that was selected as a link in the topic.
Screen Tip	Specify text that appears when users hover the cursor over the link.
Style Class	To select a link style to apply to the link text.
Target Frame	Select how the linked destination will open (such as in a new window).

6. Click **OK**. The link is added to the topic. (By default, links appear as blue underlined text.)

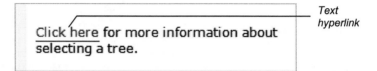

Text
hyperlink

Click here for more information about selecting a tree.

CREATING RELATED TOPICS LINKS

With related topics links, users can view information that is relevant to the current topic. Related topics links are similar to "See also" in a book index.

▶ **To insert a related topics link:**

1. Open the topic in which you want to insert the link.

2. Click in the topic where the link will be inserted (typically the bottom of the topic).

3. Select **Insert** tab → **Related Topics Control** (in the Help Control group).

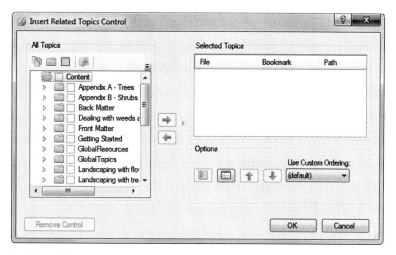

4. In the All Topics section, click a topic you want to add to the related topics link and click 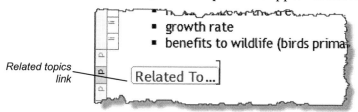. The topic is added to the Selected Topics list on the right. Repeat this step for each topic you want to add to the link.

5. Click **OK**. The link is added to the topic. (If Show Markers is turned on, related topics links appear as shown here.)

- growth rate
- benefits to wildlife (birds prima

Related topics link → Related To...

Best Practice — Apply an "online only" condition tag to the text block that contains the related topic link to prevent it from appearing as an extra line in print output. (When you build print output, Flare automatically removes Help control links from your topics, since they don't apply to print output.)

CREATING BOOKMARKS AND LINKING TO THEM

Bookmarks allow you to place a marker in a topic so you can link to that text from within the topic or from another topic. First, you insert the bookmark, then you insert links to it.

▶ To insert a bookmark:

1. Click in the topic where you want to insert the bookmark (typically at the beginning of a paragraph or heading).

2. Select **Insert** tab → **Bookmark**.

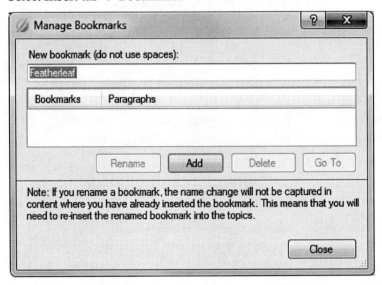

3. In the New bookmark field, type a bookmark name (without any spaces). If you clicked at the beginning of a text block, Flare places the block's first word in the New bookmark field.

4. Click **Add**. Flare marks the location with a bookmark icon and the bookmark name.

Bookmark ————

▶ **To insert a link to a bookmark:**

1. In the XML Editor, place your cursor where you want to insert the link.

2. Select **Insert** tab → **Hyperlink** or click **Insert a hyperlink** in the XML Editor toolbar.

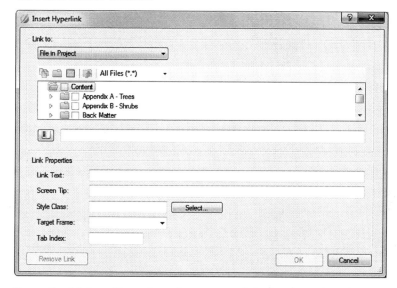

3. From the Link to list, select the source of the bookmark (**File in Project** or **Place in this Document**). Then select the file that contains the bookmark.

4. If the source is "Place in this Document," select the bookmark from the list of bookmarks in the current document.

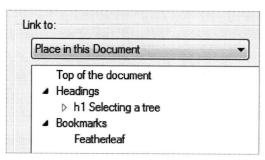

5. If the source is "File in Project," select the file that contains the bookmark, then click 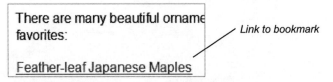 and select the bookmark from the Select Bookmark dialog.

6. Click **OK**. The link is added to the topic. (By default, links appear as blue underlined text.)

> There are many beautiful orname
> favorites:
>
> Feather-leaf Japanese Maples
>
> — Link to bookmark

TESTING YOUR LINKS

You can test your links as you develop project content or test them all after you build your output. The choice is yours.

There are two ways to test your links. You can:

- Build your output, view it, and click on each link to be sure that it jumps to the proper location (topic, bookmark, URL, email address, etc.). Test your links in every topic.

- Preview a topic in the XML Editor and click on each link in that topic. See "Previewing a topic" on page 57.

ADDING CROSS-REFERENCES

Like a text hyperlink, a cross-reference lets a user jump to a topic or bookmark in a topic. But unlike text hyperlinks, cross-references have more formatting options and can include commands for inserting items such as page numbers and topic titles in the result.

ABOUT COMMANDS

Using commands allows Flare to automatically update cross-references when the destination's title, page number etc., change.

Let's see how commands work. Suppose you create a cross-reference to a topic that includes a title and page number:

See "Adding an account" on page 23.

If you change the topic title to "Adding a user account" and build your output, Flare automatically updates the cross-reference with the new title:

See "Adding a user account" on page 23.

> **Important** — If you change a topic's title, Flare updates cross-references to it.

CROSS-REFERENCES IN PRINT AND ONLINE OUTPUT

You can add cross-references to print and online output. By using stylesheet mediums, you can create one cross-reference format for online output (e.g., without page numbers) and another for print output (e.g., with page numbers).

> **Tip** — The advantage of using cross-references instead of text hyperlinks in online output is that the text part of the link is updated when you build output.

When you create a new project, Flare creates three stylesheet mediums:

- Default

- Print

- Non-print

Cross-references use the MadCap:xref style. For the **default** and **non-print** mediums, the MadCap:xref style is set to:

See "{paratext}"

For the **print** medium, the MadCap:xref style is set to:

See "{paratext}" on page {page}

> **Note** — To use the cross-reference style defined by the print medium, select the print medium on the Advanced tab when you set up your target for print output. For more information about using mediums, see "What are mediums?" on page 92.

INSERTING A CROSS-REFERENCE

▶ ## To insert a cross-reference:

1. Open the topic in which to insert the cross-reference.

2. In the XML Editor, place your cursor where you want to insert the cross-reference.

3. Select **Insert** tab → **Cross-Reference** or click in the XML Editor's top toolbar.

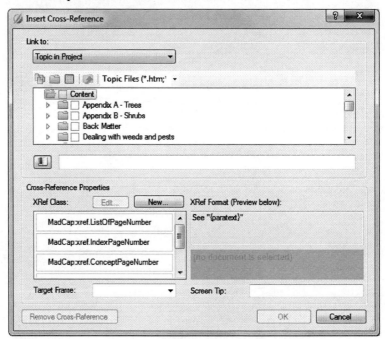

4. Select what you want to link to:

To link to ...	Do this ...
A heading or bookmark in another topic in the open project	From the "Link to" list, select **Topic in Project**. Select the topic file you want to link to and click **Bookmark**. From the Select Bookmark dialog, select the heading or bookmark you want to cross-reference.

To link to ...	Do this ...
A heading or bookmark in the current topic	From the "Link to" list, select **Place in this document**. Then select the heading or bookmark you want to cross-reference.

This example shows the Insert Cross-Reference dialog after choosing a cross-reference to a topic in the open project.

Cross-reference format for default medium 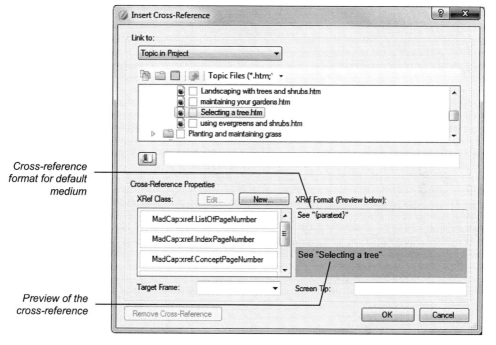 *Preview of the cross-reference*

The preview format you see depends on the medium currently selected in the XML Editor. Notice the XRef Format (See "{paratext}"). This is the format for the default medium. The format for the print medium is: See "{paratext}" on page {page}.

5. (*Optional*) From the Target Frame list, select an option for opening the linked file. If you don't select an option, the topic opens in the same window as the topic that contains the cross-reference.

6. (*Optional*) In the Screen Tip field, type the phrase you want to appear when a user hovers the cursor over the cross-reference in the output.

7. Click **OK**. The cross-reference is added to the topic.

> For information about varieties of trees, See "Selecting a tree."

8. Click **Save All** 💾 to save your work.

CHANGING CROSS-REFERENCES

You can change a cross-reference by:

- Changing the file it links to

- Changing the target frame (how the linked topic opens in the output)

- Entering or changing the screen tip

- Changing the format of the cross-reference style, which changes the format for all cross-references that use that style.

Changing a single cross-reference

Use the following procedure to change the linked file, target frame, or screen tip of a single cross-reference.

▶ **To change a single cross-reference:**

1. Open the topic that contains the cross-reference you want to change.

2. Right-click the cross-reference and select **Edit Cross-Reference**. The Insert Cross-Reference dialog appears.

3. Change the cross-reference as described in Steps 4 – 8 of the procedure for inserting a cross-reference (page 182).

Changing the format of a cross-reference style

There are two ways to change the format of a cross-reference style. Both methods *change the style in your stylesheet*. You can:

- Open a topic that contains a cross-reference that uses the style you want to change, and edit the style.

- Open the Stylesheet Editor and change the MadCap:xref style (or MadCap:xref style class, if you've created one).

You'll learn the first method here. To learn about the Stylesheet Editor, see "Changing styles with the Stylesheet Editor" on page 151.

▶ To change the format of a cross-reference style:

1. Open any topic that contains a cross-reference with the style you want to change.

2. Right-click the cross-reference and select **Edit Cross-Reference**. The Insert Cross-Reference dialog appears.

3. In the Cross-Reference Properties section, select the <MadCap:xref> style you want to change and click **Edit**.

> **Note** — These instructions show you how to change the format of the MadCap:xref tag. If you create your own cross-reference style (a class of the MadCap:xref tag) and want to change it, select it instead.

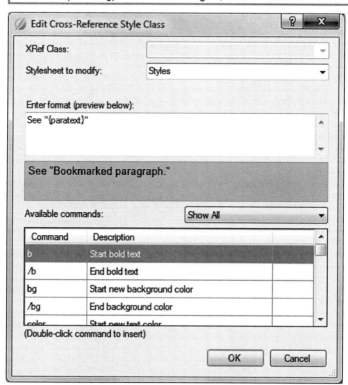

4. In the Stylesheet to modify field, select the stylesheet you want
    to change.

> **Important** — These steps change the MadCap:xref style in all three
> mediums (default, print, and non-print) for the stylesheet you select. (For
> more information about mediums, see "What are mediums?" on page 92.)

5. In the Enter format field, change the format as desired.

To insert ...	Do this ...
Text (e.g., "See" or "on page")	Type the text in the Enter format field.
A command	<ul><li>Click in the Enter format field where you want to insert the command.</li><li>In the Available commands list, locate and double-click the command you want to insert.</li></ul> **Note** — For commands such as adding boldface, you'll need to insert *both* a start and end tag into the Enter format field.

6. Click **OK**, then **Yes** to confirm that you want to redefine the
    existing style. The Insert Cross-Reference dialog shows your
    changes.

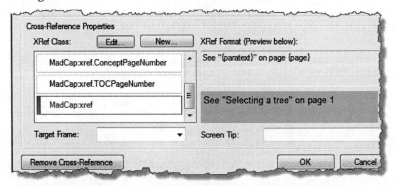

> **Note** — When you change a cross-reference style, you might not see the
> format change until you update the cross-reference.

UPDATING CROSS-REFERENCES MANUALLY

Updating cross-references manually is optional because Flare does this automatically when you build your output. However, you can update the appearance (format) and content of cross-references in the active topic at any time.

> **Tip** — When you change the format of a cross-reference, it's helpful to see what it looks like without building your output.

▶ **To update cross-references manually:**

1. Open the topic that contains the cross-reference you want to update.

2. Select **Tools** tab → **Update Cross-References**. The Update Cross-References dialog appears, listing all cross-references in the active topic.

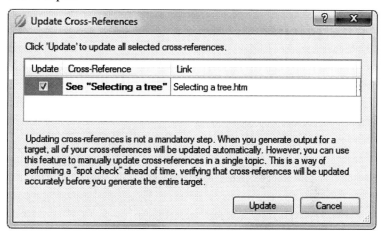

3. Click **Update**. The cross-references are updated in the active topic. Both the format and the content are updated.

ADVANCED FEATURES

You can do more with cross-references, such as:

- Creating context-sensitive cross-references in which the cross-reference link text reflects its proximity to the linked output if it appears on the same, previous, or next page.

- Using stylesheet mediums to format a cross-reference differently for print and online output. For example, a cross-reference can appear as "See 'Adding an account'" in your online output and "See 'Adding an account' on page 56" in your print output.

- Creating classes of the MadCap|xref style.

- Adding format commands.

To learn more about these features, search on "cross-references" in the Flare Help system.

CREATING INDEX ENTRIES

Index entries are created in the same way, whether you're using them for print or online output. To create index terms, you must add index keywords to your topics before building your output. The keywords are added right in the topics.

> **Tip** — You can make index keywords conditional (by applying a condition tag) so that you can include only index terms applicable to the desired target. See the procedure called "To add index terms with Index Entry mode" on page 189.

ADDING INDEX KEYWORDS

Here are two ways to add index keywords:

- Use Index Entry mode to add phrases and multi-level keywords to the open topic

- Use the lower portion of the Index window to add phrases and multi-level keywords and to assign topics to keywords

You might use a combination of these methods, depending on your needs.

This chart describes when each method might be helpful.

Table 4-2:
When to use each method

Use this option ...	When ...
Index Entry mode	<ul><li>You want to add index entries to snippets.</li><li>The index entry must be positioned close to the content it references (not at the top of the topic).</li><li>You want to add multiple index keywords to the same index marker.</li></ul>
Index window "Explorer" (the lower portion of the Index window)	<ul><li>The topic is not open.</li><li>You want to add the same index marker to multiple topics.</li><li>You want the index term to be placed at the beginning of a topic.</li><li>The top-level term already exists in the index and you want to add a second-level entry to it.</li></ul>

No matter which method you use to create index entries, the terms are added to the applicable topic within an index code marker.

> *Tip* — Index Entry mode opens the Index window. Once open, you can either type terms in the boxes at the top of the window, or you can enter terms in the index hierarchy at the bottom.

▶ To add index terms with Index Entry mode:

1. Open the topic you want to insert index keywords into.

2. Click **Toggle Index Entry Mode** in the XML Editor's top toolbar.

    The cursor changes to an index entry symbol, as shown here:

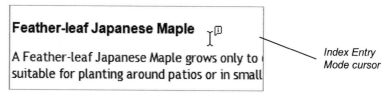

3. Click in the topic where you want to place an index entry.

4. Type the index keyword or phrase.

The Index window opens and shows your entry as you type it.

5. Press **ENTER**. The index entry is placed in your topic and the cursor moves to the next blank line at the top of the Index window. (If markers are visible, the marker appears where you clicked.)

> *Tip* — To turn on markers, see "Viewing index keywords" on page 195.

Index keyword (markers are turned on)

Feather-leaf Japanese Maple

A Feather-leaf Japanese Maple Japanese M... grows only to 6 feet tall, and is quite suitable for

6. To add more keywords to the same index marker, type a keyword on the next line and press **ENTER**. Continue adding index keywords to the same marker, as desired.

> *Note* — To create a multi-level index entry, separate the levels by a colon in the Index window. In the example above, "trees:selecting" causes the term "selecting" to be listed under "trees" in the index.

Two-level index keyword

Feather-leaf Japanese Maple

trees:select... A Feather-leaf Japanese Maple Japanese M... grows only to 6 feet tall, and is quite suitable for planting around patios or in small spaces.

7. When you're done adding entries to the index marker, click your cursor in a different spot in the topic to add another index marker.

8. When you're done adding index markers to the open topic, click **Toggle Index Entry Mode** ⊞ again, then click anywhere in the topic. Now you'll be able to continue editing in the XML Editor.

9. (*Optional*) When you're done adding index entries, close the Index window.

> ***Tip*** — You can also right-click a marker to copy it and paste it somewhere else. Then right-click the pasted marker and select **Edit Index Keyword** to revise it in the Index window.

▶ To add index terms in the Index window Explorer:

1. Open the topic you want to insert index keywords into.

2. Select **View** tab → **Index Window**.

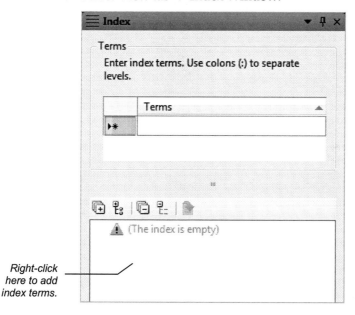

Right-click here to add index terms.

3. If the index already has some entries, right-click **Index**. If it has no entries, right-click **The index is empty**.

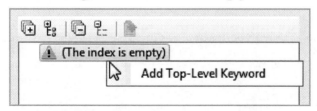

4. Select **Add Top-Level Keyword**. Flare adds a new term to the index with a temporary name ("NewTerm").

Top-level index keyword ——

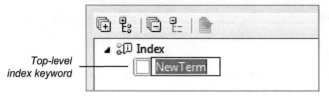

5. Type the text for the top level index term.

6. To add a sub-keyword (a second-level entry), right-click the top-level entry and select **Add Sub-Keyword**.

Sub-keyword ——

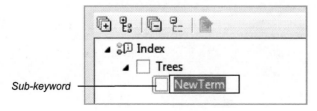

7. Type the text for the sub-keyword.

Here is an index with a few more index entries. (They have not yet been assigned to topics.)

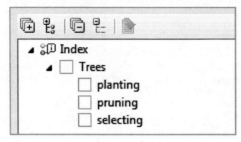

8. To assign a topic to an entry at any level, right-click the entry and select **Assign Topic**.

9. Select the file you want to assign to this index entry and click **Open**.

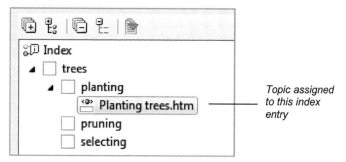

Topic assigned to this index entry

Flare places the index code marker at the beginning of the assigned topic:

Index entry in the assigned topic

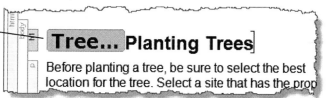

If you hover your cursor over the index marker, you'll see that "Trees:planting" is the keyword for this index entry.

This example shows two topics assigned to the same index entry:

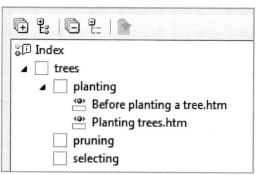

10. (*Optional*) When you're done adding index entries, close the Index window.

APPLYING CONDITION TAGS TO INDEX ENTRIES

Applying a condition tag to an index entry marker applies it to all of that marker's keywords. Just like with topic content, index entries that are tagged with condition tags can be excluded from your output. If excluded, the index is created without those entries.

▶ **To apply a condition tag to an index entry:**

1.   Open the topic that contains the index entry you want to apply a condition tag to.

2.   Right-click the index marker and select **Conditions** from the menu.

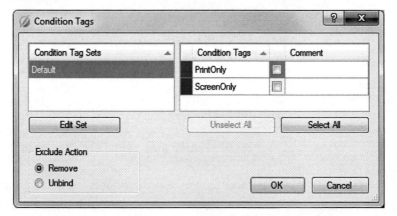

3.   Select the checkboxes for the condition tag (or tags) you want to apply to the index marker. The condition tag is applied to the marker and the color associated with that condition tag is shown on the marker in the topic.

Index marker with a condition tag applied

> ## Feather-leaf Japanese Maple
>
> ■ Trees:Japan... A Feather-leaf Japanese Maple grows only to 6 feet tall, and is quite suitable for planting around patios or in small spaces.

> **Note** — To learn more about condition tags, see "Using condition tags" on page 344.

VIEWING INDEX KEYWORDS

To see index keywords in a topic, you must have markers turned on.

▶ **To turn on markers:**

- Click the arrow on the **Show tags** button in the XML Editor's top toolbar, and select **Show Markers**.

CHANGING AND DELETING INDEX KEYWORDS

You can change the text of a marker's index keywords and remove keywords from a marker.

▶ **To change or remove a word from an index keyword:**

1. Open the topic that contains the keyword you want to change or remove. (If markers aren't visible, show them as described above.)

2. Right-click the marker to be changed and select **Edit Index Keyword** from the menu. The Index window opens and shows the keywords contained in that marker.

3. Change or remove keywords as desired and press **ENTER**. Close the Index window when finished.

DELETING INDEX MARKERS

You can delete entire index markers, but **use caution** when doing so because this removes all keywords contained in that marker.

> **Note** — This procedure applies to all markers, not just index markers.

▶ **To delete an index marker:**

1. Open the topic that contains the index marker to be deleted. (If markers aren't visible, show them as described above.)

2. Right-click the marker to be deleted and select **Delete** from the menu.

HOW INDEX ENTRIES APPEAR IN ONLINE OUTPUT

The index terms you add to your topics are shown in online output when you click the **Index** accordion bar. Index terms open the topics in which they were inserted. In the figures that follow, notice that "trees:selecting" was entered as the index keyword, which results in a two-level index entry for selecting trees.

Figure 4-2:
Index in
online
output

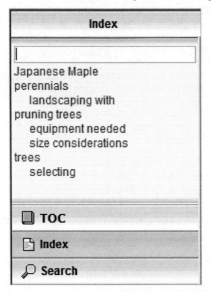

HOW INDEX ENTRIES APPEAR IN PRINT OUTPUT

The index terms you add to your topics are shown in print output as a traditional index.

Here's an example of a print index:

Figure 4-3:
*Index in
print
output*

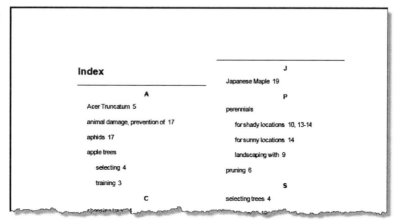

As the previous figure shows, index entries that contain multiple pages are shown as a range of pages separated by a dash. By default, index term and page numbers are left-aligned.

FORMATTING A PRINT INDEX

You can format your index with styles by using Flare's Stylesheet Editor, or by adding style rules to your stylesheet (your CSS file). This is an advanced skill to learn after you've learned Flare basics.

To complete the following tasks, you'll use the Stylesheet Editor. (See "Changing styles with the Stylesheet Editor" on page 151.) Make sure you save the stylesheet after you're done changing index styles.

> *Tip* — If "Advanced View" appears to the right of the Editor name, the editor is in Simplified View. Click **Advanced View** to open it.

Here are some of the ways to format your index:

Table 4-3: Examples of index formatting

To ...	Do this ...
Remove the line above the index columns	1. Open your stylesheet in the Stylesheet Editor in Advanced View. 2. Click the **MadCap | indexProxy** style. If not already selected, select **Show: Alphabetical List** from the list in the right pane. 3. In the right pane, scroll to the "border-top-style" property and click the field to its right. 4. Select **None** from the list.
Set the separator between the index term and page numbers	1. Open your stylesheet in the Stylesheet Editor in Advanced View. 2. Click the **MadCap | indexProxy** style. If not already selected, select **Show: Alphabetical List** from the list in the right pane. 3. In the right pane, scroll to the "mc-reference-initial-separator" property and click the field to its right. 4. Type the separator characters (such as a comma followed by a space).
Left (or right) align index headings **Note** — Index headings are centered by default.	1. Open your stylesheet in the Stylesheet Editor in Simplified View. 2. Scroll to and double-click the **p.IndexHeading** style. 3. On the Properties dialog, click the **Paragraph** tab. 4. Select the alignment as desired (**Left** or **Right**).
Change the spacing before or after index entries and index headings	1. Open your stylesheet in the Stylesheet Editor in Simplified View. 2. Double-click the style you wish to change (such as **p.Index1** or **p.IndexHeading**). 3. On the Properties dialog, click the **Paragraph** tab. 4. In the Spacing section, under Before and After, select **Length**, then set the spacing in the desired unit of measure (Point, Pixel, Inch, etc.).

Table 4-3:
(Cont.)

To ...	Do this ...
Wrap long index entries to the next line	1. Open your stylesheet in the Stylesheet Editor in Advanced View. 2. Scroll to and double-click the index style you want to change (such as **p.Index1**). 3. If not already selected, select **Show: Alphabetical List** from the list in the right pane. 4. In the right pane, scroll to the "white-space" property. (It's near the bottom of the list.) Click the field to its right. 5. Select **normal** from the list. 6. Repeat Steps 2 – 5 for each index style to be changed (p.Index2, p.Index3, etc.).
Change the font or font size of index headings and entries	1. Open your stylesheet in the Stylesheet Editor in Simplified View. 2. Scroll to and double-click the applicable style (**p.IndexHeading** or **p.Index1** for example). 3. On the Properties dialog, click the **Font** tab. 4. Select the desired font and font size.

Here's how a print index might look after changing the default formatting:

Figure 4-4:
A PDF
index
with
formatting
applied

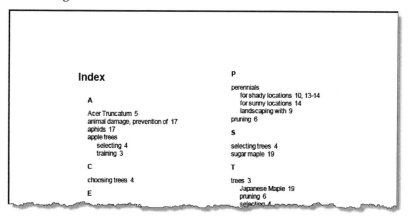

WHAT'S NEXT?

Now your Flare project is ready to be built into output. Refer to:

- Step 5A: Create Print Output (which includes PDFs)

- Step 5B: Create Online Output

- Appendix G: DITA Import and Export

- Appendix H: Create EPUB Output

You're almost there!

Step 5A: Create Print Output

STEP 5: Create Output
5A: Print Output
5B: Online Output

STEP 4: Create Nav Aids

STEP 3: Develop Content

STEP 2: Learn the XML Editor

STEP 1: Get Started

In this chapter …

➤ Learn about types of print output
➤ Create a simple print document
➤ Make upfront decisions
➤ Include front and back matter
➤ Discover page layouts
➤ Build your output

OVERVIEW

In this chapter, you'll learn how to build the following types of print output:

- Microsoft Word

- Adobe FrameMaker

- Adobe PDF

- Microsoft XPS

- XHTML

> *Note* — If you're unfamiliar with terms and concepts such as *output, build, distribute* and *target,* refer to the Document Basics chapter.

When you build print output, Flare puts the print output files in a folder in your project directory. You can then distribute those files to others. The type and number of files Flare creates depends on the type of print output you build.

KEEPING TRACK OF PRINT OUTPUT

To make it easier to track various targets and types of output, this book includes a Target Settings form (see Appendix A). As you learn to create more targets for your output, you'll find it very helpful to record the names of various Flare project files.

Keep a copy of this form handy as you proceed through this chapter and begin making it a habit to fill it out.

TYPES OF PRINT OUTPUT

This section describes the various types of print output, plus information about viewing and distributing your output.

Microsoft Word output

You can build Microsoft Word documents in DOC, XML, or DOCX format as long as you have Word installed locally or have a subscription to Microsoft Office 365.

> **Important** — If you're using only Microsoft Office 365, you must first select **File** tab → **Options** → **General** tab → **Import/Export Word Files Without MS Office** checkbox. The Word documents would be in DOCX format.

By default, Flare creates a DOC file if you have MS Word 2003 and an XML file if you have MS Word 2007 or later. Output is saved in a single file unless you set up the target to build multiple files.

> **Note** — If you want Flare to create a Word Table of Contents or an index, the content *must* be contained in a single file.

Distributing Word output

When you build your Word output, Flare does not *automatically* embed images into the DOC, DOCX, or XML file. Instead, it stores the images in the Resources\Images folder (located in a sub-folder of the Output folder). When you distribute your Word output, you must include the DOC, DOCX, or XML file *plus* the contents of the Resources folder. However, you can easily embed images into the document file so you can distribute it without the Resources folder. Just double-click your Word target in the Project Organizer, click the **Advanced** tab, and select **Embed images in output**.

> **Best Practice** — Keep this option enabled for all your Word targets.

Adobe FrameMaker output

You can create FrameMaker documents for Adobe FrameMaker 7.0 and later versions in BOOK and FM formats. FrameMaker output is saved as multiple files, which consist of a BOOK file with associated FM files.

> **Tip** — If you want to save FrameMaker output in a single file, see the topic "Specifying Chapter Breaks and Page Layouts" in the Flare Help system.

Distributing FrameMaker output

When you distribute FrameMaker output, you must include the BOOK and FM files *plus* the contents of the Resources folder (located in a sub-folder of the Output folder). The Resources folder contains ancillary files, such as the images you've inserted into your topics.

ADOBE *PDF* OUTPUT

You can build PDF output by itself or with Microsoft Word or Adobe FrameMaker output. The output is saved in a single PDF file.

Distributing PDF output

The PDF file is the only file you need to distribute.

MICROSOFT *XPS* OUTPUT

XPS (XML Paper Specification) is a fixed layout, device-independent document format developed by Microsoft. You can build XPS output by itself or simultaneously with Microsoft 2007 output. XPS output is saved in a single XPS file.

Table 5A-1:
Building
XPS
output

To build XPS output ...	You must have ...
By itself	.NET Framework installed on your computer (included in Vista, Windows 7, and Windows 8, also a free download from Microsoft).
Simultaneously with Microsoft 2007 output	Microsoft Word 2007 – and – the "Save as XPS" add-in for Microsoft Office 2007 installed on your computer (a free download from Microsoft).

Viewing XPS output

You can view XPS output from within Flare or externally by opening the XPS output file.

Distributing XPS output

The XPS file is the only file you need to distribute.

XHTML OUTPUT

XHTML is a browser-based XML document format that you can view online or print. Regardless of the number of topics, XHTML output is saved in a single file with an .htm extension.

Distributing XHTML output

When you distribute your output, you must include the HTM file *plus* the contents of the Resources folder. The Resources folder contains ancillary files, such as the images you've inserted into your topics.

BEFORE CREATING PRINT OUTPUT

Before you create print output, you should do the following:

- **Create your project**. You can build print output from any Flare project. To create the project, see "Creating a Flare project" on page 47.

- **Create and format your content**. You create and format content for print output as you would for any other output as described in Step 2: Learn the XML Editor, and Step 3: Develop Content.

- **Add navigation aids**. Use Step 4: Create Navigation Aids, to add cross-references, links, and index entries.

- **Verify that you have a target for the type of print output you want to create**. If not, add the target. See "Adding a target" on page 65.

WHAT YOU CAN INCLUDE IN A PRINT DOCUMENT

Your print output can contain any of the following front and back matter parts, which you'll learn more about later in this chapter:

- Table or Contents

- index

- glossary

- endnotes

- list of elements

- list of concepts

> ## Decision Time!
>
> Before you continue, think about the document parts your output must contain, how it should be oriented, and its size.
>
> ✓   Which front or back document parts do you need?
>
> ✓   How should the print output be oriented (portrait, landscape, or a combination of both)?
>
> ✓   What size does your document need to be (letter, legal, A5, or custom)?
>
> Appendix A contains detailed planning worksheets to help you record your decisions.

Recommendation

In this chapter, you'll learn how to create both a simple print document and a more complex one—one with multiple document parts. For the more complex document, I've provided a tutorial.

I think it's best to climb the learning curve one step at a time. Therefore, I suggest that you create a simple print document as described next before attempting to create a document with front and back matter.

If all you need is a simple print document, read only the next section. Otherwise, take a look at "Creating a more complex print document" starting on page 208.

Creating a Simple Print Document

Read this section to create only a simple print document (no title page, TOC, index, or glossary). This is the quickest way to produce print output because it requires the least amount of setup.

To create a simple print document, you'll:

- Create a topic outline (a Flare TOC), which tells Flare which topics to print and in what order.

- Edit the target for the type of print output you want.

- Build the output.

Use the following procedure to create a simple print document (one that uses the same page layout throughout) in PDF format.

▶ To create a simple PDF print document:

1. Create a TOC that includes the topics to be printed in the desired print order. See "Creating a Table of Contents" on page 164. Flare uses this TOC as an outline when building the output.

   > **Note** — Your TOC can be as simple as a list of topics if that's all you need.

2. Add a new target and select **PDF** for its Output Type. (See "Adding a target" on page 65 for more information.)

   The Flare Target Editor opens.

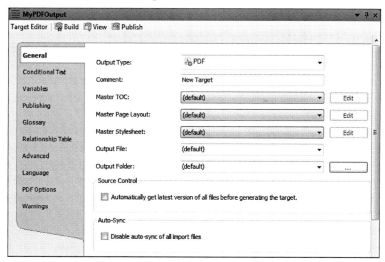

3. Click the **General** tab.

4. In the Master TOC field, select the TOC to use as an outline.

5. (*PDF and XPS only*) If your output includes redacted text, click the **Advanced** tab and select the redaction method (**Blackout, Highlight, Display as normal text**).

6. (*Optional*) Click the **PDF Options** tab and select the desired PDF options for image compression, document properties, PDF tagging, initial view, and security).

7. Click **Save All** to save your selections.

8. In the Project Organizer under **Targets**, right-click the target you just set up and select **Build <target name>** from the menu.

    Flare builds the output according to the selections you made. If your project is large, this might take several seconds.

9. View the output when prompted or view it later.

    When you're ready to distribute your output, you'll find it in a folder under your project's Output folder. By default, the file is in a folder named for the target used to build output.

Now that you've created a simple print document, let's get more ambitious!

CREATING A MORE COMPLEX PRINT DOCUMENT

I've developed a tutorial to show you how to create a document that's more complex—one with front and back parts.

Keep in mind that there are many ways to accomplish the same result. How you set up print output depends in part on how you arrange content in your Flare topic files. For instance, one person might put a document's title and copyright text into a single topic and another might put them into two separate topics.

In this tutorial, you'll learn one way of setting up a more complex document.

HOW TO USE THIS TUTORIAL

There's a lot to learn here. Because it's so easy to focus intently on a tutorial's detailed instructions, you can miss the significance of what you're doing. It might be helpful to for you to go through this tutorial a few times. The real learning happens after you step back from the details and can see the big picture.

So, let's get to it!

This tutorial teaches you how to create a PDF document that contains a title, copyright text, Table of Contents, two chapters, and an index. You should **set aside at least two hours** to complete this entire tutorial.

SAMPLE DOCUMENT

Our sample output will have these characteristics:

- portrait orientation

- page size of 8.5 x 11 inches

- page margins of one inch on three sides (top, bottom, outside) and 1.5 inches on the inside. (The Flare page layout templates you're going to use for this tutorial have a 1.5 inch inside margin.)

- two-column index

- chapters starting on an odd page

- chapters ending on an even page (whether the page has content or not)

The following illustrations show what you'll be creating in the tutorial.

Figure 5A-1:
Title page

Specs: First page in the document starts on the right; no header, footer or page number.

Figure 5A-2:
Copyright
page

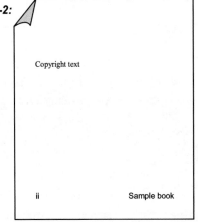

Specs: Second page in the document starts on the left; no header. Footer contains the words "Sample book." Roman numeral page number.

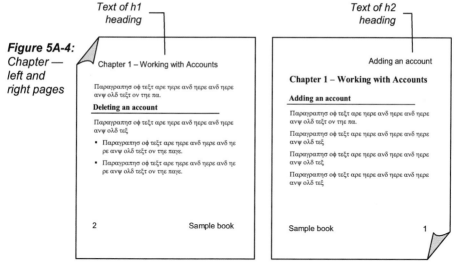

Figure 5A-3:
Table of Contents — left and right pages

Contents

Topic 3 11
   Sub-topic 1 12
   Sub-topic 2 15
   Sub-topic 3 17
   Sub-topic 4 18

Topic 4 19
   Sub-topic 1 22
   Sub-topic 2 23
   Sub-topic 3 25

iv   Sample book

Contents

Topic 5 27
   Sub-topic 1 28
   Sub-topic 2 29
   Sub-topic 3 31
   Sub-topic 4 33

Topic 6 38
   Sub-topic 1 40
   Sub-topic 2 43
   Sub-topic 3 45

Sample book   v

Specs: *Header contains the word "Contents." Footer contains the words "Sample book." Roman numeral page numbers.*

Text of h1 heading

Text of h2 heading

Figure 5A-4:
Chapter — left and right pages

Chapter 1 – Working with Accounts

Παραγραπησ οφ τεξτ αρε ηερε ανδ ηερε ανδ ηερε ανψ ολδ τεξτ ον τηε πα.

Deleting an account

Παραγραπησ οφ τεξτ αρε ηερε ανδ ηερε ανδ ηερε ανψ ολδ τεξ

- Παραγραπησ οφ τεξτ αρε ηερε ανδ ηερε ανδ ηε ρε ανψ ολδ τεξτ ον τηε παγε.
- Παραγραπησ οφ τεξτ αρε ηερε ανδ ηερε ανδ ηε ρε ανψ ολδ τεξτ ον τηε παγε.

2   Sample book

Adding an account

Chapter 1 – Working with Accounts

Adding an account

Παραγραπησ οφ τεξτ αρε ηερε ανδ ηερε ανδ ηερε ανψ ολδ τεξτ ον τηε πα.

Παραγραπησ οφ τεξτ αρε ηερε ανδ ηερε ανδ ηερε ανψ ολδ τεξ

Παραγραπησ οφ τεξτ αρε ηερε ανδ ηερε ανδ ηερε ανψ ολδ τεξ

Παραγραπησ οφ τεξτ αρε ηερε ανδ ηερε ανδ ηερε ανψ ολδ τεξ

Sample book   1

Specs: *Header text uses h1 style (left page) and h2 style (right page). Footer contains the words "Sample book." Decimal (1, 2, 3) page numbers.*

Figure 5A-5:
Index —
left and
right pages

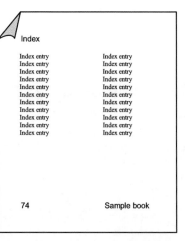

Specs: Header contains the word "Index." Footer contains the words "Sample book."
Decimal (1, 2, 3) page numbers.

Complete all of the tasks in this tutorial to learn how to set up and build a more complex document with front and back matter. Read on to learn about the tasks you're going to complete.

TUTORIAL TASKS

- **Task 1**: Create a topic for each front and back matter part to be included in the output (e.g., Table of Contents, glossary, index). These topics are placeholders for content.

- **Task 2**: Create a topic outline (Flare TOC), which tells Flare which topics to print and in what order.

- **Task 3**: Add a page layout for each document part.

- **Task 4**: Delete unneeded pages from page layouts.

- **Task 5**: Customize footers.

- **Task 6**: Customize headers.

- **Task 7**: Link page layouts to topics in the Flare TOC.

- **Task 8**: Set up the print target.

- **Task 9**: Build the print output.

TUTORIAL SETUP

Before you begin this tutorial, make sure you have completed these setup tasks:

- Create a project. (See "Creating a Flare project" on page 47.) Select **MyPDF** for the target.

- Add topics with these names (See "Adding a topic" on page 53):
    - **Title**
    - **Chapter 1**
    - **Overview**
    - **Starting your application**
    - **Chapter 2**
    - **Adding accounts**

TASK 1: CREATE PLACEHOLDER TOPICS

In this tutorial, you'll create two special topics:

- Table of Contents

- Index

These topics are different from regular Flare topics because you don't type content (other than a topic heading) into them. Instead, Flare inserts a placeholder, called a **proxy**, into the topic.

When you build your output, the proxy is automatically replaced with the actual content. Flare builds the print Table of Contents from your headings (styles h1 – h6) and the index from index markers you'll place in your topics.

> **Note** — Although Flare includes a feature that automatically generates a table of contents, an index, and a glossary, this book shows you how to generate them manually for more control over the layout, the headings, and number of index columns in the output. For information about automatically generating these elements, search Flare's Help system for "auto-generating proxies". For new print targets, the auto-generate feature is enabled by default. To turn it off, open your print target, select the **Advanced** tab, and clear these checkboxes: **Generate TOC Proxy**, **Generate Index Proxy**, and **Generate Glossary Proxy**.

You'll start by creating a topic for the printed Table of Contents.

1. Select **Project** tab → **New**. On the Add File dialog, do the following:

    a. If not already selected, select **New from template**.

    b. Under the **Factory Templates** folder, select **TopicForTOC.htm**.

    c. Type **Print TOC** for the File Name.

    d. Type **Contents** for the 1st Heading.

    e. Click **Add**. The new topic is copied to the Content Explorer.

    > **Best Practice** — Give the TOC a meaningful file name such as **<your project name> Print TOC** to distinguish it from any other TOCs you might have in your project.
    >
    > This is a good example of when you might *type* the 1st heading instead of leaving it blank. If left blank, Flare uses the File name for the 1st heading.

    When you build your output, Flare builds the print Table of Contents from heading styles in your topics.

    > **Tip** — To prevent the h1 heading in the Table of Contents topic from being listed in the print Table of Contents, use a style other than h1 – h6 for the heading. For example, you might create a class of the "p" paragraph style and set its formatting to look like the h1 style.

2. With the new topic (Print TOC) open, delete the text shown before the output toc proxy.

    The XML Editor page should now look like this:

The Table of Contents will go here when you build your output.

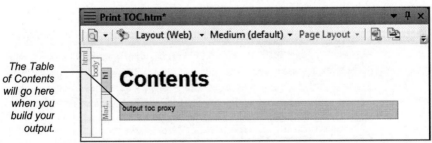

3. Click **Save All** 🖫 to save your work.

Now you'll create a topic to hold the index.

4. Select **Project** tab → **New**. On the Add File dialog, do the following:

    a. If not already selected, select **New from template**.

    b. Under the **Factory Templates** folder, select **TopicForIndex.htm**.

    c. Type **Print Index** for the File Name.

    d. Type **Index** for the 1st Heading.

    e. Click **Add**. The new topic is copied to the Content Explorer.

5. With the new topic (Print Index) open, delete the text shown before the output index proxy.

    The XML Editor should now look like this:

The index will go here when you build your output.

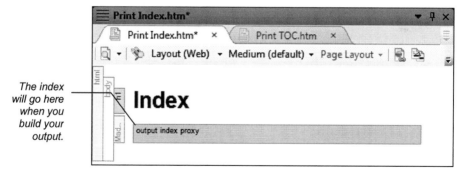

6. Click **Save All** 💾 to save your work.

Creating the topic for the index isn't the only thing you need to do to create an index. You also need to add index keywords, which are used to create the index entries. (To create index keywords, see "Creating index entries" on page 188.)

TASK 2: CREATE A TOPIC OUTLINE

In this task, you'll create a topic outline that contains all of the topics you want to include in your output.

Using Flare's TOC feature, you'll add the regular topics (Title Page, Chapter 1, Overview, Starting your application, Chapter 2, and Adding accounts) to the TOC plus you'll add TOC entries for the Table of Contents and index topics you just created.

> **Important** — The TOC entries in the topic outline *do not* become the Table of Contents in your print output. *Flare uses them only to locate the topics to include and build them in the proper order.* The Table of Contents generated from the TOC proxy is built from heading styles h1 – h6 in your topics. To exclude specific heading styles from the print Table of Contents, change the "mc-heading-level" property in your stylesheet to zero (0) for each heading style to exclude. (Search for "mc-heading-level" in Flare's Help.)

Now you'll create the topic outline for your print (PDF) output.

1. In the Project Organizer, expand the TOCs folder and double-click **Master (Master)**. The TOC Editor opens with the beginnings of a TOC, which includes a starter topic called "Topic."

2. In the Master TOC, right-click **Topic** and select **Delete** from the menu.

3. Click **Save All** ![icon] to save your changes.

   Now you have an empty TOC, and you're ready to build your topic outline.

4. Open the Content Explorer to view the list of topics in your project. You should see the eight topics you created (Chapter 1.htm, Chapter 2.htm, Overview.htm, Starting your application.htm, Adding accounts.htm, Print Index.htm, Print TOC.htm, and Title.htm) plus the starter topic (Topic.htm) that Flare added when you created your project.

   Let's get rid of the starter topic.

5. In the Content Explorer, right-click **Topic.htm** and select **Delete** from the menu. Click **OK** in response to the confirmation

message. (If the Link Update dialog appears, click **Remove Links**.)

Now you'll add your topics to the TOC in the order you want them to appear in your print output.

6. Drag **Title.htm** to the TOC Editor. Next, drag each topic to the TOC Editor and drop it in the order shown here:

    > **Print TOC**
    > **Chapter 1**
    > **Overview**
    > **Starting your application**
    > **Chapter 2**
    > **Adding accounts**
    > **Print Index**

    Your Master TOC should now look like this.

    If your topics aren't all at the same level, that's okay. You'll see how to fix that next with the "Move item ..." buttons in the TOC Editor's toolbar.

    Now you'll change the hierarchy of topics in the TOC.

7. In the TOC Editor, select the topic called **Overview** and click

    Move item to the right in the TOC Editor toolbar. Notice that the Chapter 1 topic becomes a book when Overview is indented beneath it.

Next move the topics **Starting your application** and **Adding accounts** to the right using the same method.

Your TOC Editor should now look like this:

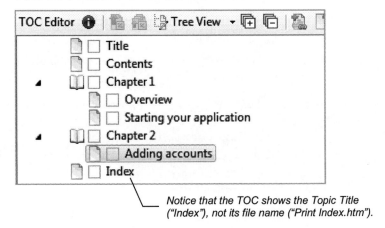

Notice that the TOC shows the Topic Title ("Index"), not its file name ("Print Index.htm").

The order in which the topics are arranged in the TOC Editor dictates their order in the output.

8. Click **Save All** to save your work.

   Next, you'll rename the TOC. This next step isn't necessary, but it will help you keep things straight as your project grows.

9. In the Project Organizer, expand the **TOCs** folder (if necessary), right-click **Master (Master)** and select **Rename** from the menu. Then type **Outline for PDF output** and press **ENTER.**

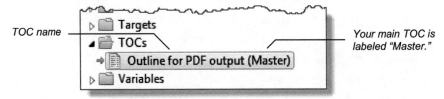

TOC name ⎯ Targets / TOCs / Outline for PDF output (Master) / Variables

Your main TOC is labeled "Master."

Let's close all open documents before moving on to Task 3.

10. Select **Window** tab → **Close All Documents**. The middle pane is now empty.

> **Note** — To create multiple output documents with different topic outlines, you can create one TOC for each topic outline or you can apply condition tags to TOC items.

Next you'll specify **page layouts**, which are files that store your layout choices.

TASK 3: ADD PAGE LAYOUTS

You'll create a page layout from a page layout template provided by Flare, starting with the Title page.

1. Select **Project** tab → **New** arrow → **Add Page Layout**.

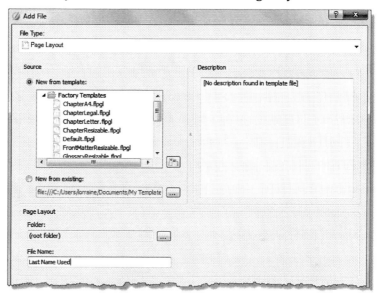

2. Make sure that **New from template** is selected.

3. Under Factory Templates, select the **FrontMatterResizable.flpgl** template. (See page 237 for a description of each template.)

> **Note** — The template you're selecting is a page-layout template. Don't confuse this with a topic template.

4. Type **Title Pg Layout** in the File Name field.

5.   Click [...] to the right of the Folder field and select the
     (Resources) **PageLayouts** folder, (or the desired folder).

6.   Click **Add**.

     The file is copied to the folder you selected in Step 5 above
     (Content/Resources/PageLayouts in our example). For this
     tutorial, ignore the default page layout if you see one listed. It's
     added automatically when you create a new project.

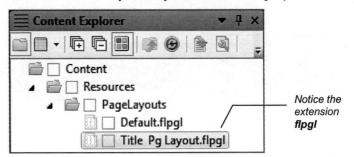

     Notice the
     extension
     flpgl

     The page layout you created opens in the Page Layout Editor.

     Now you need to create three more page layouts—one for the
     TOC, one for chapters, and one for the index.

7.   Repeat Steps 1 – 6 in this procedure three times, using this chart
     as a guide. On the Add File dialog:

Select this template ...	Type this File name ...
FrontMatterResizable.flpgl	TOC Pg Layout
ChapterResizable.flpgl	Chapter Pg Layout
IndexResizable.flpgl	Index Pg Layout

When you're done, your four page layouts are listed in the Content Explorer, as shown here:

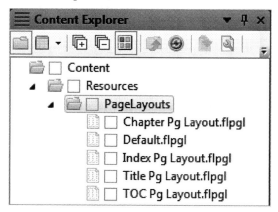

All page layouts are open in individual tabs in the middle pane.

TASK 4: DELETE PAGES FROM PAGE LAYOUTS

Page layout templates provide a starting point only. You'll probably need to customize the page layouts the first time you create print output. After that, you can reuse them each time you print the same output.

> *Tip* — You can also copy page layouts, so that once you set up the layouts for one output document, you can replicate the layouts for others.

Page layouts can contain up to ten page types (such as First, Title, Left, Right, etc). (See page 238 for more information about page types.) You won't need some of the pages on some of the layouts.

You'll work in the Page Layout Editor to customize the page layouts you just created. First, you'll remove the pages you don't need.

> *Best Practice* — Remove the pages you don't need to keep your page layouts tidy and eliminate uncertainty about which pages you're using.

1. If you don't see all four tabs in the middle pane, click ▤ to the right of the Page Layout Editor tabs to view a list of open files. Select **Title Pg Layout.flpgl** from the list or click its tab to make it active.

2. At the right side of the Page Layout Editor, right-click the **Title** ("T") page and select **Remove Page**.

> **Note** — To store title page and copyright text in *different* topics, create a layout that has only T (title) and E (empty) pages as discussed in the Flare Help system. To *combine* title page and copyright text into one topic, use the F (first) page for the title and the L (left) page for the copyright page as shown in this tutorial.

3. Remove the **R** (right) page and **E** (empty) pages by the same method.

    What remains is the **F** (first) page and the **L** (left) page, which you'll use for the copyright text.

4. Remove these pages from these page layouts:

From this page layout ...	Remove these pages ...
TOC Pg Layout.flpgl	F (first) and T (title)
Chapter Pg Layout.flpgl	F (first)
Index Pg Layout.flpgl	F (first)

    Notice that you didn't delete the **E** (empty) pages from these layouts. In this tutorial, we want Flare to start each part (chapter, index, etc.) on an odd (right) page. If your layout includes the **Empty** page, Flare will pad the end of the previous chapter with an empty page if necessary in order to begin this chapter on an odd page.

5. Click **Save All** 💾 to save your work.

There are two more tasks for you to do to finish setting up the page layouts—customizing the header and footer frames.

Task 5: Customize footers

You'll continue working with the Page Layout Editor to customize the footer frames of the page layouts you just created.

Let's start with the chapter page layout (see Figure 5A-4 on page 211). Once you've set up the left and right footers, you'll copy them to the other layouts to save yourself some time.

For this tutorial, this is what you want the left footer to look like.

1. Click the **Chapter Pg Layout.flpgl** tab and complete the following tasks:

   a. Click the Left page. Scroll down to the footer frame and select it.

   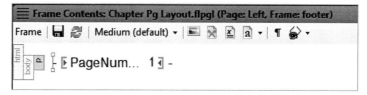

   The footer frame contains a centered page number, which is not what you want for this tutorial, so you need to edit it.

   b. Press **F2** to open the Frame Contents window.

   ![Frame Contents: Chapter Pg Layout.flpgl (Page: Left, Frame: footer). Frame toolbar with Medium (default) dropdown. PageNum... 1]

   You'll use the Frame Contents window to add and change content in page layout frames. It contains some of the XML Editor tools just for this purpose. Notice that the frame contains the variable PageNumber (but not in a two-column table), so you'll delete it.

   c. In the Frame Contents window, triple-click the text block to select the PageNumber variable and the dashes that surround it. Then press **Delete**.

Flare normally aligns all of the text within a footer as either left, right, centered, or justified. However, this tutorial example is more complex (but also quite typical). We want the page number left aligned and the words "Sample book" right aligned. How can you do this? With a two-column table in the footer!

d.   Select **Table** tab → **Insert Table**, and set these properties on the General tab of the Insert Table dialog:

Set this property ...	To ...
Number of columns	2
Number of rows	1
Number of header rows	0
Number of footer rows	0
AutoFit Behavior	Fixed column width
Fixed column width	3.00 in

> **Note** — Here's how the 3-inch column width was calculated:
>
> ```
>     8.5 inches   (page size)
>  −  1.0 inch     (right margin)
>  −  1.5 inch     (left margin)
>  =  6.0 inches   (space for text)
>  Divided by 2 columns = 3 inches per column
> ```

e.   Click **OK**.

Now you'll insert the page number variable into the table.

f.   Click inside the left cell of the table. From the Frame Contents window's toolbar, select **Insert a variable** .

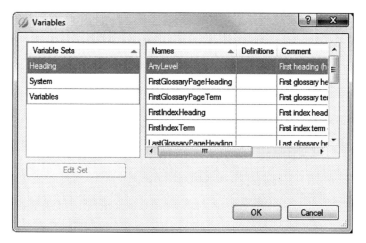

g. Select **System** for the Variable Set and **PageNumber** for the
    variable name, then click **OK**. The PageNumber variable is
    shown in the cell of the table.

    Don't worry about the format or starting page number for
    now. You'll set these in Task 7 when you link your page
    layouts to topics in the topic outline.

h. Click in the right cell of the table and type **Sample book**.

    Right-align the text by clicking **Right** ≡ on the **Home**
    ribbon. Your footer should now look like this:

i. Save the frame by clicking **Save File** 🖫 in the Frame
    Contents window, then close the Frame Contents window.

    Leave the Chapter Pg Layout's Left page footer frame in
    view. You're going to use it again.

2. Since all left pages of this tutorial use this same footer, you'll
    copy and paste the footer you just created to other left pages.
    Copying is faster than recreating the footer everywhere you
    need it.

To copy the footer:

a. On the **Chapter Pg Layout Left** page, select the footer frame and press **CTRL + C** to copy it.

b. Click the **Title Pg Layout.flpgl** tab, click the Left page, scroll down and select the footer frame, then press **Delete**. Now press **CTRL + V** to paste the frame you just copied.

c. Click **Save All** ⊞ and close the Title Pg Layout. You're done setting it up.

d. Paste the Chapter Pg Layout Left-page footer frame to these layouts in the same manner. (Don't forget to delete the frame you don't want before pasting the new one.)

In this page layout ...	Paste into these pages ...
Chapter Pg Layout	Empty page
TOC Pg Layout	Left page and Empty page
Index Pg Layout	Left page and Empty page

3. Next you're going to create the right page footer by copying the left page footer and swapping the contents of the table cells.

This is what you want the footer to look like.

| Sample book | 1 |

Complete the following tasks:

a. Click the **Chapter Pg Layout** tab and copy its Left page footer frame. Select the **Right** page, delete its footer, and paste in the **Left** page footer frame. Then press **F2** to open the Frame Contents window.

b. Switch the contents of the cells so the words "**Sample book**" are in the left table cell and the page number is in the right table cell.

c. Save the frame ⊟ and close the Frame Contents window.

   d. Copy and paste the right footer frame into the **Right** pages of
       the **TOC Pg Layout** and the **Index Pg Layout**.

4. Click **Save All** to save your work.

Now that both the left and right footers are set up for all pages in
your page layouts, you'll set up the header frames.

TASK 6: CUSTOMIZE HEADERS

Both the Table of Contents and Index have headers that contain text
you type (no variables). You'll set up the Table of Contents header
first. For our example, the word "Contents" should appear on both
left and right pages.

1. Click the **TOC Pg Layout.flpgl** tab and complete the following
    tasks:

    a. Click the **Left** page, scroll up and select the header frame,
        and press **F2**.

    b. In the Frame Contents window, type **Contents**. Then save

        the frame and close the Frame Contents window.

    c. Copy the **Left** page header frame you just created, and paste
        it into the **Empty** page. (This way, if Flare needs to pad the
        end of a chapter with an empty page, the page will have a
        header.)

    d. Click the **Right** page, select the header frame, and press **F2**.

    e. In the Frame Contents window, type **Contents**. Then save
        your work and close the Frame Contents window.

    f. Close the **TOC Pg Layout**. You're done setting it up.

Next, you'll set up the header for the Index.

2. Click the **Index Pg Layout.flpgl** tab and complete the following tasks:

    a. Click the **Left** page, scroll up and select the header, and press **F2**.

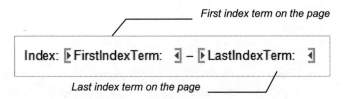

The variables for first and last index terms came from the index template. Although these variables can be used when creating PDF output, you're not using them for this tutorial, so you'll delete them.

    b. In the Frame Contents window, select the entire text block and press **Delete**.

    c. Type **Index**. Then save the frame 💾 and close the Frame Contents window.

    d. Copy the **Left** page frame you just saved and paste it into the **Empty** page.

    e. Click the **Right** page, select the header, and press **F2**.

    f. Repeat steps 2b and 2c listed previously.

    g. Close the **Index Pg Layout**. You're done setting it up.

One more layout to finish—the Chapter Pg Layout.

The Chapter Pg Layout needs headers that show h1 heading text on left pages and h2 heading text on right pages.

3. Click the **Chapter Pg Layout.flpgl** tab and complete the following tasks:

    a. Click the **Right** page and scroll to the upper right to see what's in the header frame.

Although it's partially covered, the right page header frame contains the variable Heading.Level1, which places the text of the first h1 heading on the page in your running header. We'll delete this and insert Heading.Level 2 (the variable for the h2 heading).

b. Select the header frame, press **F2**, right-click the variable, and select **Delete** from the menu. From the Frame Contents window's toolbar, select **Insert a variable** [x].

c. From the Variables dialog, select **Heading** for the Variable Set and **Level2** for the Name, and click **OK**. Then save the frame [save] and close the Frame Contents window.

d. Now click the Left page, scroll to the left to see the header frame.

The ChapterResizable template contains a variable that places a "Chapter" number in the left page header.

What Flare calls a chapter is not necessarily what you might call a chapter. Flare's "chapter number" represents the order of the topic files in your topic outline. In this example, Flare would consider the Title page topic to be "Chapter 1" and the Table of Contents to be "Chapter 2." It would consider the real Chapter 1 to be "Chapter 3."

In this example, we want the text of the first heading in Chapter 1 to appear in the header of left pages. You'll insert the Level 1 variable to do this.

e. Select the header frame, press **F2**, select all, and press **Delete**.

f.   From the Frame Contents window's toolbar, select **Insert a variable** ▣.

g.   From the Variables dialog, select **Heading** for the Variable Set and **Level1** for the Name, then click **OK**. Save the frame ▣ and close the Frame Contents window.

Notice that Heading.Level 1 now appears in the header frame.

h.   Select the header frame you just set up and copy it. Click the Empty page and paste the frame into it.

4.   Click **Save All** ▣ and close the Chapter Page Layout.

Whew! You're done setting up page layouts. It seems like a lot of work, but once you get comfortable with using Flare's page layout features, you'll find that shortcuts (such as copying and pasting frames) make setup quicker. Plus, once your page layouts are set up the way you want them, you won't have to do it again unless you want to change them.

> *Tip* — You can copy page layouts to the Content\Resources\PageLayout folder of another Flare project to use them with other documents (or store them in a global project).

TASK 7: LINK PAGE LAYOUTS TO TOPICS IN THE TOC

Now you'll tell Flare where each document part begins (chapter breaks) and which page layout to use for each document part. We're using the term "document part" to mean each major section, such as a title page, Table of Contents, chapter, glossary, or index. Flare uses the term "chapter" generically to refer to these document parts.

In this task, you'll link the applicable page layout to the first topic in each "chapter." When you build your output, Flare uses that layout for the remaining topics until it encounters another chapter break.

If you have TOC entries for topics within a chapter, you need to link only the first TOC entry that uses the page layout you are assigning to that chapter.

Let's look at the TOC outline you created in Task 2.

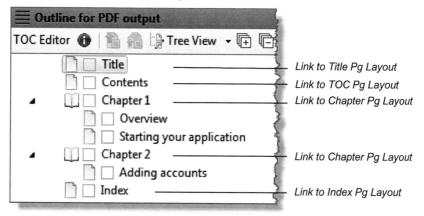

Notice that you *don't* need to link the topics called "Overview" and "Starting your application" to page layouts because they will use the Chapter Pg Layout, which is linked to the Chapter 1 topic. Also notice that you *do* need to link the first topic in Chapter 2 to Chapter Pg Layout, but you don't need to link its second topic, "Adding accounts."

Okay, let's see how to set chapter breaks and link to page layouts.

1. In the Project Organizer, expand the **TOCs** folder and double-click **Outline for PDF output (Master)**.

2. In the TOC Editor, select **Title**, then click **Display properties for the selected item** ⬚ on the top toolbar.

3. On the Properties dialog, select the **Printed Output** tab.

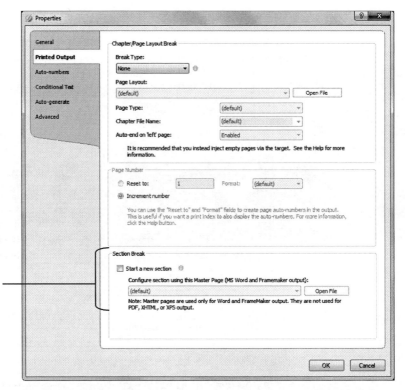

This section applies only if you're using master pages for print output. Ignore it when using page layouts.

4. In the Chapter/Page Layout Break section, select **Chapter Break**.

> **Note** — For Word documents, when you select **Chapter Break**, Flare inserts a section break before the chapter whose properties you are setting up. The section break is Odd or Even depending on if you select Right or Left for the Page Type.

5. From the Page Layout list, select **/Title Pg Layout**.

6. From the Page Type list, select **First**. (This is the page type we want Flare to use for the first page of the Title "chapter.")

7. In the Page Number section, select **Reset to** and verify that the number is **1**. Then select **roman (i, ii, iii)** from the Format list.

8. Click **OK**.

9. You do the rest, using the following chart for help.

For TOC entry ...	Assign page layout ...	Select page type ...	Set the page numbers to ...
Contents	TOC Pg Layout	Right	Increment number
Chapter 1	Chapter Pg Layout	Right	Reset to 1 Format: Decimal (1, 2, 3)
Chapter 2	Chapter Pg Layout	Right	Increment number
Index	Index Pg Layout	Right	Increment number

Notice that you're using "Right" for the page type. That's because you want each chapter to start on an odd page. By selecting "Right," you're telling Flare to use the Right page type for the first page of each chapter.

10. Click **Save All**  to save your work.

11. Close the TOC.

TASK 8: SET UP THE PRINT TARGET

Now you'll define what you want to build—your print output—by setting up the print target. You're almost there!

1. In the Project Organizer, expand **Targets** and double-click **MyPDF** or **MyPDF (Primary)**. The target opens in the Target Editor.

2. Click the **General** tab.

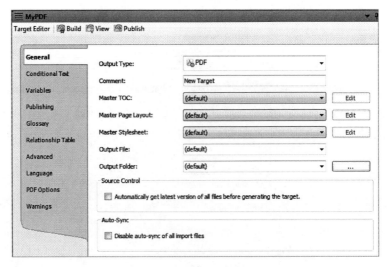

3. If not already selected, select **PDF** as the Output Type.

4. In the Master TOC field, select **Outline for PDF output**.

5. Click the **Advanced** tab and do the following:

   a. Select **Inject empty pages as needed to ensure TOC nodes start on their selected pages**. This option pads the end of chapters with an empty page if needed (*applies to PDF and XPS targets only*).

   b. Clear the checkboxes to generate proxies for the TOC, Index and Glossary. (This tutorial does not use these options.)

6. (*Optional*) Click the **PDF Options** tab and set PDF options as desired. For information about accessibility options, see "Options for accessibility" on page 241.

   For this tutorial, no other options need to be set.

7. Click **Save All** to save your work.

8. Close the Target Editor.

Because you saved the target settings, you can build your output at any time. Let's try that now.

TASK 9: BUILD THE PRINT OUTPUT

Building the print output is the easiest part of this process. Although it's the last task before distributing your output, you'll likely build your output many times before you're done setting up layouts and developing your project's content.

> *Tip* — Build your output as you set up your page layouts, so you can see the results and make sure that you're getting what you want.

1. In the Project Organizer, under Targets, right-click **MyPDF (Primary)** and select **Build 'MyPDF'** from the menu.

   A Build Progress window opens as Flare builds the output for the target you selected. If your project is large, this might take several seconds.

2. Click **Yes** to view the output when prompted. Your default PDF viewer opens and displays your output.

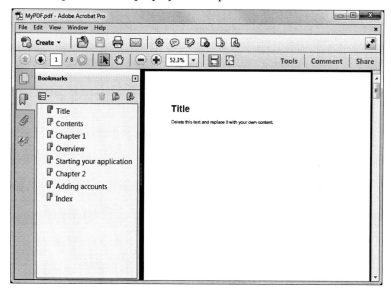

> *Tip* — By default, a thin black line appears above the Table of Contents and index entries in the PDF file. In the Styles stylesheet, the proxy styles used in the index and Table of Contents are defined as having a one-pixel black line at the beginning of the proxy content. To change this, see "Changing styles with the Stylesheet Editor" on page 151. Change the "border-top-style" property to "None" for the "MadCap|indexProxy" and "MadCap|tocProxy" styles.

Congratulations! You've survived the process of creating a more complex print document!

When you're ready to distribute your PDF file, you'll find it in a folder under your project's Output folder. The file is in a folder named for the target you built (**MyPDF** in this tutorial).

To view and distribute other types of print output, see "Types of print output" on page 202.

LEARN MORE

This section contains more information about the features you used in the tutorial part of this chapter. Refer to it as needed.

PAGE LAYOUTS

In Flare, a **page layout** is a file you create to specify the layout for the pages in a part of your document. You'll create one layout for each unique combination of these page characteristics, including:

- Page orientation
- Page size
- Page number format
- Inclusion of a header on the first page
- Header contents and placement
- Footer contents and placement

For many writers, this means creating one layout for each of the following document parts:

- Title page

- Table of contents

- Chapter (one page layout for each different chapter format)

- Glossary

- Index

> **Best Practice** — Use page layouts to define headers and footers for *print* output. Use master pages to define headers and footers in *online* output.

Page layout templates

To simplify print output, Flare includes templates for standard page layouts. You'll create a page layout by using one of these templates as a starting point. (These are not the same as *topic* templates, which you use when creating a new topic.)

Flare provides the following page-layout templates.

Table 5A-2: Flare page layout templates

Page layout template	Use this template for ...
ChapterA4	Page sizes that conform to the A4 international standard, which is 21 x 29.7 cm (8.27 x 11.69 in.).
ChapterLegal	Legal documents (8.5 x 14 in.).
ChapterLetter	Letter-size documents (8.5 x 11 in.). Frames in this layout are not anchored.
ChapterResizable	Letter-size documents (8.5 x 11 in.) that use frames.*
Default	The body of a document or simple letter-size documents that need a header, body, and footer. Margins are set to one inch all around.
FrontMatterResizable	Front matter, like Tables of Contents (8.5 x 11 in.).*
GlossaryResizable	Glossaries (page size is 8.5 x 11 in.).*

Table 5A-2:
(Cont.)

Page layout template	Use this template for ...
IndexResizable	Indexes (page size is 8.5 x 11 in.).* This option includes the variables "Heading.FirstIndexTerm" and "Heading.LastIndexTerm" in the header. (Available only for PDF, XPS, and XHTML output.)
NormalResizable	The body of a document or simple letter-size documents that need a header, body, and footer. This option is identical to the "default" layout except that frames are anchored.* Margins are set to one inch all around.

* Frames are anchored. Anchored frames maintain their distance from the edge of the page if you change the page size of the layout.

Page types

For each page layout, you can define ten types of pages (First, First Left, First Right, Title, Normal, Right, Left, Empty, Empty Left, and Empty Right). The page buttons on the right represent each page type contained in that particular page layout.

Figure 5A-6:
Page layout showing frames and page types

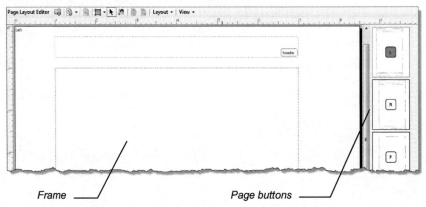

Frame   Page buttons

Page buttons

Clicking a page button opens that page in the Page Layout Editor.

Each button icon displays a letter indicating its type. For example, the Left page button displays "L" and the First Left page button displays "FL" as shown here:

Table 5A-3: *Flare page* *types*	**Use this** **page type ...**	**When ...**
	First or First Right	The first page of a chapter begins on the right and has a different layout from other right pages in the chapter.
	First Left	The first page of a chapter begins on the left and has a different layout from other left pages in the chapter. (Helpful for right-to-left languages.)
	Title	The document needs a title page layout.
	Normal	There are no differences between left and right chapter page layouts.
	Right	Specifying the page layout for right (odd) pages in a chapter.
	Left	Specifying the page layout for left (even) pages in a chapter.
	Empty or Empty Left	Chapters must end on a *left* empty page (if needed) when the next chapter begins on the right (First or First Right).
	Empty Right	Chapters must end on a *right* empty page (if needed) when the next chapter begins on the left (First Left). (Helpful for right-to-left languages.)

Page frames

Each page type contains **frames** that act as placeholders for content. Page layouts can contain these types of frames:

- Header

- Footer

- Body

- Decoration (not supported by Word or FrameMaker)

- Image

Frames also indicate where the content should be placed on the printed page. To arrange content, you can insert, move, and resize frames. You can also set up a frame's characteristics. For example, a frame can have one or more columns, a background color, and borders.

> *Tip* — Within each frame, content is bounded by the frame size. If you're setting up headers and footers, make sure the frame is large enough to hold the content. (If you're using variables, you might not know this until you build output.) If your headers or footers are cut off, stretch the length of the frames, or reduce the size of the font until the content fits the frame size.

There is much more you can do with frames in Flare. We're just scratching the surface to get you started.

Editing frames

You can edit the contents of all frames except body frames. You edit frames in the Frame Contents window, which has some of the same features as the XML Editor.

> *Note* — Flare uses styles from the Print medium to display frame contents.

Body frames

You cannot change the content in body frames. When you build your output, Flare automatically places your topic content into the body frames.

However, you can insert more body frames on a page to control the flow of content and how it is formatted. You can even rotate body frames so your content flows from a vertical frame to a horizontal frame.

Arrows indicate the direction in which the
text flows from one body frame to another.

Figure 5A-7:
*Multiple
body
frames on
a page*

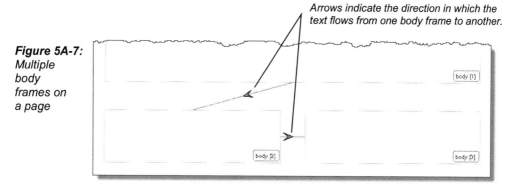

body [1]

body [2]

body [3]

Header and footer frames

You set up header and footer frames with the content you want. To
get content into headers and footers:

- Type text into them

- Insert snippets

- Insert variables (such as page numbers or heading text from
  topics)

OPTIONS FOR ACCESSIBILITY

Flare includes options that make PDF documents (and WebHelp)
more accessible for people with disabilities, and allows writers to
comply with Section 508 disability laws.

For PDF files, the Target Editor's PDF Options tab contains an option
Generate tagged PDF that if checked, inserts tags into your PDF file.
Tags indicate a document's structure based on its heading levels.
Screen readers can then interpret the document structure and
present the content in an alternative format for sight-disabled
people.

The "Warnings" tab in the Target Editor lets you choose which
accessibility features you want Flare to check for when you build
PDF output. For example, Flare can check for and identify images
that are missing alternate text and tables that are missing a caption,
summary, and header rows.

If you need to add alternate text to an image that is used in multiple places, open a topic that includes that image, right-click the image, and select **Edit Image**. On the Edit Image dialog, select the **Apply the alternate text and screen tip to all image references** checkbox.

WHAT'S NEXT?

At this point, you could continue adding content to your project. Since setup is done, you can also re-build the document at any time. Just remember:

- **If you add topics to your project**, you must add linked TOC entries for those topics.

- **If any of those topics will begin a new chapter**, you must designate them as chapter breaks in the TOC and link them to page layouts (see Task 7 starting on page 230).

You've now gone through an entire project cycle, from creating the project to building output! If you keep working with Flare and try other, more advanced features, it won't be long before you're a bona fide Propeller Head or even a Propellus Maximus (these are titles granted to frequent posters on the Flare user forum).

In addition:

- To develop online output, take a look at Step 5B: Create Online Output.

- To create DITA output, see Appendix G.

- To create EPUB output, see Appendix H.

- To explore other features of Flare, check out the appendixes.

Step 5B: Create Online Output

STEP 5: Create Output
5A: Print Output
5B: Online Output

STEP 4:
Create
Nav Aids

STEP 3:
Develop
Content

STEP 2:
Learn the
XML Editor

STEP 1:
Get Started

In this chapter ...

➤ Learn about online output types
➤ Add breadcrumbs
➤ Add a master page
➤ Add and edit a skin
➤ Set up a target
➤ Build online output
➤ Test and troubleshoot
➤ Distribute online output

OVERVIEW

This step explains how to create and distribute online output, such as Help systems and knowledge bases.

Before you begin using the procedures in this chapter, make sure you have done the following:

- **Create your project**. You can create online output from any Flare project. To create the project, see "Creating a Flare project" on page 47.

- **Create and format your content**. You create and format your content as you would for any other output as described in Step 2: Learn the XML Editor, and Step 3: Develop Content.

- **Add navigation aids**. Use Step 4: Create Navigation Aids, to add links and create index entries for navigation.

> **Note** — If you're unfamiliar with terms and concepts such as *output*, *build*, *distribute* and *target*, refer to the Document Basics chapter.

KEEPING TRACK OF ONLINE OUTPUT

To make it easier to track various targets and types of output, this book includes a Target Settings form (see Appendix A). As you create more targets, you'll find it very helpful to record the names of the Flare project files each target uses.

It's a good idea to keep a copy of this form handy as you proceed through this chapter and make it a habit to fill it out.

Types of Online Output

With Flare, you can create the following types of online output.

Table 5B-1:
Types
of online
output

Output Type	Description
HTML5	A web-based Help format that supports the HTML5 specification. Has a more modern appearance and offers additional features not found with other WebHelp formats. You can create standard HTML5 output or server-based HTML5 output, (which supports searching non-XHTML content and automatic runtime merging of Flare projects).
	Output is frameless, which improves search engine results because the output can be more easily indexed for search engines (useful for output that is not restricted to a particular application).
	Also features "responsive output"— output display adjusts to fit the size of your browser window or device, allowing you to create one output for multiple devices.
	Note — Some browser versions, especially older versions might not support all features of HTML5.
WebHelp	A web-based Help format based on HTML4 that can be run on any Internet browser or platform (Figure 5B-3).
WebHelp AIR	A web-based Help format based on HTML4 and created by Adobe that can be run via a single file from a desktop rather than a server (Figure 5B-3).
	To create online documents in WebHelp AIR:
	▪ You and users must install Abobe AIR (go to http://get.adobe.com/air/ for a free download).
	▪ You must install Java Runtime Environment (go to http://java.sun.com/javase/downloads/index.jsp for a free download).
WebHelp Plus	A web-based Help format based on HTML4 that provides enhanced functionality (Figure 5B-3). For more information, see "About WebHelp Plus Output" in Flare's Help system.
WebHelp Mobile	A standalone web-based Help format based on HTML4 and designed for viewing on mobile devices. WebHelp Mobile should reside on a web server; it is not intended to be part of an application (Figure 5B-4). For more information, see "About WebHelp Mobile Output" in Flare's Help system.

Table 5B-1:
Continued

Output Type	Description
Eclipse Help	A Help format that can be used as an Eclipse Help plug-in to extend the existing Help that comes with an Eclipse Integrated Development Environment (IDE). Requires that you install the latest Java Runtime Environment (JRE) and Java version.
HTML Help	An HTML-based Help format created by Microsoft that is used to develop Help systems for Windows desktop applications (Figure 5B-2).
DotNet Help	A Help format created by MadCap Software.

For more information about each of these output types, see Flare's Help system.

Here are a few examples of output types:

Figure 5B-1:
HTML5
sample

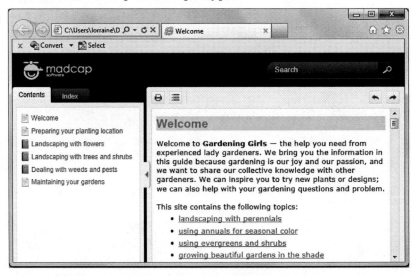

Figure 5B-2:
HTML
Help
sample

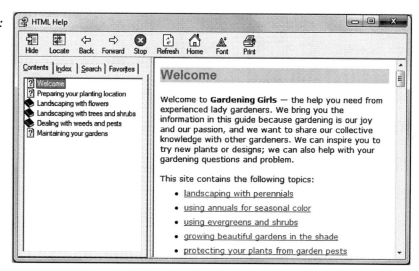

Figure 5B-3:
WebHelp,
WebHelp AIR,
and WebHelp
Plus sample

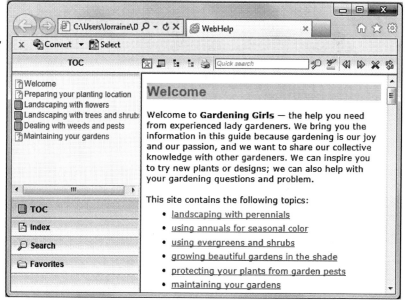

Figure 5B-4:
WebHelp
Mobile sample

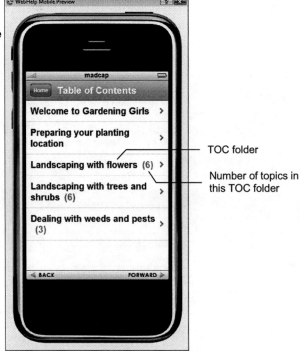

TOC folder

Number of topics in
this TOC folder

ABOUT RESPONSIVE OUTPUT

Flare's responsive output feature allows you to display the same
HTML5 output on multiple devices in a format that fits each device
type. This can be helpful if you need to create output that can be
accessed from a smart phone, a tablet, and a web browser on a
computer. Flare simplifies the process of creating output that can be
viewed on each device.

You set up and build only one target and set up one skin. (You don't
need to create a WebHelp Mobile target.) And you deliver only one
HTML5 output.

When users view the output from their tablet or smart phone, the
display of that output is automatically adjusted for the device they
are using. When they view the output in a computer's browser
window and make the window smaller, the display changes when
the browser reaches the width in pixels (Tablet-Max-Width or

Mobile-Max-Width) that you previously set up in the HTML5 skin. You can also set up styles for three display sizes: web, tablet, and mobile by using mediums in the HTML5 Skin Editor.

> ***Important*** — Responsive output is enabled by default in new HTML5 skins. If you don't need this feature, you can turn if off by clearing the **Enable responsive output** checkbox on the HTML5 Skin Editor's **Setup** tab.

Here's an example of HTML5 output on a tablet in Flare's Preview window.

Figure 5B-5:
HTML5 Tablet output generated as "responsive output"

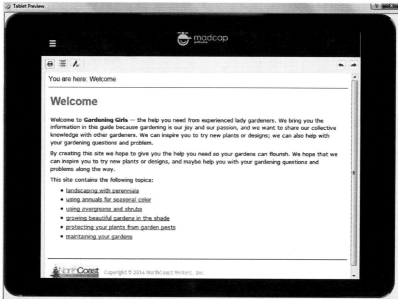

THE BASIC STEPS

Here's a list of the steps you'll take to create online output:

- Create a TOC. See "Creating a Table of Contents" on page 164.

- Add index keywords in topics. See "Creating index entries" on page 188.

- (*Optional*) Add a master page to include a header, footer, and breadcrumbs in your online output.

- Set up your target.

- Build your online output.

- Test and troubleshoot.

- Distribute online output.

> **Note** — When creating online output, you may want to create browse sequences, which are a type of navigation aid. To learn about them, search the Flare Help system for "browse sequences."

ABOUT BREADCRUMBS

Breadcrumbs are an optional navigation aid that shows the path through the TOC to the topic currently open in a Help system session. The breadcrumb trail appears just above the open topic in the output as shown in the following screen.

Figure 5B-6: Breadcrumb trail

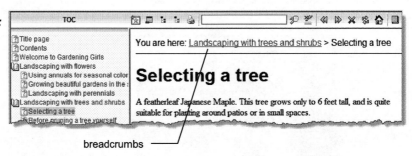

breadcrumbs

To show breadcrumbs, you must use a breadcrumbs proxy in a master page and select that master page when you set up your target. If you add a master page to your project (described next) by selecting the MasterPage Factory Template, you automatically get a breadcrumbs proxy.

> **Note** — If you don't want the breadcrumb trail, simply delete it from the master page. From the Content Explorer's Resources\MasterPages folder, open the master page, right-click the proxy, and select **Edit → Delete**.

ADDING A MASTER PAGE

Master pages let you add headers, footers, and breadcrumbs to all topics in online output.

▶ To add a master page:

1. Select **Project** tab → **New**. Select **Master Page** for the File Type.

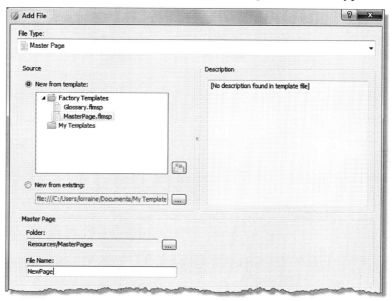

2. If not already selected, select **New from template**.

3. Under the **Factory Templates** folder, select **MasterPage.flmsp**. (The breadcrumbs proxy is automatically used with this template.)

4. Click [···] to the right of the Folder field and select the (Resources) **MasterPages** folder, (or the desired folder).

5. In the File Name field, type a name for the master page.

> **Best Practice** — Record the name of the Master Page on the Target Settings form provided in Appendix A.

6. Click **Add**.

The master page file (.flmsp) is added to the folder you selected in Step 4 above (Content\Resources\MasterPages in our example) and the master page opens in the XML Editor.

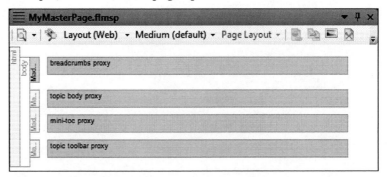

7. (*Optional*) To include a header in your online topics, place your cursor *before* the **topic body proxy** and type text or include content. (You can quickly move your cursor between proxies with your keyboard's **UP** and **DOWN** arrow keys.)

> **Note** — You can insert any type of content in master page headers and footers, including images, snippets, variables, and even text hyperlinks.

8. (*Optional*) To include a footer in your topics, place your cursor *after* the **mini-toc proxy** and type text or include content.

9. (*Optional*) To remove a proxy from the master page, right-click it, then select **Delete**.

10. Click **Save All** to save your work.

    After you create a master page, you must select it when you set up your target. (See "Setting up an online target" on page 253).

> **Note** — You can add multiple master pages to your project, but you can associate only one master page with each target.

ADDING AND EDITING SKINS

A skin defines the appearance of online output—its interface. A skin file stores the interface settings, such as its buttons, colors, and accordion bars or tabs.

New projects include a default skin, which you can edit. You can also add skins. WebHelp Mobile and HTML5 require their own unique skins. You'll need to add skins for them to your project before you build their output.

▶ To add a skin:

1. Open the Project Organizer and right-click the **Skins** folder.

2. Select **Add Skin**.

3. On the Add File dialog, select a skin from the factory template list, type a File Name for the skin, and click **Add**.

▶ To edit a skin:

1. Open the Project Organizer and expand the Skins folder.

2. Double-click the skin you want to edit. The Skin Editor opens.

3. On the General tab, select the interface features you want (such as TOC and Index). Other tabs and options vary, depending on the type of skin you are editing. For WebHelp and HTML5 skins, select the toolbar buttons you want (such as Print, ExpandAll, and NextTopic).

4   On the Styles tab, change styles as desired (colors, fonts, etc.) for the parts of the interface (accordion items, buttons, text, background colors, etc.).

See Figure 5B-1 through Figure 5B-4 for examples of skins.

For more information about using skins, search for "skins" in the Flare Help system.

SETTING UP AN ONLINE TARGET

Now that you've finished creating the content, TOC, and index keywords, you'll tell Flare what you want to build—the output—by setting up an online target.

Use the following procedure to set up a target you've already added to your project. (To add a target, see "Adding a target" on page 65.)

▶ To set up a target:

1. In the Project Organizer, expand the **Targets** folder and double-click the target you want to set up.

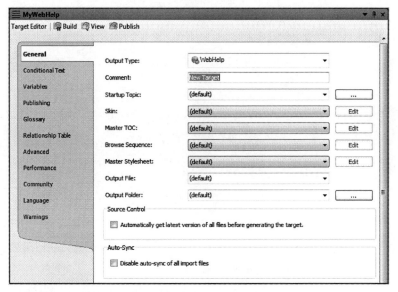

2. Click the **General** tab to open it (if necessary).

3. When you created your project, you should have selected the desired online output type. If you didn't, select the Output Type now. (See "Types of online output" on page 245 for online output types.)

4. In the Startup Topic field, select or browse for the topic you want opened when a user opens the online output. (If you're creating a WebHelp Mobile target, you cannot define a startup topic.)

5. In the Master TOC field, select the desired TOC for this target.

6. In the Master Stylesheet field, select the stylesheet to apply to this target. If you select **default**, the Styles stylesheet will be used.

7. In the Output File field, type a name for the file that will launch the online output.

> **Best Practice** — Check with the software developer to see if there are any requirements for the Output File name. If not, an easy way to keep track of your projects is to enter your project name and the target type (plus the appropriate file extension) as your Output File name. Example: "MyProjectWebHelp.htm"
>
> Don't forget to record the target name, TOC name and Output File name on the Target Settings form in Appendix A. (You'll need to remember the Output File name when you distribute your output.)

In Flare, the Output File is also called the Main Entry file.

8. In the Skin field, select the desired skin. For WebHelp Mobile and HTML5, if you don't see the applicable skin in the list, add one to your project. (See page 252.)

9. (*Optional*) To exclude content tagged with a condition tag, click the **Conditional Text** tab.

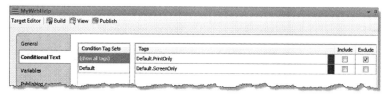

On this tab, make sure the **Basic** button is selected so the checkboxes are visible, then select the checkboxes for the condition tags you want to exclude from your output. The corresponding conditional expression is shown in the box under the Basic button (for display purposes only). (The "Advanced" button lets you build complex conditional expressions—an advanced feature not covered in this book.)

> **Important** — Unless excluded, all content tagged with a condition tag *is automatically included* in output.

10. (*Optional*) If you are using variables in your topics, click the **Variables** tab if you want to change the definitions of variables for this target only.

11. (*Optional*) If you are creating a target for context-sensitive help, click the **Advanced** tab and select an Alias File. See "Adding an alias file" on page 320.

12. (*Optional*) If you are using a master page, click the **Advanced** tab and select the Master Page you want to use to build this target.

13. Click **Save All** to save your work.

Because you saved the target settings, you can build the online output at any time, even immediately. Let's try that now.

BUILDING ONLINE OUTPUT

You'll probably build often as you develop content to see how it will look. Fortunately, building online output is a snap.

> **Best Practice** — Build frequently, especially when you're using condition tags. Doing so will help you verify that the TOC structure is correct—plus you can fix any broken links as you develop content.

WHAT CONTENT IS INCLUDED IN OUTPUT?

By default, all project content is included in output unless you specifically exclude it! Even topics that are not included in your TOC are included in your output. That means that those topics can be found when a user searches for terms in your Help system, knowledge base, or Mobile output.

Why create a topic that you don't want included in output? There can be any number of reasons. Maybe the topic is a work-in-progress for some future version, or maybe you want a place to keep notes about your project, but you don't want that information available in output for users to see.

Options for excluding topics from output and search

You have a few options for excluding topics from output or from being searched.

Table 5B-2: Options for excluding topics from output or from being searched

To exclude ...	Do this ...
A *specific topic* from being searched (but not from output)	Right-click the topic in the Content Explorer, select **Properties →Topic Properties** tab, and clear the checkbox **Include topic when full-text search database is generated** in the Properties dialog.
A *specific topic* from output	Apply a condition tag to the topic and exclude that condition tag in your target.
From output, *all topics* that are not linked (either directly or indirectly) to the target (not included in the TOC and not hyperlinked to a topic that *is* included in the TOC)	Open the target you want to exclude the topic from, and click the **Advanced** tab. Select the checkbox **Exclude content not linked directly or indirectly from the target**.

Procedure for building output

▶ To build online output:

1. In the Project Organizer, under Targets, right-click the desired target and select **Build 'target name'** from the menu.

   A Build Progress window opens as Flare builds the output according to the selections you made. If your project is large, this might take several seconds.

   If there are warnings or errors, a message appears:

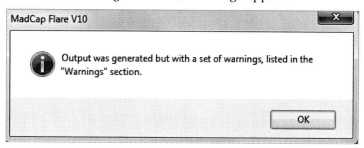

> *Important* — Errors stop the build from finishing; warnings do not.

2. Resolve any errors or warnings and build again. See "Testing and troubleshooting," the next topic.

3. To save the error log in the Project Organizer's Reports folder, click **Save Log**.

4. If there aren't any errors, you'll be asked if you want to view output. Do one of the following:

   - Click **Yes** to view the output in your default browser.

   - Click **No** to choose a browser. In the Build Progress window, click the arrow on the right of the **View Output** button View Output ▼ and select the desired browser from the list.

   Your online output is opened.

For samples of online output, see "Types of online output" on page 245.

TESTING AND TROUBLESHOOTING

When you built your output, Flare checked it for errors. During a build, errors will be listed in the Build Progress window.

One of the most common types of errors is broken links. This and other problems are described in Appendix E: Track and Troubleshoot, which starts on page 327, along with information about using the internal analyzer that comes with Flare.

When you make any changes to your content, remember to re-build your output.

> *Best Practice* — Always test your links after building online output to verify that they connect to the correct content.

WHAT IS PUBLISHING?

Publishing is *optional*. It is simply is a way of distributing online output—typically WebHelp—after it is built. When you publish, you define a destination where Flare should place the output. The destination can be a website, Intranet location, FTP server, or local hard drive folder. You define that destination from the Publishing tab of the Target Editor.

This author doesn't encourage the use of publishing for beginners unless you are publishing to your local hard drive. It is much safer to distribute online files manually as described in the next topic than to place them directly on the Web. Besides, software developers and webmasters might prefer that you *not* copy files directly to the web server. Read on to learn about alternatives to publishing.

DISTRIBUTING ONLINE OUTPUT

Distributing your output simply means sending your project to others after it is built. However, *how* you distribute and *what* you distribute differs depending on the type of output you have created and your preferences.

HOW TO DISTRIBUTE

In most cases, you will provide the software developer with the output files so they can be linked to an application. When using the application, users will access your output via the Help menu or context-sensitive help buttons and links.

There are various ways to distribute online output:

- Use an FTP application to upload output files to an FTP site.

- Use Windows Explorer to copy output to another location, such as a folder on a network. This method is quick and easy!

- Publish your output to a website or Intranet location (not recommended for beginners) or to a hard drive. See "What is publishing?" previously for details.

WHAT TO DISTRIBUTE

To distribute your output, you must supply:

- The name of the Output File (the file that launches the online output—defined when you created the target). See "Setting up an online target" on page 253 for details.

- Specific files and folders as defined in Table 5B-3.

> **Note** — You distribute only *output* files; you don't distribute your project's source files (the files contained in the Content folder under your project name).

Use Table 5B-3 as a guide to when you're ready to distribute your output.

Table 5B-3:
What to
distribute

To distribute ...	Include ...
DotNet Help	All *output* files and folders under Output\<your user name>, starting with the folder named for the target, plus the MadCap Help Viewer (a free download from MadCap Software).
HTML Help	The CHM file (such as YourProject.chm).
HTML5, WebHelp, WebHelp Plus, or WebHelp Mobile	All *output* files and folders under Output\<your user name>, starting with the folder named for the target.
WebHelp AIR	The AIR file (such as YourProject.air). Users must also install Adobe AIR™ (a free download at http://get.adobe.com/air/).
Eclipse Help	Either all files in the output folder or the JAR (Java Archive) file.

Where are the project's output files?

If you use the default locations for storing your project files, you'll find your project's output files in the My Projects\Documents folder.

The output files for each target are located in the "Output" folder under your project name.

Example:
Documents\My Projects\Gardening Girls\Output\<user name>\<target name>

Figure 5B-7:
Default location of project output as seen in Windows Explorer

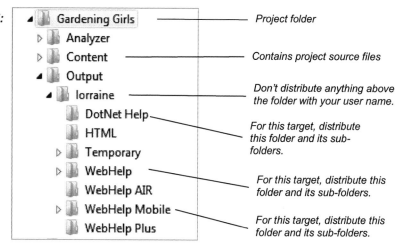

You'll need to give the software developer the name of the Output File and its location. The application needs to run this file.

About the Output File

The Output File was created when you defined the target. This is the file that launches your online output. The Output File uses the following file extensions:

Table 5B-4:
Output File extensions

Extension	Type of output
.mchelp	DotNet Help
.htm	HTML5
.chm	HTML Help
.htm	WebHelp, WebHelp Plus, and WebHelp Mobile
.air	WebHelp AIR
.jar	Eclipse Help

You'll need to give the software developer the name of the Output File and its location. The application needs to run this file.

For each type of online output listed above, you can find the Output File in the following folder (if you accepted the default project location when you created your project):

My Projects\<project name>\Output\<user name\<target name>

WHAT'S NEXT?

At this point, you could continue adding content to your project. Since setup is done, you can also re-build the document at any time. Just remember that **if you add topics to your project, you should add linked TOC entries for those topics**.

You've now gone through an entire project cycle, from creating the project to building output! If you keep working with Flare and try other, more advanced features, it won't be long before you're a bona fide Propeller Head or even a Propellus Maximus (these are titles granted to frequent posters on the Flare user forum).

In addition:

- To develop print output, look at Step 5A: Create Print Output.

- To create DITA output, see Appendix G.

- To create EPUB output, see Appendix H.

- To explore other features of Flare, look at the appendixes.

Appendix A:
Planning
Worksheets

In this chapter ...

> Part 1: Source of content
> Part 2: Types of output
> Part 3: Content Structure and
  Management
> Part 4: Content reviews
> Part 5: Project Conventions
  and Documentation
> Part 6: Start a new project
> Part 7: Target settings

PART 1: SOURCE OF CONTENT

Use this worksheet to define where your content will come from. Copy this worksheet as needed.

If your content is …	Decide …
Not in electronic form	• Which topics will you create? _____ _____ _____ _____ _____ _____ _____ • Which images will you create? _____ _____ _____ _____

Word or FrameMaker documents	How will you maintain the content?
	  ☐ By using Flare ☐ By using your source application
	
	If maintaining with source application, do you want Flare to *automatically* re-import? (The alternative is that *you initiate* the re-importing.)
	  ☐ Yes ☐ No

HTML files	Do you want to keep the style of your source content or use a Flare stylesheet?
	  ☐ Keep style of source content ☐ Use a Flare stylesheet
	        Name of Flare stylesheet: _____

If your content is …	Decide …
DITA files	How will you maintain the content?
	☐ By using Flare ☐ By using your source application
	If maintaining with source application, do you want Flare to *automatically* re-import? (The alternative is that you *initiate* the re-importing.)
	☐ Yes ☐ No
	Do you want to import all files into one folder?
	☐ Yes ☐ No
	Do you want Flare to preserve element IDs when it converts DITA content?
	☐ Yes ☐ No

PART 2: TYPE OF OUTPUT

Use this worksheet to define the output to be built by Flare. Copy this worksheet as needed.

To create …	Decide …
Online output	▪ Type of output: (*Check all that apply. Indicate if you want to create multiple outputs of one type—for different versions, etc.*)
	☐ WebHelp ☐ WebHelp Mobile ☐ HTML5
	☐ WebHelp Plus ☐ HTML Help ☐ Eclipse Help
	☐ WebHelp AIR ☐ DotNet Help
	▪ How will you structure the Help TOC (books, sub-books, with topics in each)? Write this structure on a separate sheet and list the topics in each.

To create …	Decide …
Online output *(continued)*	▪ How do you want your final output to look? Body text font: _____ Size: _____ Color: _____ Heading 1 font: _____ Size: _____ Color: _____ Heading 2 font: _____ Size: _____ Color: _____ ▪ Which skin (interface) will you use? ☐ Default: _____ ☐ Custom: _____ ☐ Mobile: _____ ☐ HTML5: _____ ▪ (WebHelp only) Which buttons do you want on the toolbar? _____ ▪ (HTML Help only) Which Help buttons do you want? _____ ▪ Which features do you want? (TOC, Index, Search, etc.) _____ (Features appear as tabs in HTML Help and as accordion bars in Mobile and WebHelp.) Heading 2 font: _____ Size: _____ Color: _____
Print output	▪ Type of output: ☐ Word ☐ FrameMaker ☐ PDF ☐ XHTML ☐ XPS (requires Microsoft .NET Framework or Word 2007 with the Office 2007 "Save as XPS" add-in) ▪ For the output selected above, choose which of the following will be included: ☐ TOC ☐ Mini-TOC ☐ Glossary ☐ Endnotes ☐ List of concepts ☐ List of elements (table of figures or images) ☐ First page header: _____ ☐ Right page header: _____ ☐ Left page header: _____ ☐ First page footer: _____ ☐ Right page footer: _____ ☐ Left page footer: _____ *(If you have multiple front and back matter parts, you might need a separate page to document the headers and footers.)*

To create …	Decide …
Print output (*continued*)	Start each document part on the right (odd) side? ☐ Yes ☐ No
	End each document part on a left page that is empty if necessary? ☐ Yes ☐ No
	▪ For the output selected above, identify:
	Page size: _____ Page orientation: ☐ Portrait ☐ Landscape
	Page margins: Left: _____ Right : _____ Top: _____ Bottom: _____
	Unit of measure (inches, pixels, points, etc.): _____
DITA output (code)	▪ How will you structure the Help TOC (books, sub-books, with topics in each)? Write this structure on a separate sheet and list the topics in each.
EPUB output	▪ Choose which of the following will be included:
	☐ TOC ☐ Mini-TOC ☐ Glossary
	☐ Endnotes ☐ List of concepts ☐ List of elements (table of figures or images)

PART 3: CONTENT REVIEWS

Use this worksheet to determine how content will be reviewed. Copy this worksheet as needed.

Select one	If reviewers use …	Reviews will proceed like this …
☐	Flare or MadCap Contributor	▪ You send reviewers Flare topics.
		▪ Reviewers view topics with Flare or MadCap Contributor and annotate them.
		▪ You view comments in Flare and accept or dismiss them in your Flare topics.
☐	Word, FrameMaker, or PDF	▪ You give reviewers Word, FrameMaker, or PDF documents that contain the topics to review.
		▪ You type changes directly into your Flare topics.

PART 4: CONTENT STRUCTURE AND MANAGEMENT

Use this worksheet to determine how content will be structured, managed, and shared. Copy this worksheet as needed.

If you need …	Do this …
To reuse common project elements in multiple projects	▪ Identify the common elements (to be stored in a global project). Identify the projects that will use elements from the global project. (You might even create a simple structure chart to show information dependencies.)
To use resources (spreadsheets, graphs, PDF files) that are external to your project ("external resources")	▪ Define which resources are needed. _____ ▪ Identify where the resources are stored. _____ ▪ Decide who will create and maintain the resources.
To track development progress, especially in a team environment	▪ Decide what file tags to use to track author progress and topic status. For example: ☐ Not started ☐ In progress ☐ Ready for review ☐ Needs research ☐ Complete ☐ Ready for translation ☐ Other _____

PART 5: PROJECT CONVENTIONS AND DOCUMENTATION

Decide and document …
▪ Conventions for naming project elements (prefixes, suffixes acronyms) Example: "CSH" for context-sensitive Help topics Projects: _____   Folders: _____ Topics: _____   Context-sensitive topics: _____ TOCs: _____   Targets: _____ Stylesheets: _____   Condition Tags: _____ Other: _____

Decide and document ...

- How to document project design decisions _____

_____

_____

PART 6: START NEW PROJECT

Use this worksheet before you begin using the Start New Project Wizard. Copy this worksheet as needed.

Note — If you choose to create the project and import the content simultaneously, you do not need to use the Start New Project Wizard. For simplicity, this book doesn't cover that feature. However, the Flare Help system does an excellent job describing how to use it. Just search for "Creating a project by importing."

If you want to ...	Decide ...		
Store your project in a location other than the default folder	Where your project will be stored: _____		
	_____		
Use your project with a source control application	Identify the type of source control application:		
	☐ Visual Source Safe	Location of INI file: _____	
		Folder used to store Flare project: _____	
	☐ Team Foundation Server	Location: _____	
	☐ Subversion	Location: _____	
	☐ Perforce	Location: _____	
	☐ Other: _____	Location: _____	

PART 7: TARGET SETTINGS

Use this form to record the settings for the target to be built by Flare. Copy this form as needed.

Product Names/Acronyms: _____

Target	Master TOC	"Master" Page Layout	Master Page (Advanced tab)	Medium	Condition Tags	Output File (Main Entry File)
					Excl:	
					Excl:	
					Excl:	
					Excl:	
					Excl:	
					Excl:	

SAMPLE TARGET SETTINGS FORM (TWO PRODUCTS)

Product Names/Acronyms: Widget Professional (WPRO) Widget Home (WHME)   Both products (WIDG)

Target	Master TOC	"Master" Page Layout	Master Page (Advanced tab)	Medium	Condition Tags	Output File (Main Entry File)
WPRO PDF	WPRO Print TOC	WIDG Pg Layout	—	WIDG PrintMed	**Excl:** Comments, WHome, Online	WPRO help topics.pdf
WPRO WebHelp	WPRO Online TOC	—	WIDG Master Page	—	**Excl:** Comments, WHome, Print	WPRO Ver2-1 Help.htm
WPRO Word	WPRO Print TOC	WIDG Pg Layout	—	WIDG PrintMed	**Excl:** Comments, WHome, Online	WPRO help topics.doc
WHME PDF	WHME Print TOC	WIDG Pg Layout	—	WIDG PrintMed	**Excl:** Comments, WPro, Online	WHME help topics.pdf
WHME WebHelp	WHME Online TOC	—	WIDG Master Page	—	**Excl:** Comments & WPro, Print	WHME Ver2-1 Help.htm
WHME Word	WHME Print TOC	WIDG Pg Layout	—	WIDG PrintMed	**Excl:** Comments, WPro, Online	WHME help topics.doc

Stylesheet for all: WIDG Help Styles
Startup topic for WPRO and WHME WebHelp: Welcome
Skin for WPRO and WHME WebHelp: WIDG Skin

Appendix B:
Import Content

In this chapter ...

➤ What you can import
➤ Import Word and Frame files
➤ Import CHM files

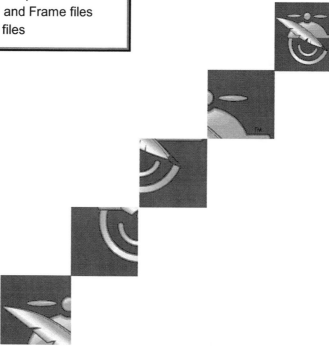

OVERVIEW

In Step 1: Get Started, you learned how to create content (topics) from scratch. Now you'll learn how to import content into a Flare project. Not only is importing a fast way to add content, but it's also the best way to get legacy content into a Flare project.

There are two ways to import content into Flare:

- By adding an import file to an existing Flare project and then importing the content, or

- By creating a Flare project and importing the content at the same time using an Import Wizard.

Since you've already learned how to create a Flare project, this appendix will cover only the first method. Let's start by looking at what you can import into Flare.

WHAT YOU CAN IMPORT

You can import the following into Flare:

- Microsoft Word and Microsoft Office 365 documents (DOC, DOCX, and RTF files)

- Adobe FrameMaker documents (BOOK, FM, and MIF files)

- CHM files (HTML Help files)

- HTML files

- RoboHelp projects (MPG and XPJ files)

- Content and project files from other Flare projects (global project linking)

- Microsoft HTML Help projects (HHP files)

- DITA files (DITA and DITAMAP files; see Appendix G)

- An existing Flare project from a source control application

When Flare imports content, it converts it to XHTML format.

WHAT THIS APPENDIX INCLUDES

This appendix covers these import options:

- Importing Word files

- Importing FrameMaker files

- Importing CHM files

You may also find it handy to copy and paste small pieces of text into your topics, which is done without importing. See "Copying and pasting content into a topic" on page 105 for details.

WHAT THIS APPENDIX DOES NOT INCLUDE

As mentioned earlier, this book addresses the needs of new Flare users who have little experience with document authoring tools. Consequently, it doesn't discuss how to import:

- RoboHelp projects. RoboHelp users transitioning to Flare can find instructions by searching for "robohelp project" in the Flare Help system.

- Microsoft HTML Help projects (HHP files)

- Importing HTML files

- Flare projects from source control applications

> **Note** — Importing DITA files is covered in Appendix G. Importing files from other Flare projects is discussed in Appendix F. See "Using global project linking" on page 365.

GETTING STARTED

Use the following chart to help you decide which parts of this appendix to read. (There's no need to read this entire appendix unless you need to import all the file types listed in this chart.)

Table B-1: *Which sections to read*

If you have ...	Do this ...	See these sections ...
Content in Word files	Import the Word files Use heading styles to break the content into topics	Importing from Word and FrameMaker files, next
		A bird's-eye view of the import process (page 277)
		Dividing one document into many topics (page 279)
		Choices for importing styles (page 280)
		Choices for maintaining content (page 281)
		Importing a Word document (page 283)
Content in FrameMaker files	Import the FrameMaker files Use heading styles to break the content into topics	Importing from Word and FrameMaker files (page 276)
		A bird's-eye view of the import process (page 277)
		Dividing one document into many topics (page 279)
		Choices for importing styles (page 280)
		Choices for maintaining content (page 281)
		Importing a FrameMaker document(page 291)
Content in CHM files	Import the CHM files	Importing CHM files (page 302)

IMPORTING FROM WORD AND FRAMEMAKER FILES

You might think of importing as simply a method of getting content into a project, but with Flare you have the option of not only importing the content, but also linking it to its source.

This means you can import content from Word or FrameMaker and then keep it updated in Word or FrameMaker!

By linking your imported content to its source, you can re-import the content at any time or choose to have Flare automatically check for updates to the source. The bottom line is that you don't have to use

Flare's XML Editor to make updates if you prefer doing so in Word or FrameMaker.

A BIRD'S-EYE VIEW OF THE IMPORT PROCESS

Now that you know what's possible, let's take a high-level look at the entire process, starting with what to do before you import the content.

Before importing

DECISION TIME!

Before you import a document, decide:

✓ Which documents will you import?

✓ Where do you want to divide the content into topics?

✓ How do you want Flare to handle styles when it converts your Word or FrameMaker documents?

✓ Will you maintain the content with Flare or with your original source program (Word or FrameMaker)?

Prepare your content

After you've made these decisions, **prepare your content for importing**. The cleaner your source files are, the smoother the import will be. Don't expect the import to be perfect; it won't be. No matter how clean your source files are, you will end up doing some formatting in your Flare project after you import your content.

For best results, take these steps before importing:

- **Use styles to control formatting** rather than local formatting in your source files. Don't use toolbar buttons and shortcut keys to apply formatting such as bold and italics.

- **Clean up the styles in your Word or FrameMaker document**. It's easy to have a proliferation of style variations. See "Choices for importing styles" on page 280 for more information about why this is important.

- **Make sure that the text of each topic is contiguous**. Choose a heading style to divide topics in Flare. Then edit your document to make sure that *the content of each topic* immediately follows that heading style. See "Dividing one document into many topics" to learn more.

- **Remove page breaks**. Page breaks divide a topic into multiple files when imported, which is probably not what you intended. As you'll see, it's better to use a heading style to break up content into topics.

> **Note** — If you don't want Flare to automatically create page layouts when you import, then also remove section breaks.

- **Remove headers and footers**. Instead of importing them, set up headers and footers in Flare using page layouts or master pages.

- Update fields in your source doc and **fix or delete bad cross-references**. (In Word, search for "Error! Reference source not found" and "Error! Bookmark not defined".)

- **Format lists as normal paragraphs** in your source files before importing, then format them as lists in Flare.

- **Don't include empty topics in your source.** If you want to import some headings without text after, then create a few paragraphs of placeholder text, which you can change later in Flare. Otherwise, clear the "Avoid Creating 'Empty' Topics" checkbox on the Options tab when you're setting up the import with the Import Editor.

Import tasks

Importing content from Word or FrameMaker into Flare (if you don't use the wizard) is a two-part process:

- First, **set up an import file**. Using Flare's Import Editor, you'll select options for the decisions you made about importing, such as if you want to link your Flare topics to source files and which style begins each topic.

> **Note** —Flare import files are saved in the Imports folder of the Project Organizer. For Word imports, the file's extension is .flimp; for FrameMaker imports, its extension is .flimpfm.

- Next, **import the content** into your project, using the import file.

Recommendation

Before you import *all* your content files, set up the import file and try importing a small sample file. Select a sample file that's somewhat representative of your other content files.

If you're not satisfied with the result, you might have to clean up your source files further, or tweak the import settings in your Flare import file until you have all the settings the way you want them. It might take a few test imports to get the settings just right.

> **Tip** — To change a Flare import file, simply open the **Imports** folder (in the **Project Organizer)** and double-click the Flare import file you want to change.

Let's look more closely at some of the choices you'll make when you set up the import file.

DIVIDING ONE DOCUMENT INTO MANY TOPICS

As mentioned earlier, if a source file will be imported into more than one Flare topic, you must decide *where* each topic should begin in the source file.

A Word or FrameMaker document typically contains paragraphs of text separated by headings. Generally, Heading 1 is used for a major topic, and lower-level headings (Heading 2 or Heading 3) are used to divide sub-topics in the Heading 1 topic.

Before you import files, choose a heading style at which to break topics. Then edit your document to make sure that the content for each topic follows the heading style you chose.

> **Note** — You can import multiple source files; each can contain content for one or more topics.

An example

Suppose you chose the Heading 2 style as the dividing point between your topics. When you import your document, each unit of content between each Heading 2 style will be converted into a Flare topic, as shown in the following illustration.

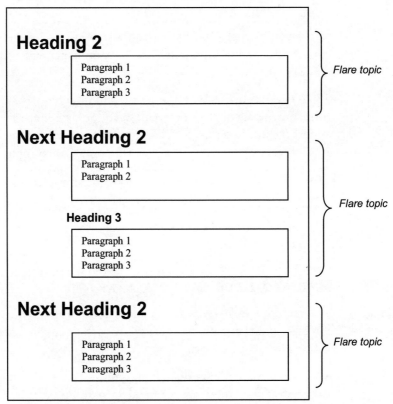

When you import this document, you'll end up with three Flare topics, as shown above.

CHOICES FOR IMPORTING STYLES

You should carefully consider the state of your documents' styles when deciding if you want to preserve them during import. Examine your source document(s) and ask:

- Do you use local formatting (not controlled by styles) in your Word or FrameMaker files?

- Are there lots of variations of styles? For example, do you have Heading 1, Heading 1 + bold, Heading 1 centered, Heading 1 underlined? Or are the styles clean (one type of Heading 1; one type of Heading 2, etc.)?

Then use this chart to help you decide the best Flare import option.

Table B-2: Choices for importing styles

If ...	Use this import option ...
You want to retain the styles in your source document *and* you don't have a proliferation of style variations - or - You want to retain local formatting (Word only).	**Preserve MS Word (or FrameMaker) Styles** With this option, Flare converts all Word or FrameMaker styles, including every style variation and custom style, to styles in a Flare stylesheet.
You want to use *only* styles from a Flare stylesheet	**Don't Preserve MS Word (or FrameMaker) Styles**

CHOICES FOR MAINTAINING CONTENT

Before you import your content, you'll need to decide where you will maintain it. You have two choices:

- **Option 1** — Use Flare to maintain your content after import. You will import your content just once and maintain it in Flare after that.

- **Option 2** — Use Word or FrameMaker to maintain your content after import. With this option, your Flare topics will be linked to the source files from which they were created, and **you will not change your topics in Flare.**

So how will Flare topics get updated if you choose Option 2?

DECISION TIME!

If you choose Option 2, you will select one of these options:

✓ Have Flare check your source files and remind you when they have changed. It's then up to you to update your Flare topics by re-importing your Word or FrameMaker files.

✓ Have Flare check your source files for changes when you build the output, automatically re-import them, and update the corresponding Flare topics before building the output. This option is called **Easy Sync**.

Use this chart to help you decide on the right options for you.

Table B-3:
Options for
maintaining
content

Choose ...	When ...
Option 1: Maintain content in Flare	You don't need to keep the source files current.
	Changes are made by only one or two people (who have access to Flare).
Option 2: Maintain content in Word or FrameMaker	Some of the people editing content have Word or FrameMaker, but not Flare.
Easy Sync (available with Option 2)	You make frequent changes to your content.
	Changes are made by many people.

About Easy Sync

With Easy Sync, you don't have to guess if and when your content has changed. All changes to the source files will be incorporated before the Flare output is built.

> **Important** — When you use Easy Sync, don't change your topics in Flare! Your changes will be lost with the next automatic re-import.

What if you change your mind after importing the content?

No problem! You can switch between linking your files and not linking them by using the Link Generate Files to Source Files checkbox on the Source Files tab in the Import Editor. If you unlink the source files, you must then begin updating your content with Flare instead of with Word or FrameMaker.

> **Tip** — You can turn Easy Sync on and off to control when changes are re-imported into Flare.

IMPORTING A WORD DOCUMENT

You can import Word documents in DOC, DOCX, or RTF (Rich Text) format that were created with Microsoft Word or with Microsoft Office 365.

> **Important** — To import from Microsoft Office 365, you must first select **File** tab → **Options** → **General** tab → **Import/Export Word Files Without MS Office** checkbox.

Flare can import the following items from Word files:

- text
- images
- formats
- index entries
- links
- cross-references
- bookmarks

About Word drawing objects and images

Flare handles drawing objects and images in Word as follows:

- Flare puts imported images into sub-folders in your project's Resources\Images folder, in the Content Explorer.

- Flare does *not* import drawing objects such as lines, and arrows. (Although Flare imports the text of callouts, they are not imported as drawing objects; they are imported as flat text.)

- The text of floating text boxes can be imported, but the text will be anchored instead of floating.

If your Word file contains drawing objects, consider taking these actions before you import your Word files.

Table B-4:
Actions to take before importing Word drawing objects

If your Word file contains ...	Do this ...
Callouts and other drawing objects that annotate images	• Incorporate callouts into the image files before import *or* • Use MadCap Capture to re-create the drawing objects.
	Tip — If you want to edit callouts after import, use Capture to add the callouts after importing the image. Capture stores graphic elements in layers, so you can easily edit callouts later.
Drawings that do not annotate images	Import the drawings as raster or vector images.

How Flare creates TOCs from a Word document

Flare creates a new TOC from the topics you import. The TOC has the same name as the Word import file. If you already created a TOC, Flare does *not* add your imported topics to the existing TOC. To consolidate the new TOC with an existing one, simply copy the new TOC items into the existing TOC.

How to import content from Word documents

Follow these steps to import content from a Word document into a Flare project. This procedure includes instructions for creating the Word import file *and* for importing the content.

▶ To import content from a Word document:

1. Make sure that the Flare project you want to import into is open with the Project Organizer in view.

2. *If you previously imported Word documents into this project,* expand the **Imports** folder and double-click the Flare import file you want to use for this import. The Word Import Editor opens. Skip to Step 4.

3. *If you have not previously imported Word documents into this project,* create a Flare import file to store your import settings as follows:

    a. In the Project Organizer, right-click the **Imports** folder.

    b. Select **Add MS Word Import File** from the menu.

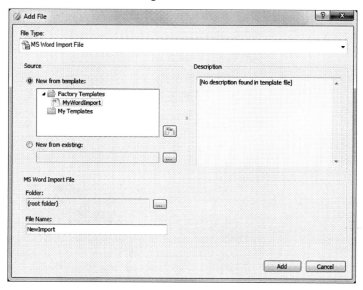

    c. If not already selected, select **New from template**.

    d. To use a template provided by Flare, select **MyWordImport** under the **Factory Templates** folder. To use one of your own templates, select **My Templates** for the folder and select the template you want to use from the list of templates on the right.

    e. Type a File Name. (Flare will add an extension of .flimp to the Word import file.)

    f. Click **Add**. The File Name you typed is listed in the Imports folder and the Word Import Editor opens.

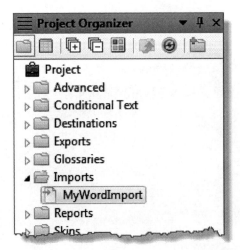

The Word Import Editor opens.

4. On the Source Files tab, do the following:

a. Click **Add Files** and select the Word documents you want to add. (You can choose DOC, DOCX, or RTF files.)

> *Note* — DOCX (Word's XML format) is available only with Word 2007 and later.

b. If you want to update your content from Flare instead of from Word after import, clear the **Link Generated Files To Source Files** checkbox. (See "Choices for maintaining content" on page 281 for options.)

> *Note* — If your imported topics are linked to your source files, a link icon appears next to the topic's file name on the XML Editor tab. (If you're using source control, the source control icon appears instead.)

c. If you've selected multiple Word documents to import, you can change the order in which they're listed by clicking **Move Up** and **Move Down**.

> *Note* — The document order shown here determines the topic order in the TOC that Flare creates.

5. If you're splitting your documents into multiple topics, do the following:

    a. Click the **New Topic Styles** tab. On the left, Flare shows the styles used in the Word documents being imported.

    b. In the Used Word Styles column, double-click the style you want to start each new topic. The style appears in the right column.

6. If you want Flare to incorporate changes from your linked Word documents each time you build output, do the following:

    a. Verify that the **Link Generated Files To Source Files** checkbox (Source Files tab) is checked.

    b. Click the **Options** tab and select the **Auto-reimport before 'Generate Output'** checkbox. (This feature is called "Easy Sync" in the Flare Help system.)

7. *(Optional)* On the Options tab, select these options as desired:

To ...	Use this option ...
Split long topics based on the number of characters (instead of using heading styles) and have Flare create a link called "Topic Continued" at the end of each page that is continued. You can also edit the link's format of the link.	Add "Topic Continued" links when appropriate
Split long topics based on the number of characters and have Flare create a link called "Topic Continued From" at the top of each page that continues a split topic. You can also edit the format of the link.	Add "Topic Continued From..." links when appropriate
Split long topics when a specified number of characters in the topic is reached. Enter the number of characters to use as a threshold. If a topic exceeds the threshold, it will be split.	Split Long Topics

To ...	Use this option ...
Prevent Flare from creating topics for empty sections in your Word documents. Enter the threshold of empty characters. If a source topic exceeds the threshold, Flare will not create a topic for it.	Avoid Creating 'Empty' Topics

> ***Important*** — Clear this option if you have any topics that are shorter than 50 characters (the default threshold). If selected, Flare consolidates topics that are shorter than the threshold instead of creating separate topics. (Instead of clearing this option, you could also increase the threshold.)

To ...	Use this option ...
Specify a length for the file names Flare will create when it splits long topics.	Approximate Filename Length
Set imported tables to Auto-Fit to Contents so no table width is set.	Convert all tables to "Auto-Fit to Contents"
Create Flare page layouts from the headers and footers in each section of the imported Word document.	Create a Page Layout for each section header/footer
Use the first heading in the topic as the topic title (a topic property) and automatically update the topic title whenever the heading changes.	Automatically set topic title

> ***Note*** — To learn more about these options, search for "importing Word" in the Flare Help system.

8. Click the **Stylesheet** tab and do the following:

   a. If you want the imported topics to be linked to a Flare stylesheet, click the **Stylesheet** button and select a stylesheet to apply to the imported topics. (If you select a stylesheet already in your project, Flare creates a new stylesheet from it, and appends the number "1" to its name.)

   b. Under **Source Styles**, select the desired button to either preserve or not preserve Word styles. (See "Choices for importing styles" on page 280.)

c. To create Flare styles for local formatting in your Word documents, select the **Convert inline formatting to CSS styles** checkbox; otherwise, clear this checkbox. (This option is available only if you preserve Word styles.)

> **Note** — In Word, you can apply formats by using toolbar buttons and menu options instead of character styles. In Flare, you'll hear the terms "local" formatting and "inline" formatting used to describe this.

9. (*Optional*) If you want your Word *paragraph* styles to take on the characteristics of your Flare styles, map the styles by doing the following:

a. Click the **Paragraph Styles** tab.

b. For each Word style you want to map, select the style in the MS Word Style column, select a style (in the Flare Styles column) to map to it, then click **Map**. The Flare styles you select appear to the right of the Word styles you mapped them to, as shown here:

MS Word Style	Flare Style	
Bodytext	p	
Heading 1	h1.Heading 1	
Word style —— Heading 3	h3.Heading 3 ——	*The Flare style it is mapped to. (In this example, we preserved Word styles.)*
Procedure		

> **Note** — If you chose to preserve Word styles (on the Stylesheet tab), and you then map a Word style to a Flare style, Flare creates a style class of the Flare style. For example, if the Word style is called "Heading 1" and it's mapped to the Flare style "h1," the style class is "h1.Heading 1."

In the following example, paragraph styles are mapped and Word styles are not preserved. Notice how the resulting Flare style name is a Flare style name (h1), not a combination of the Word style (Heading 1) and the Flare style. (Flare did not create a new style.)

MS Word Style	Flare Style
Bodytext	p
Heading 1	h1
Heading 2	h2

Word style —— (pointing to Heading 2 row, MS Word Style column)

The Flare style it is mapped to. (In this example, we did not preserve Word styles.) —— (pointing to h2)

10. (*Optional*) If you want your Word *character* styles to take on the characteristics of your Flare styles, map the styles as follows:

   a. Click the **Character Styles** tab.

   b. For each Word style you want to map, select the style in the MS Word Style column, select a style in the Flare Styles column to map it to, then click **Map**.

11. Do one of the following:

   ▪ If you want to import the content now, proceed to Step 12.

   ▪ If you don't want to import the content now, click **Save All** [icon], then close the Word Import Editor.

12. Select **Import** (under the tab name). Then click **Yes** when prompted to save changes to the Flare import file.

   The Accept Imported Documents dialog lists the documents to be imported (on the left) and a preview of the currently selected document (on the right).

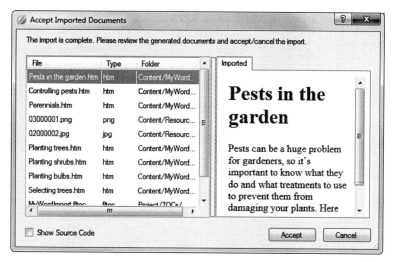

13. If you're satisfied with how the topic previews look, click **Accept** to import the files. The files are added to your Flare project.

14. Close the Word Import Editor.

Where are my imported topics?

You may notice that your imported topics aren't listed in the Content Explorer with your other project topics. That's because Flare put your imported topics together in a folder in the Content Explorer. That folder has the same name as the Word import file you created.

Flare placed any imported images under the Resources folder, in a folder named the same as your Import file.

Figure B-1:
Where Flare stores your imported Word topics

Imported topics

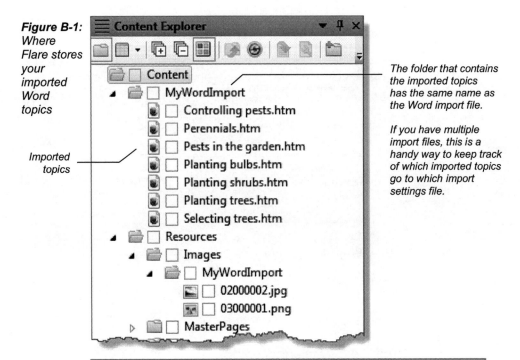

The folder that contains the imported topics has the same name as the Word import file.

If you have multiple import files, this is a handy way to keep track of which imported topics go to which import settings file.

> **Important** — If you re-import content, Flare writes over files (topics, TOC, etc.) you previously imported unless you've changed them in Flare.

Re-importing content

If you re-import content, Flare writes over only those files (topics, TOC, etc.) that you have previously imported that, but have not changed in Flare. It also alerts you about files that you *have* changed, and lets you choose whether to overwrite them. If you choose not to overwrite them, Flare creates a file by the same name with a number appended to the end of its name (starting with the number "1").

IMPORTING A FRAMEMAKER DOCUMENT

You can import FrameMaker documents that were created with FrameMaker Versions 7.0 and newer in BOOK, FM, or MIF formats.

As already discussed, when you import a document, you can split it into multiple topics. Flare uses FrameMaker's heading styles as the division points.

Flare can import the following items from FrameMaker files:

- text

- images (with or without callouts)

- formats

- master pages (imported as Flare page layouts)

- variables

- conditionals

- auto-numbering

- index entries

- hypertext links

- cross-references

> **Best Practice** — If you have a FrameMaker book, it is better to import the book rather than individual files. Flare will identify and import the files that are part of the book.

About FrameMaker images

Flare handles images in FrameMaker as follows:

- Flare puts imported images in the same folder as imported topics. If you prefer, you can later move the images to the Resources\Images folder, which is the default folder for new images.

- For anchored frames with images, you can choose to import the images with or without callouts. If imported with callouts, Flare creates both an image file and a PROPS file so you can edit them in MadCap Capture.

- After import, you might need to resize or re-position images, since Flare does not anchor them in frames.

Before importing FrameMaker documents

When Flare imports your FrameMaker files, it uses the file name of the first FrameMaker source file as the file name of the first topic file it creates. If you want the file name to be the same as the text of the first heading, you must insert a marker in your first FrameMaker source file before you import the file.

> **Best Practice** — Insert a marker in every FrameMaker source file to be imported, not just the first one. (After all, you might later decide to rearrange the order in which you import the FrameMaker files.)

Add the marker at the *end* of the first heading in each FrameMaker file you want to import, not at the beginning of the heading. The marker should be a custom marker type called "Filename." For the text of the marker, type the file name for the first topic to be created from this source file. (For specific instructions, search the Flare Help system for "Specifying custom file names for FrameMaker imports.")

How to import content from FrameMaker documents

Follow these instructions to import content from a FrameMaker document into a Flare project. This procedure includes instructions for creating the FrameMaker import file *and* importing the content.

▶ To import content from a FrameMaker document:

1. Make sure that the Flare project you want to import into is open with the Project Organizer in view.

2. *If you previously imported FrameMaker documents into this project,* expand the **Imports** folder and double-click the Flare import file you want to use for this import. The Frame Import Editor opens. Skip to Step 4.

3. *If you have not previously imported FrameMaker documents into this project,* create a Flare import file to store your import settings as follows:

   a. In the Project Organizer, right-click the **Imports** folder.

   b. Select **Add FrameMaker Import File** from the menu.

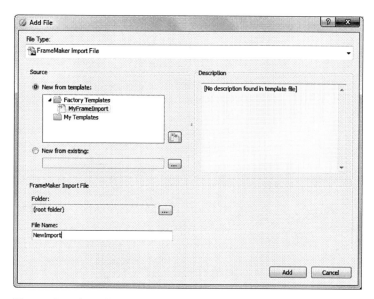

c. If not already selected, select **New from template**.

d. To use a Flare template, select **MyFrameImport** under the **Factory Templates** folder. To use one of your own templates, select **My Templates** for the folder and select the desired template from the list of templates on the right.

e. Type a File Name. (Flare will add an extension of .flimpfm to the import file.)

f. Click **Add**. The file is added to the Imports folder.

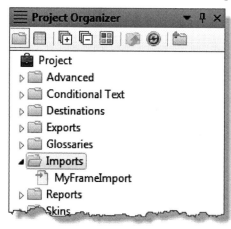

The Frame Import Editor opens.

4.   On the **Source Files** tab, do the following:

   a.   Click **Add Files** ⊞ and select the FrameMaker documents
        you want to add. (You can choose BOOK, FM, or MIF files.)

   > **Best Practice** — If you're importing a FrameMaker book, it is better
   > to import the book rather than individual FM files. Flare will identify and
   > import the files that are part of the book.

   b.   If you want to update your content from Flare instead of
        from FrameMaker after import, clear the **Link Generated
        Files To Source Files** checkbox. (See "Choices for
        maintaining content" on page 281 for options.)

   > **Note** — If your imported topics are linked to your source files, a link
   > icon ⬚ appears next to the topic's file name on the XML Editor tab. (If
   > you are using source control, the source control icons appear instead.)

   c.   If you've selected multiple FrameMaker documents to
        import, you can change the order in which they're listed by
        clicking **Move Up** ⬆ and **Move Down** ⬇.

   > **Note** — The document order shown determines the order of topics in
   > the TOC that Flare creates.

5.   If you're splitting your FrameMaker documents into multiple
     topics, do the following:

   a.   Click the **New Topic Styles** tab. FrameMaker opens. Styles
        you use in the FrameMaker documents being imported are
        shown on the left.

   b.   In the Used FrameMaker Styles column, double-click the
        style that will mark the beginning of each new topic. The
        style is listed in the right column.

6. (*Optional*) On the **Options** tab, select from among these tasks:

To ...	Do this ...
Import anchored frames with images	Select the desired option: **Generate Images Without Callouts**, **Generate Images With Callouts**, or **Generate Flattened Images**.
Incorporate changes in your linked FrameMaker documents each time you build Flare output	Select the **Auto-reimport before 'Generate Output'** checkbox. (called "Easy Sync" in the Flare Help system.) (Make sure that the **Link Generated Files To Source Files** checkbox is checked on the Source Files tab.)
Preserve the size of resized images in your FrameMaker documents	Select the **Preserve Image Size** checkbox.
Enable passthrough markers (if used) in your FrameMaker documents	Select the **Enable 'Passthrough' Markers** checkbox and select the format (text, fragment, or XML) of the passthrough markers. FrameMaker passthrough markers indicate text (such as JavaScript code) that requires special treatment when imported.
Create Flare table styles from the formats used in tables in your FrameMaker topics	Select the **Convert Table Styles** checkbox. Table formatting will be imported even if you don't select this option.

7. (*Optional*) On the **Options** tab, select these options if you have topics that are shorter than 50 characters, want to avoid creating empty topics, or want to split long topics in FrameMaker documents:

To ...	Do this ...
Split long topics when a topic reaches a specified number of characters	Select the **Split Long Topics** checkbox and enter the number of characters to use as a threshold. When a topic exceeds the threshold, it will be split.

To ...	Do this ...
Create a link called "Topic Continued" at the end of each Flare page that is continued	Select the **Add "Topic Continued" links when appropriate** checkbox. You can also edit the format of the link.
Create a link called "Topic Continued From" at the top of each Flare page that continues a split topic	Select the **Add "Topic Continued From..." links when appropriate** checkbox. You can also edit the format of the link.
Specify a length for filenames Flare will create when it splits long topics.	Type a length in the **Approximate Filename Length** field.
Prevent Flare from creating topics for empty sections in your FrameMaker documents	Select the **Avoid Creating 'Empty' Topics** checkbox and enter the threshold of empty characters. When a source topic exceeds the threshold, Flare will not create a Flare topic for it. *Important* — Clear this checkbox if you have any topics that are shorter than 50 characters (the default threshold). If selected, Flare consolidates topics that are shorter than the threshold instead of creating separate topics. (Instead of clearing this option, you could increase the threshold.)
Convert MathFullForm equations to MathML	Select the **Convert equations to MathML** checkbox.

Note — To learn more about these options, search for "importing framemaker" in the Flare Help system.

8. On the **Stylesheet** tab, do the following:

    a. Apply a stylesheet to the imported topics. Either select a stylesheet from list of stylesheets in this project, or click the **Stylesheet** button and select a stylesheet outside of your project.

b. Under **Source Styles**, select the desired button to either preserve or not preserve FrameMaker styles. (See "Choices for importing styles" on page 279.)

c. To specify the characteristics for each style's property group, click the **Conversion Styles** button to open the Import Styles Editor. Click the field to the right of each characteristic to select a value.

9. (*Optional*) If you want your FrameMaker *paragraph* styles to take on the characteristics of your Flare styles, map the styles by doing the following:

a. Click the **Paragraph Styles** tab.

b. For each FrameMaker style you want to map, select the style in the FrameMaker Style column, select a style (in the Flare Styles column) to map to it, then click **Map**. The Flare styles you select appear to the right of the FrameMaker styles you mapped them to, as shown here:

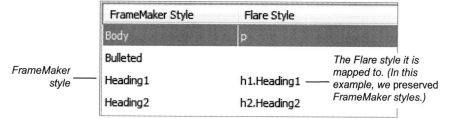

FrameMaker style

The Flare style it is mapped to. (In this example, we preserved FrameMaker styles.)

Note — If you chose to preserve FrameMaker styles (on the Stylesheet tab), and you then map a FrameMaker style to a Flare style, Flare creates a style class of the Flare style. For example, if the FrameMaker style is called "Heading1" and it's mapped to the Flare style "h1," the style class is "h1.Heading1."

In the following example, paragraph styles are mapped and FrameMaker styles are not preserved. Notice how the resulting Flare style name is purely a Flare style name (h1), not a combination of the FrameMaker style (Heading1) and the Flare style. (Flare did not create a new style.)

FrameMaker Style	Flare Style
Body	p
Bulleted	
Heading1	h1
Heading2	h2

FrameMaker style ——— (pointing to FrameMaker Style column)

h1 ——— *The Flare style it is mapped to. (In this example, we did not preserve FrameMaker styles.)*

10. (*Optional*) To make your FrameMaker *character* styles take on the characteristics of your Flare styles, map the styles by doing the following:

    a.   Click the **Character Styles** tab.

    b.   For each FrameMaker style you want to map, select the style in the FrameMaker Style column, select a style in the Flare Styles column to map to it, then click **Map**.

11. (*Optional*) To make your FrameMaker *cross-references* take on the characteristics of a Flare style, map the styles by doing the following:

    a.   Click the **Cross-Reference Styles** tab.

    b.   For each FrameMaker style you want to map, select the style in the FrameMaker Style column, select a style in the Flare styles column to map to it, then click **Map**.

12. Do one of the following:

    ▪   If you want to import the content now, proceed to Step 13.

    ▪   If you don't want to import the content now, click **Save All**, then close the Frame Import Editor.

13. Select **Import** (under the tab name). Then click **Yes** when prompted to save changes to the Flare import file.

The Accept Imported Documents dialog lists the documents to be imported (on the left) and a preview of the currently selected document (on the right).

14. If you're satisfied with how the topic previews look, click **Accept** to import the files. The files are added to your Flare project.

15. Close the Frame Import Editor.

Where are my imported topics and images?

You may have noticed that your imported topics aren't listed in the Content Explorer with your other project topics. That's because Flare put your imported topics in a folder in the Content Explorer. This folder has the same name as the FrameMaker book file (if you imported a FrameMaker book) or as the first document listed at the top of the Source Files tab.

Flare placed any imported images under the Resources folder, in a folder named the same as your import file.

Figure B-2: Where Flare stores your imported Frame-Maker topics

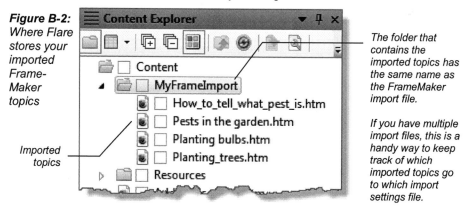

The folder that contains the imported topics has the same name as the FrameMaker import file.

If you have multiple import files, this is a handy way to keep track of which imported topics go to which import settings file.

Imported topics

Re-importing content

If you re-import content, Flare writes over previously imported files (topics, TOC, etc.) that you have not changed in Flare. It also alerts you about files that you *have* changed, and lets you choose whether to overwrite them. If you choose not to overwrite them, Flare creates a file by the same name with a number appended to the end of its name (starting with the number "1").

Importing CHM Files

You can create a new Flare project by importing "decompiling" Microsoft HTML Help output (a CHM file) directly into Flare. All associated files (including images) are imported.

This feature is especially helpful if (1) you don't have the source from which a CHM file was created; (2) you want to maintain the content in Flare so you can create online output a newer format; or (3) you want to take advantage of Flare's single-sourcing features.

▶ To create a project from a CHM file:

1. Select **File** tab → **New Project** → **HTML Help File (CHM)**

2. Select and open the desired CHM file.

3. Proceed through the import wizard and click **Finish** when you're ready to create the project.

    Flare automatically creates a TOC, skin, stylesheet, and Content Explorer folders to match the TOC structure—all from the CHM.

Appendix C:
XML Editor
Reference

In this chapter ...
➤ Toolbars
➤ Cursor types
➤ Shortcuts when working with text
➤ Navigational shortcuts

TOP TOOLBAR

Click ...	To ...
(Preview as primary target icon) **Preview as primary target**	See how the topic will look when compiled. To learn more, see "Previewing a topic" on page 57.
(Conditional expression icon) **Select the conditional expression to apply to the document**	Hides content that is tagged with the condition tags you exclude so you can see and edit a topic in the XML Editor without seeing the content tagged with the excluded condition tags.
Layout (Web) ▾ or **Layout (Print)** ▾ **Layout Mode**	Toggle between **Web Layout** and **Print Layout** modes. (See "Task 7: Viewing layout modes" on page 91.) Click the down arrow to select two additional choices: ■ **Edit Page Layout Document** — Opens the Page Layout Editor so you can edit the page layout associated with this topic. ■ **Edit Master Stylesheet** — Opens the Stylesheet Editor so you can edit the stylesheet associated with this topic (if there is one).
Medium (default) ▾ **Medium** **(default, non-print, print)**	Select a medium to use when viewing your topic. (Flare uses the "default" medium for web layouts and the "print" medium for print layouts.) The XML Editor shows the topic in the styles associated with the medium you select. For more info, see "What are mediums?" on page 92.
Page Layout ▾ **Page Layout**	Select a page layout in which to view your topic when Print Layout mode is selected.
(Hyperlink icon) **Insert a hyperlink**	Open the Insert Hyperlink dialog to add a hypertext link. Links can open topics within your project or external to your project, files, email addresses, websites, documents, or headings and bookmarks within the active topic.
(Cross-Reference icon) **Insert a Cross-Reference**	Open the Insert Cross-Reference dialog to add a cross-reference to your topic. By default, the cross-reference inserts the word "See" plus the text of the block you are cross-referencing within quotes. You can create a cross-reference to a topic in the project, a file, a document, or a heading or bookmark within the active topic.

Click ...	To ...
[icon] Insert an image	Open the Insert Image dialog to insert an image or graphics file. You can also type a screen tip that will appear when you hover your cursor over the image in output.
[icon] Insert a snippet	Open the Insert Snippet Link dialog so you can select a snippet to insert in your topic.
[icon] Insert a variable	Open the Insert Variables dialog so you can select a variable to insert in your topic or snippet.
[icon] Character	Open the Character dialog for tasks pertaining to characters (such as setting a default quick character). The drop-down list contains choices for inserting quick, favorite, and recently used characters, and non-breaking spaces or hyphens.
[icon] Toggle Index Entry Mode	Toggle index entry mode on or off. Also contains a drop-down list of options for creating index keywords. To learn more about index entry mode, see "Adding index keywords" on page 188.
[icon] Toggle Concept Entry Mode	Toggle concept entry mode on or off. Use to add concept markers in topics. You can then insert concept links (links to related topics) into other topics.
[icon] Show/Hide Spaces	Toggle on or off the display of spaces and the end of block character [icon] for the active topic.
[icon] Show tags (displayed as "Toggle show tags" after clicked)	Toggle on or off the display of the *active* topic with its XML tags. (This is not editable code. If you want to edit a topic's code, you need to use a text editor such as Notepad or Flare's Internal Text Editor.) The drop-down list contains additional choices for various items such as variable names, bookmark names, and conditional indicators.
[icon] Send this file to the text editor	Open the active topic in Flare's Internal Text Editor so you can edit the topic's XML tags and content.

BOTTOM TOOLBAR

Click ...	To ...
Words: 55 Word count	Displays the number of words in the topic.
⊟ Smaller Font (*Web Layout only*)	Lower the magnification of fonts in the *active* topic. Each time you click, the magnification is lowered by 10%. (You cannot reduce the magnification to below 100 %.) **Note** — This option does not reduce the size of images.
▣ Reset font scaling to 100% (*Web Layout only*)	Reset the magnification of fonts in the *active* topic to 100%. (Does not change the font size.)
⊞ Larger Font (*Web Layout only*)	Raise the magnification of fonts in the *active* topic. Each time you click, the magnification is raised by 10%.
100% ▼ (*Web Layout only*)	Select a percentage by which to magnify the fonts in the *active* topic.
⏮ Go to the first page (*Print Layout only*)	Show the first page of the topic.
◀ Go to the previous page (*Print Layout only*)	Show the previous page of the topic.
▶ Go to the next page (*Print Layout only*)	Show the next page of the topic.
⏭ Go to the last page (*Print Layout only*)	Show the last page of the topic.

Click ...	To ...
Page: 1 of 2 (*Print Layout only*)	Select the page number you want to view.
Zoom/scale (*Print Layout only*) ***Note*** — This button changes to reflect the current zoom/scale choice.	Specify how to magnify the page for the *active* topic: **100 %** — Scales the content to 100% magnification. **100 % (2 pages)** — Shows two pages at 100%. **Fit Width** — Scales the content to fit the window width. **One Page** — Scales the content to show one page. **Two Pages** — Scales the content to show two pages. **Four Pages** — Scales the content to show four pages. **Eight Pages** — Scales the content to show eight pages.
Hide/show Conditional Indicators	Toggle on or off the highlighting of condition tags that have been applied to text in the *active* topic. See "Using condition tags" on page 344 for information about using condition tags in your topics.
Toggle show blocks	Toggle on or off tag bars in the *active* topic. Tag bars show the tag for each block in your topic. If you click inside a table, tag bars also show tags applied to the table's cells. You can resize or rearrange a table's rows by dragging its tag bars. To learn more about tag bars, see page 95.
Toggle show spans	Toggle on or off span bars for the *active* topic. Span bars appear across the top of the content area and show the tags for formats applied to text. For example, if you apply bold to a word, a span bar labeled "b" appears above your topic. They also show column bars if your cursor is inside a table. (You must click inside a table to see its column bars.) You can resize or rearrange a table's columns by dragging its column bars. To learn more about span bars, see page 95.
Toggle show the horizontal ruler	Toggle on or off a horizontal ruler across the top of the *active* topic. Click the ruler to select the units of measure (pixels, points, centimeters, or inches) used.

Click …	To …
Toggle show the vertical ruler	Toggle on or off a vertical ruler at the left side of the *active* topic. Click the ruler to select the units of measure (pixels, points, centimeters, or inches) used.

Cursor Types

There are other cursor shapes that are not discussed here, but these are the most common ones you'll see when viewing topics in the XML Editor. Refer to Figure C-1 when reading about cursor types.

Before we talk about cursors, let's first discuss another way to look at the tags behind your topics.

Open a topic and click **Show tags** in the top toolbar. This option gives you a quick view of your topics' structure and tags.

Figure C-1:
Examples
of tags

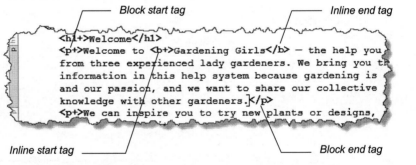

Cursor looks like this …	When it is …
[	Placed at a start tag. A start tag might be at the beginning of a text block or within a text block (an inline tag). For example, you might have applied bold to text within a text block. That text will be nested with its own tag set, as shown in Figure C-1.
]	Placed at an end tag.
I	Floating over text in a text block.

Cursor looks like this ...	When it is ...
I	Anchored within a text block. (You clicked the mouse or used the keyboard to move the cursor in a text block.) When the cursor looks like this, you can edit text at the cursor's location.
I	Placed at the start of an inline tag. When the cursor looks like this, you can insert text in the parent tag after the nested end tag.
—	Placed between the end tag for a text block and the next start tag. For example, the cursor might be positioned after an end paragraph tag </p> and before the next start paragraph tag <p>. When the cursor looks like this, you can insert text at the beginning of the next start tag. This cursor appears only when you use the keyboard (not the mouse) to navigate in your topic.
✥	Placed on the **Resize Picture** button at the lower right corner of an image. When the cursor looks like this, you can resize the image.
🖑	Placed over a tag or span bar. Right-click the tag or span bar to open a menu of choices that pertain to the text block associated with the tag bar or content associated with the span bar.

> **Note** — The last three cursors in this table appear only when you're not viewing tags.

SHORTCUTS WHEN WORKING WITH TEXT

SELECTING TEXT

To select ...	Do this ...
A word	Double-click the word.
A block of text	Either triple-click anywhere within the text block or click the text block's tag bar.
The entire topic	Either select **Home** tab → **Editing** → **Select All**, or click four times in fast succession.

To select ...	Do this ...
The table cell after the one your cursor is in	Press **TAB**.
The table cell before the one your cursor is in	Press **SHIFT + TAB**.

DELETING TEXT

To ...	Do this ...
Delete the character to the right of the insertion point	Press **DELETE**.
Delete the character to the left of the insertion point	Press **BACKSPACE**.
Delete several consecutive words	Select the words. Then either press the **DELETE** key or select **Home** tab → **Delete**.
Delete an entire text block	Select the text block. Then either press the **DELETE** key or right-click the block's tag bar and select **Delete**.
	Note — The start and end tags for the text block are also deleted.

COPYING AND PASTING TEXT

You can copy (**CTRL + C**) and paste (**CTRL + V**) text as you would in most word processing applications, but you can also right-click the tag bar (left) to open a menu that contains copy and paste options. (For more info, see "Copying and pasting content into a topic" on page 105.)

MOVING TEXT WITHIN A TOPIC

Use the following procedures to move a word, several consecutive words, or entire blocks of text.

▶ **To move a one word or several consecutive words:**

1. Select the words to be moved. (See the chart on page 309 for assistance.)

2. Cut the selected text (**CTRL + X**) and paste it (**CTRL + V**) where desired.

▶ **To move a text block:**

Do one of the following:

- Select the text block to be moved. (See the chart on page 309 for assistance.) Cut the text block (**CTRL + X**) and paste it (**CTRL + V**) where desired.

- Make sure that tag bars are in view. (If not, click **Toggle show blocks** .) Drag and drop the text block's tag bar to the desired place in the topic.

> *Note* — To learn more about tag bars, see "Toggling tag and span bars" on page 97.

SHORTCUTS FOR INSERTING CONTENT

To insert a ...	Do this ...
Non-breaking space	Press **SHIFT + SPACE**.
Bookmark	Press **CTRL + SHIFT + K**.
Cross-reference	Press **CTRL + SHIFT + R**.
Hyperlink	Press **CTRL + K**.
Image	Press **CTRL + G**.
Snippet	Press **CTRL + R**.
Variable	Press **CTRL + SHIFT + V**.

NAVIGATIONAL SHORTCUTS

To move to ...	Do this ...
The top of the topic	Press **CTRL + HOME**. A blinking left bracket [appears before the first word in the block.
The end of the topic	Press **CTRL + END**. A blinking right bracket] appears after the last word in the block.
The beginning of the line your cursor is in	Press **HOME**
The end of the line your cursor is in	Press **END**
The next page of print output (*in Print Output mode*)	Press **PAGE DOWN**.
The previous page of print output (*in Print Output mode*)	Press **PAGE UP**.
The next word	**CTRL + →**
The previous word	**CTRL + ←**

MISCELLANEOUS SHORTCUTS

To ...	Do this ...
Save the active file	Press **CTRL + S**.
Save all open files	Press **CTRL + SHIFT + S**.
Create a new topic	Press **CTRL + T**.
Undo the last action	Press **CTRL + Z**.
Redo the last action	Press **CTRL + Y**.

Appendix D: Context-Sensitive Help

In this chapter ...

➤ Learn about context-sensitive help
➤ Create a header file
➤ Create an alias file
➤ Set up an alias file
➤ Test your context-sensitive help

OVERVIEW

This appendix pertains to Help systems only. Further, it applies only if the application you are writing Help for will have help buttons on its windows and dialogs.

Creating context-sensitive help involves collaboration between you (the help author) and the software developers of the application you are writing Help for. When you develop context-sensitive help, you'll work closely with software developers to make it happen.

WHAT IS CONTEXT-SENSITIVE HELP?

Context-sensitive help links an application's window or dialog to a help topic that explains it. Users can access a help topic by clicking a help button or pressing **F1** from the associated window or dialog.

With context-sensitive help, a software developer places help buttons on the windows and dialogs where Help is needed. As the help author, you'll write the help topics that the help buttons will open—plus you'll indicate ahead of time which topics go with which dialogs. This process is called **mapping**, and it uses two kinds of files:

- Header file
- Alias file

HEADER FILE

Header files (also called map files) assign a unique identification number (map number) to each window and dialog that will open a help topic. The choice of which windows and dialogs will have context-sensitive help is a decision you and the software developers will make and depends on the content of your Help system.

Header files are text files, readable in Notepad. They have an extension of .h or .hh, which is added automatically by Flare.

Software developers may provide the header file, but if they don't, you can use Flare to create it, and then add topic IDs (called "Identifiers" in Flare) used by an application and map numbers to it. If you create the header file, you'll need to discuss with the software developers what it should contain, because the map numbers and topic IDs must match what's used in the application. For more information about this, see "Creating a header file" on page 318.

Here's an example of a header file. (Header files typically have more than five lines, but for the sake of space, I show just five here.)

Figure D-1:
Header file

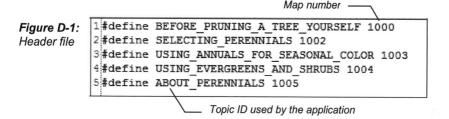

Map number ⎯

```
1 #define BEFORE_PRUNING_A_TREE_YOURSELF 1000
2 #define SELECTING_PERENNIALS 1002
3 #define USING_ANNUALS_FOR_SEASONAL_COLOR 1003
4 #define USING_EVERGREENS_AND_SHRUBS 1004
5 #define ABOUT_PERENNIALS 1005
```

Topic ID used by the application

ALIAS FILE

An alias file is used to assign each identifier and map number to a topic in your Flare Help project. You'll create alias files from Flare in a format readable only by Flare (you cannot view them in Notepad). Alias files have a .flali extension.

In addition to assigning windows and dialogs to help topics, you can also assign a **skin** to each help topic so you can change the appearance of the context-sensitive help. For example, you might want context-sensitive topics to open in a smaller window than your regular help topics.

Think of an alias file as the "go-between" that connects a software application and your Help system.

AN EXAMPLE OF MAPPING

Suppose that your application contains an Add dialog, a Change dialog, and a Properties dialog, each of which need to open context-sensitive help. In addition, assume that ...

Table D-1:
Example
of mapping

This dialog's help button ...	Should open this topic ...
Add dialog	Adding a widget
Change dialog	Changing a widget
Properties dialog	Widget properties

The header and alias files in our example would contain:

```
Header file

Add_acct_dialog        1
Change_acct_dialog     2
Properties_dialog      3
```

```
Alias file

Add_acct_dialog        1    Adding a widget
Change_acct_dialog     2    Changing a widget
Properties_dialog      3    Widget properties
```

HOW FLARE USES CONTEXT-SENSITIVE HELP

Let's look at how Flare uses help buttons to open Flare help topics:

Flare uses this button to open a topic that contains information about this dialog.

Figure D-2:
Help
buttons on
a dialog

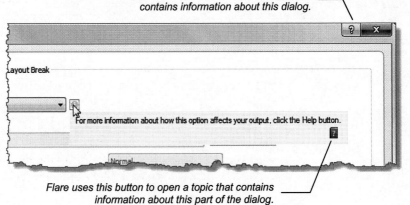

For more information about how this option affects your output, click the Help button.

Flare uses this button to open a topic that contains information about this part of the dialog.

YOUR TASKS

To create context-sensitive help, you'll need to complete these tasks:

- **Planning**. Talk to the software developer and decide which windows and dialogs require context-sensitive help and whether context-sensitive help topics will open in windows that are sized or positioned differently than regular help topics.

- Verify that your **project contains a header file**.

  If the software developer gives you a header file, you must import it into your project. (You can find instructions for importing a header file in the Flare Help system by searching on "header files" and opening the topic called "Importing Header Files.") Alternately, you can copy the header file into the Project Organizer's Advanced folder (<project name>\project\advanced).

  If the software developer doesn't give you a header file, use Flare's default header file, or create your own in Flare. See "Creating a header file" next.

- **Add an alias file** to your project (or use Flare's default alias file). See "Adding an alias file" on page 320.

- **Set up the alias file**. This involves creating topic IDs and map numbers (only if you didn't get a header file from the software developer), mapping topic IDs to help topics, and optionally assigning a skin to topic IDs. See "Setting up an alias file" on page 321.

- **Select the alias file when you set up the target**. (Open the target in the Target Editor. On the **Advanced** tab, select the alias file.)

- *If you create the header file,* **give it to the software developer**. (For instructions, search on "header files" in the Flare Help system and open the topic called "Providing a Developer with a Header File.")

- **Test the context-sensitive help links** using Flare.

- **Build the output** and **give output files to the software developers**.

CREATING A HEADER FILE

If you do not get a header file from the software developer, you'll need to create one in Flare or use the default one provided by Flare. Follow these steps:

- (*Optional*) **Add a header file to your project**. Skip this step if you already have a header file in the Advanced folder of the Project Organizer.

    Flare creates a default header ("HeaderFile.h") when you create a new project. If you want to use that header file, you don't need to add another one to your project.

Figure D-3:
Default
header file

The default header file contains one line:

Figure D-4:
Contents of
the default
header file

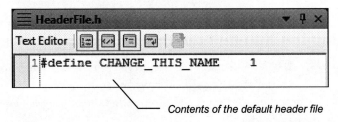

- **Add content to the header file**—This involves creating one line for each window or dialog that will link to a help topic. Each line contains a topic ID (such as add_acct_dialog) and a unique map number. *You'll add content to the header file when you set up the alias file.*

ADDING A HEADER FILE TO YOUR PROJECT

If you don't want to use the default header file, complete the following procedure to add a new header file to your Flare project.

▶ **To add a header file:**

1. In the Project Organizer, expand the **Advanced** folder, right-click the **CSH** folder and select **Add Header File**.

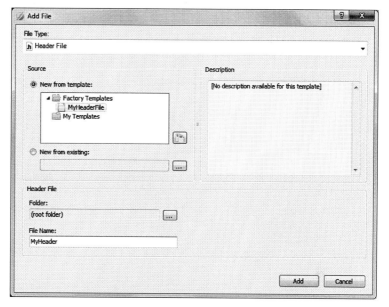

2. If not already selected, select **New from template**.

3. Under the **Factory Templates** folder, select **MyHeaderFile**.

4. Type a File Name for the header file.

5. Click **Add**. The header file is added to the Project Organizer's CSH folder.

ADDING CONTENT TO THE HEADER FILE

Adding content means adding a line for each window or dialog that will open a help topic. Each window or dialog will be a separate line, and each line will contain a **topic ID** and a unique **map number** for that window or dialog as show in Figure D-1.

Flare automatically adds content (topic IDs and map numbers) to the header file when you assign help topics to windows and dialogs in the Alias Editor, as described next.

ADDING AN ALIAS FILE

Before adding an alias file, make sure that your project already has a header file (see the previous topic). You do not need to add an alias file if you want to use the default alias file provided in the Advanced folder of the Project Organizer.

▶ To add an alias file to your project:

1. In the Project Organizer, expand the **Advanced** folder, right-click the **CSH** folder and select **Add Alias File**.

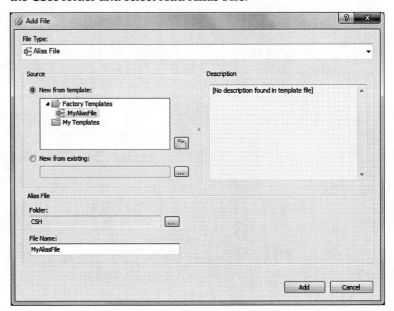

2. If not already selected, select **New from template**.

3. Under the **Factory Templates** folder, select **MyAliasFile**.

4. Type a File Name for the alias file.

5. Click **Add**. The alias file opens in the Alias Editor and is added to the Project Organizer's CSH folder.

Identifiers are listed here.

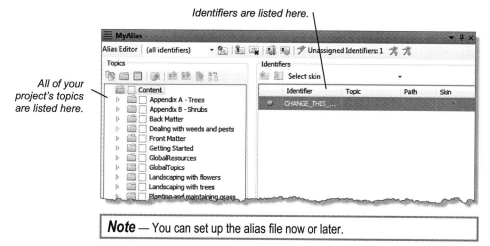

All of your project's topics are listed here.

Note — You can set up the alias file now or later.

6. If you don't want to set up the alias file now, close the Alias Editor.

SETTING UP AN ALIAS FILE

Setting up an alias file involves these tasks:

- (*If you created the header file*) **Creating identifiers (topic IDs) and unique map numbers**. You don't need to complete this task if you received a header file from a software developer.

- **Mapping.** This involves assigning a help topic to each identifier, which simultaneously creates the topic IDs and map numbers in the header file.

- (*Optional*) **Assigning a skin to topic IDs**.

Use the following procedure to set up an alias file.

▶ **To set up an alias file:**

1. If the alias file is not open in the Alias Editor, open it now by double-clicking it in the Project Organizer's Advanced\CSH folder.

    The right side of the Alias Editor lists the contents of your header files: identifier (topic ID) and value. If you have more than one header file, it lists the identifiers from all of them.

2. If you have more than one header file, click the down arrow to the right of "all identifiers" and select the appropriate header file from the list.

    New and default header files contain a placeholder identifier ("CHANGE_THIS_NAME").

    > **Note** — If you received a header file from the software developer, the right side of the Alias Editor will contain many lines (one for each identifier/value combination). Otherwise, the right side will show only what's in the header file you created ("CHANGE_THIS_NAME" if it's a new header file that you've done nothing with).

3. (*Optional, but recommended*) In the Alias Editor's toolbar, click

    Change the identifier options 🔲. Then set up default identifier options. (This will save you time, especially if you assign a default skin).

    > **Tip** — To save time, and for easy reference, select the default option **Include topic name in identifier name**. Otherwise, identifiers will be named NEW, NEW1, etc.

4. Complete the tasks listed in the following chart as applicable. For a topic to be context-sensitive, minimally it must have an identifier and it must be mapped to a topic.

To ...	Do this ...
Create a new identifier (a new row)	In the Alias Editor toolbar, click **Create a new identifier** 🔲.

To ...	Do this ...
Create a new identifier and map a topic to it	Select a topic. In the Topics toolbar, click **Assign the selected topic to a new identifier** 📷. Flare assigns an identifier name, value, and skin from the identifier options you set up in Step 3. If you set up a prefix, it is automatically appended to the beginning of the topic name to create the identifier.
Delete an identifier	Select the identifier and click **Delete the selected identifiers** 🗑 (in the Alias Editor toolbar).
Map a topic to an identifier	Select the identifier and select the topic (from the left) to map to the identifier. In the Topics toolbar, click **Assign the topic to the selected identifiers** 📷.
Map a skin to an identifier	Select the identifier. From the "Select skin" list, select a skin to map to the identifier. Click **Assign skin** <selected skin> (in the Identifiers toolbar).
Sort a column in the list of identifiers	Click the column. (Each click toggles between ascending and descending order.)
Change the text of an identifier	Click the identifier and change the name or type a new name. (Identifiers cannot contain spaces; to separate words, use underscores instead.)
Change the value	Click the value and type the new value. (Values can be decimal or hexadecimal.)

5. When you're done creating and mapping identifiers, click **Save All** 💾 to save the alias and header files.

Here's what the Alias Editor might show after you've created some identifiers and mapped topics to them.

Figure D-5:
Identifiers in the Alias file

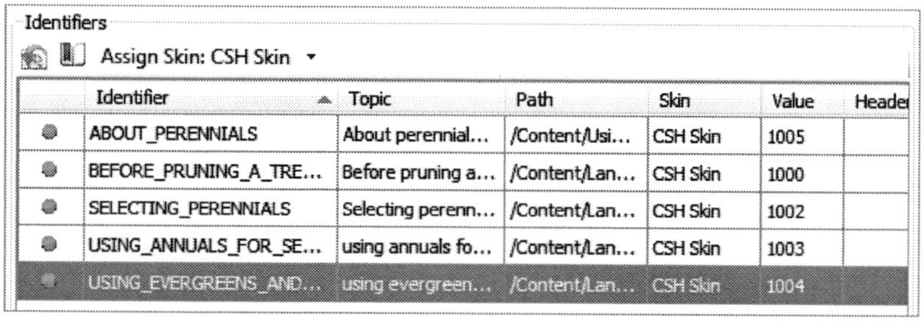

	Identifier		Topic	Path	Skin	Value	Header
●	ABOUT_PERENNIALS		About perennial...	/Content/Usi...	CSH Skin	1005	
●	BEFORE_PRUNING_A_TRE...		Before pruning a...	/Content/Lan...	CSH Skin	1000	
●	SELECTING_PERENNIALS		Selecting perenn...	/Content/Lan...	CSH Skin	1002	
●	USING_ANNUALS_FOR_SE...		using annuals fo...	/Content/Lan...	CSH Skin	1003	
●	USING_EVERGREENS_AND...		using evergreen...	/Content/Lan...	CSH Skin	1004	

A green symbol ● appears to the left of identifiers that have been assigned a topic; an orange symbol ● appears if an identifier has not been assigned a topic; and a red symbol ● appears if there is a syntax error.

Flare automatically updates the header file when you change the alias file.

Figure D-6:
Header file
after
mapping

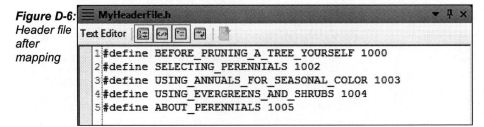

Multi-select and assign identifiers

To make the process of assigning identifiers faster, Flare includes the ability to automatically create identifiers, assign values and assign skins to multiple project files simultaneously.

▶ To multi-select and assign identifiers:

1. Click **Show All Files in Project** 🖺 (Topics toolbar). A list of files appears in a grid format.

2 Use the **SHIFT** and **CTRL** keys to select multiple files.

3. Click **Assign the selected topic to a new identifier** 🖺 to create and map the identifiers.

Auto-generate identifiers

Another time-saver—handy if most or all of your topics need to be context-sensitive—is the ability to automatically generate identifiers for an entire project.

▶ **To automatically generate identifiers:**

1. Click **Generate identifiers for this project** ⬛.

2 On the Generate Identifiers dialog, select identifier options.

3. Either select an existing header file or select a template from which to create a new header file, and click **Create**.

Both the alias and the header files are automatically populated with identifiers for all topics.

SETTING UP THE TARGET

You'll set up your target as you normally would, except for one additional task: before building, click the Target Editor's **Advanced** tab and select the alias file from the list at the bottom of the tab. (For more information see "Setting up an online target" on page 253.)

TESTING YOUR CONTEXT-SENSITIVE HELP

It's a good idea to test your context-sensitive help links in two ways:

- **From the software application** after you've built your Help system and given it to the software developer to link into the application. Click the help button from each window or dialog that is linked to a help topic.

- **From Flare** (discussed next).

TESTING CONTEXT-SENSITIVE HELP FROM FLARE

Use the following procedure to test context-sensitive links after you have mapped topics to identifiers and built the Help.

▶ To test your help links from Flare:

1. Build the output for the Help system (see Step 5B: Create Online Output).

2. Right-click the Help target and select **Test CSH API Calls <target name>** from the menu.

   The Context Sensitive Help (CSH) API Tester dialog appears.

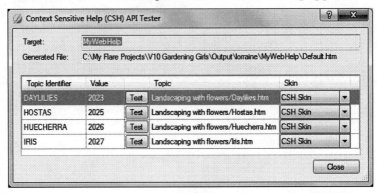

3. For each Topic Identifier, click 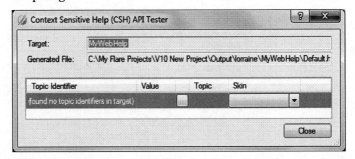. The help topic linked to the identifier opens in a separate window. If the correct topic does not appear, you'll need to check its mapping in the alias file.

   If you see the message "found no topic identifiers in target," check to make sure that the alias file is set up and that you selected it on the Advanced tab of the Target Editor for your Help target.

4. When you are done testing links, click **Close**.

Appendix E:
Track and
Troubleshoot

In this chapter ...
➤ Broken links
➤ Unlinked TOC items
➤ Image issues
➤ Build errors
➤ Analyzer
➤ Track project development
➤ Create project reports

OVERVIEW

In this appendix, you'll learn what kinds of problems can occur in your projects and how to avoid and fix them. You'll also learn more about Flare features that help you manage and track the development of your work and the work of other authors.

Here are some common problems that can occur in your projects:

- Broken links

- Broken bookmark links

- Build errors

- Unlinked TOC items

- Unlinked TOC books. (This is not a problem if you choose not to link TOC books by design.)

> **Note** — Don't confuse unlinked items with broken links. A *broken link* is one that no longer works because the file or path to it is no longer valid. An *unlinked TOC item* is not linked to anything.

Continue reading to find out why these problems occur and how to fix them.

BROKEN LINKS AND UNLINKED ITEMS

Flare attempts to help you avoid broken links. For example, if you try to delete a file (topic, image, page layout, master page, stylesheet or skin, for example) that something else links to, Flare lets you know and asks how you want to handle the links.

Figure E-1:
Flare warns you when you try to delete files that are linked.

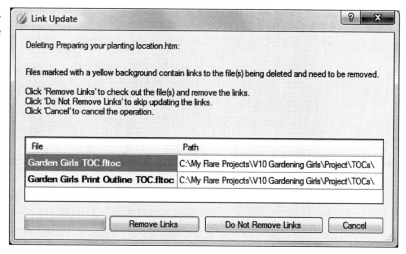

However, you can still end up with broken links in your project. For example, broken links can occur if you:

- Move a linked topic or project file to a different folder from Windows Explorer.

- Delete a linked topic or project file from Windows Explorer.

> **Important** — Do not move or delete topic or project files from Windows Explorer! Do this only from Flare's Content Explorer.

- Delete a file that was linked to another file (topic, table of contents, or target, for example), and you selected **Do Not Remove Links** when prompted.

HOW BROKEN LINKS AND UNLINKED ITEMS APPEAR IN THE TOC

The TOC Editor marks broken links with this symbol 🐾 and unlinked items and books with this symbol 🖋 . Unlinked books are not necessarily a problem. You might intentionally choose to not link TOC books to topics.

Figure E-2:
Broken links and unlinked items in a TOC

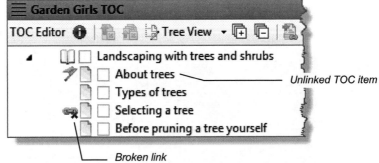

The following table describes how you can view a summary of and locate problems in your TOC.

Table E-1:
Tasks related to broken links and unlinked items

To ...	Click this ...
View a summary of broken links and unlinked items	1 Broken Link(s) in the TOC Editor toolbar
Show or hide unlinked books	
Navigate to the next broken link or unlinked item in your TOC	
Navigate to the previous broken link or unlinked item in your TOC	

Tip — The navigate buttons are especially useful when your TOC is long or the TOC books are collapsed.

UNLINKED TOC ITEMS

You'll end up with *unlinked TOC items* if you add a new TOC item by clicking **New item** in the TOC Editor toolbar and then don't link the TOC item to a topic.

Best Practice — To avoid unlinked TOC items, create a TOC item and topic simultaneously by clicking **Create a new topic and link to it** in the TOC Editor toolbar.

▸ **To fix an unlinked TOC item:**

1. Right-click the TOC item and select **Properties** from the menu.

2. On the **General** tab of the Properties dialog, click the **Select Link** 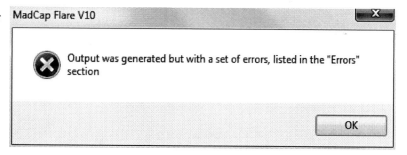 button.

3. Select the desired topic, click **Open**, then click **OK**.

   The item is linked and the unlinked symbol disappears.

IMAGE ISSUES

It's typical to add images (photographs, screen captures, and illustrations) to topics. However, be careful when converting an image from one format to another before you insert it into a Flare topic. You can easily corrupt an image file without even knowing it. If one or more of your images don't appear when you view WebHelp output, it's possible that you have corrupt images in your project.

BUILD ERRORS

When Flare builds your output, it checks for errors. If it finds any errors that prevent it from building output, the following message appears:

Figure E-3:
Build error

MadCap Flare V10   X

> ⊗ Output was generated but with a set of errors, listed in the "Errors" section
>
>   OK

Problems that don't prevent a build are listed in the Warnings tab. Click the applicable tab to view the errors or warnings.

Figure E-4: Build Progress Warnings tab

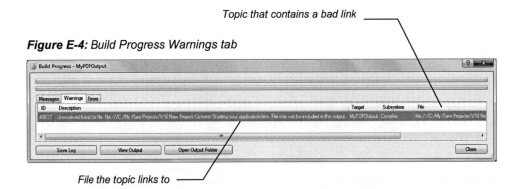

Topic that contains a bad link

File the topic links to

You can also click **Save Log** to save these messages as an error report. The log is saved in the Project Organizer's Reports folder.

> **Tip** — If you always want to save the build log, set the global option to save it automatically. (**File** tab → **Options** → Build tab → **Save log on build**)

> **Best Practice** — Save errors in a log so you can keep it open while fixing topics. (You cannot open topics to fix errors until you close this dialog.)

OPENING THE LOG FILE

Use the following procedure to open a build log that you saved after building output.

▶ **To open the log file:**

1. In the Project Organizer, expand the **Reports** folder and double-click the log file you previously saved. The log file opens in the middle pane.

2. Scroll to the right (if necessary) to view the file that contains the problem (in the "File" column).

3. Double-click a row to open the referenced topic.

Fixing bad links

Use this chart as a guide to help you fix missing linked files.

If the problem is a ...	Do this ...
Missing linked source file in a TOC	<ul><li>Right-click the TOC item.</li><li>Select **Link to Topic.**</li><li>Select the topic to link to.</li><li>Save the TOC.</li></ul>
Missing related topic	<ul><li>Right-click the **Related Topics** Help control.</li><li>Select **Edit Related Topics Control**.</li><li>On the Insert Related Topics Control dialog, select the correct file to link to.</li><li>Save the topic.</li></ul>
Missing linked source file in a topic	<ul><li>Right-click the bad link.</li><li>Select **Edit Hyperlink.**</li><li>On the Insert Hyperlink dialog, reselect the topic (file, document, etc.) to link to.</li><li>Save the topic.</li></ul>

To analyze your project for errors *before* building output, read the next section.

ANALYZING YOUR PROJECT

Flare offers two analyzers that help diagnose problems in your projects:

- **Internal analyzer** (provided with Flare)
- **External analyzer** ("MadCap Analyzer," purchased separately)

This section discusses the internal analyzer.

WHAT YOU CAN ANALYZE

With the internal analyzer, you can examine your Flare project for
the following problems:

- Broken links and bookmarks

- Topics that aren't included in a TOC (a specific TOC you select
  or to any TOC in your project)

- Topics that do not contain any index markers

- Files that contain tracked changes.

- Files that have annotations

- Database errors (project files that are not scanned for errors
  because they are incompatible with the analyzer)

> *Important* — If your project has database errors, submit a bug report to
> MadCap Software Technical Support. To do so, click **Feature Requests** at the
> bottom of the Start Page.

SELECTING ANALYZER SCANNING OPTIONS

You can decide which options you want Flare's internal Analyzer to
scan for before you open the Analyzer and start a scan. You may be
able to improve the performance of internal analyzer scans by
disabling some types of information collected during a scan or
setting limits for the number of results returned by the Analyzer.

▶ To select internal analyzer scan options:

1. Select **File** tab → **Options** (lower right corner).

2. On the Options dialog, click the **Analyzer** tab.

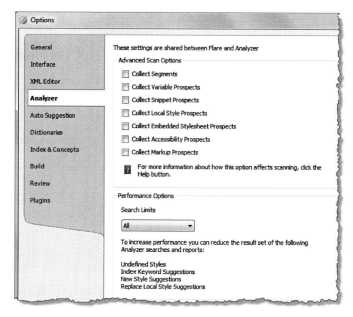

3. Select or clear Advanced Scan Options. Use the following table as a guide.

Use this scan option …	To view …
Segments	Segments of text that occur frequently, potential index keywords
Variable prospects	Text you might want to convert to variables
Snippet prospects	Text you might want to convert to snippets
Local style prospects	Instances of local formatting where you may want to use styles instead
Embedded stylesheet prospects	Embedded styles in <style> elements
Accessibility prospects	Text to which you might want to add accessibility options, such as captions or alternate text
Markup prospects	XHTML markup issues, such as extra spaces. Open the Internal Text Editor ⊞ to fix. (Some issues might be fixed in the XML Editor.)

4. Set Performance Options. To limit the number of Analyzer results, select the desired value (100, 500, 1000, or 5000) from the Search Limits list. (Selecting "All" does not limit the results.)

5. Click **OK**.

ANALYZING YOUR PROJECT

Use the following procedure to analyze your project with Flare's internal analyzer.

▶ To analyze your project:

1. Select **View** tab → **Project Analysis**. From the submenu, select the option for the problem you want to analyze. The Project Analysis window opens in the left pane.

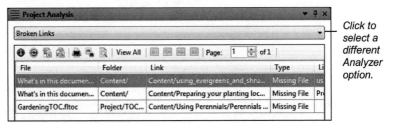

Click to select a different Analyzer option.

2. To analyze a different problem, click the down arrow and select an option from the list.

To ...	Select this from the list ...
Check your project for broken links	**Broken Links**
Check your project for broken bookmarks	**Broken Bookmarks**
View a list of files with database problems	**Database Errors**
View a list of files with tracked changes.	**Files With Changes**
View a list of files that contain annotations	**Files With Annotations**

To ...	Select this from the list ...
See which topics don't have index entries	**Topics Not in Index**
See which topics have not been linked to a TOC	**Topics Not in Selected TOC** Then select the TOC from the list.

3. (*Optional*) Double-click a file to open its topic.

4. To open MadCap Analyzer (a separate software product), select **Tools** tab → **MadCap** → **MadCap Analyzer**. Analyzer opens in a new window.

> **Note** — This book describes how to analyze a project with Flare's internal analyzer. It does not cover MadCap Analyzer.

5. When you're done analyzing your project, close the Project Analysis window.

ASSIGNING FILE TAGS

Flare's file tagging feature helps you to track the status of your project's development and the work of multiple authors. You'll apply file tags to project files to assign a status or to assign an author to a file. If you change author assignments, simply change the file tag associated with the authors' files. As your project content is developed, assign the applicable status to each topic or file. You can then use Flare's Reports feature to show project files by status or by author (or by your own custom category of file tags). The next topic discusses Flare's Reporting feature.

> **Note** — You can assign a file tag to any project file (topics, snippets, images, page layouts, targets, TOCs, etc.) except for reports.

FLARE'S DEFAULT FILE TAGS AND TAG SETS

When you create a new project, Flare automatically installs its factory file tags for tracking authors and file status in the Project Organizer's Advanced folder (File Tags sub-folder).

Figure E-5:
*File Tag
Sets in the
Project
Organizer*

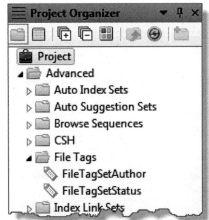

Double-clicking a file tag set causes it to open in the FileTagSet
Editor in the middle pane.

Figure E-6:
*Factory
Author File
Tag Set*

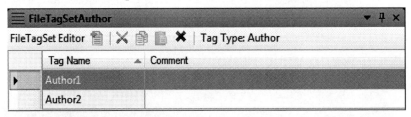

Figure E-7:
*Factory
Status File
Tag Set*

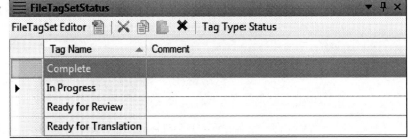

You can change the default tags and also add your own custom file
tags to the set.

▶ To assign a file tag to a topic:

1. Right-click the topic in the Content Explorer and select
   Properties. (You can also right-click a topic that's open.)

2. On the Properties dialog, select the **File Tags** tab.

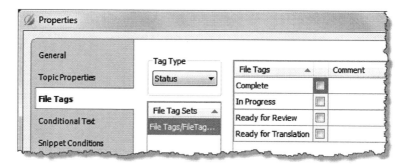

3. Select the Tag Type (Author, Status, or your own custom set type) from the list on the left.

4. Select the file tag(s) you want to assign to the topic (and clear those that no longer apply).

OTHER TASKS

Here are some other things you can do with file tags:

Table E-2:
Tasks you can do with file tags

To ...	Do this ...
Add a File Tag Set	1. Right-click the **Advanced\File Tags** folder in the Project Organizer, and select **Add File Tag Set**. 2. If not already selected, select **New from template**. 3. Under the **Factory Templates** folder, select a template (like **MyAuthorFileTagSet**). 4. In the File Name field, type a name for the file tag set. 5. In the Tag Type field, type your own custom name for the type of tag set you are adding. 6. Click **Add**.
Add a new tag	In the FileTagSet Editor's toolbar, click **New item** 📄. A new row appears, and Flare assigns a temporary name.
Rename a tag	1. Select the tag's row and press **F2**. 2. Select the existing name and type a new tag name.
Rename a tag	1. Select the tag's row and press **F2**. 2. Select the existing name and type a new tag name.

After tagging some project files, you'll want to see how content development is progressing. That's where reports come in.

CREATING PROJECT REPORTS

You've already read a little bit about reports earlier in this chapter in the section about saving a build progress error log. Now you'll learn how you can create your own reports by selecting the information about your project.

Flare's internal Analyzer stores lots of information about your project. Here are just a few of the many things that Flare has information about:

- Files with condition tags

- Files with file tags (You can select specific tags.)

- Topics that are not assigned a context-sensitive help ID

- Topics with broken links

- Unused images

- Broken snippet links

- Duplicate styles

- Unused styles

- Places where variables are used (topics, snippets, page layouts)

Creating a report basically involves two tasks: setting up the report (select what you want reported), and generating it.

▶ To set up and generate a report:

1. In the Project Organizer, right-click the **Reports** folder and select **Add Report File**. The Add File dialog opens.

2. If not already selected, select **New from template**.

3. Under the Factory Templates folder, select a factory report (which is ready to be generated) or select **Empty Report** to create your own custom report.

4. In the File Name field, type a name for the report.

5. Click **Add**. The report file is added to your Project Organizer's Reports folder and the report opens immediately in the Report Editor in the middle pane.

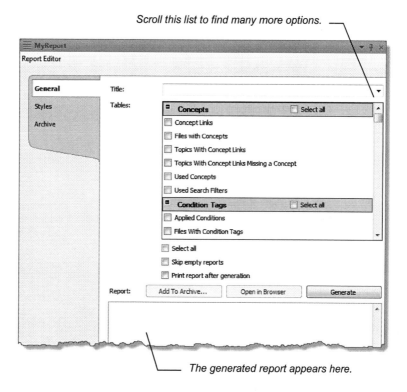

Scroll this list to find many more options.

The generated report appears here.

6. (If you selected an Empty Report in Step 3 above), select the options for the information you want the report to show. (You'll need to scroll the list to find all the options. There are many!)

    If you want a report that shows the files to which you've applied file tags, scroll to the File Tags section and select the desired category of file tags.

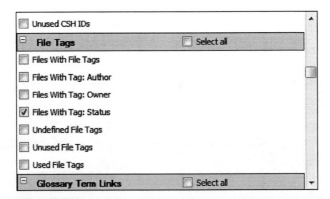

7. (*Optional*) To print the generated report, select **Print report after generation**.

8. (*Optional advanced feature*) Use the Report Editor's **Styles** tab to change the appearance of the report.

9. Click **Generate**.

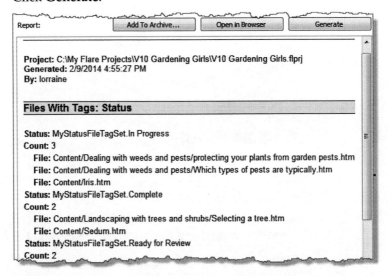

10. (*Optional*) To save a copy of the report in an archive folder so you can view it later, click **Add To Archive**. To access the report later, click the Report Editor's **Archive** tab.

Appendix F:
Single-
Sourcing

In this chapter …

➤ Create Condition tags
➤ Create Snippets
➤ Create Variables
➤ Link projects with global project linking

OVERVIEW

Single-sourcing can be summarized in one phrase: **Create once, use many!** With Flare, you create content once and reuse it in any number of topics and outputs.

Flare provides these features for single-sourcing your content:

- **Condition tags**, which mark content for a particular target.

- **Snippets**, which are small units of content you reuse in multiple topics.

- **Variables**, which store changeable content (such as customer names and version numbers) that you can use in multiple topics. When you build your output, Flare substitutes the variable value everywhere it is used.

- **Global project linking**, which allows you to single-source content among multiple Flare projects.

- **Multiple targets** from the same content (commonly called "multi-channel publishing"). Targets are described in the Document Basics chapter, Step 5A: Create Print Output, Step 5B: Create Online Output, and Appendix G: DITA Import and Export.

Read the rest of this chapter to find out how to use condition tags, snippets, variables, and global project linking in your Flare project.

USING CONDITION TAGS

A condition tag is a marker you apply to content so that content shows up in some of your outputs but not in others.

Condition tags let you create output that contains variations of a project's content. In a *single* project, you can store the common content and the variations of it. No need to spend time and money creating different documents that duplicate common content for different needs.

With condition tags, you tag only the variations of content, not the common content that is reused for all outputs. When you set up your target, you specify which condition tags to exclude for that target.

> **Note** — You can apply condition tags to topics, snippets, images, stylesheets, blocks of content (paragraphs), text within blocks, table rows and columns, TOC entries, index keyword markers, and project files (targets, skins, glossaries, etc.).

AN EXAMPLE

Suppose you need to create two Help systems, one for an insurance program in NY and another for an insurance program in CA. Here's what you'd do:

1. Create all the content for both Help systems in one project (instead of two separate projects).

2. Create one condition tag called "Insurance NY" and another called "Insurance CA."

3. Apply the "Insurance NY" condition tag to the content that belongs only in the Help system for NY insurance users.

4. Apply the "Insurance CA" condition tag to the content that belongs only in the Help system for CA insurance users.

5. Create two targets: one for Insurance NY and one for Insurance CA.

6. Set up the Insurance NY target to exclude the Insurance CA condition tag.

7. Set up the Insurance CA target to exclude the Insurance NY condition tag.

TERMS YOU SHOULD KNOW

Before you continue, let's clarify the difference between a couple of Flare terms:

- **Condition tag set** — A named group of condition tags. Condition tag sets are listed in the Project Organizer's

Conditional Text folder. You can create as many sets as you want.

> **Note** — To create a condition tag set, right-click the **Conditional Text** folder in the Project Organizer and select **Add Condition Tag Set**.

- **Condition tag** — A color-coded marker that you apply to content. Condition tags are contained in a condition tag set. You can create multiple tags in a single set.

CREATING CONDITION TAGS

Use the following procedure to add or change a condition tag (not a condition tag set).

▶ **To create a condition tag:**

1. Open the Project Organizer.

2. Expand the **Conditional Text** folder, which shows existing condition tag sets. Flare includes a default condition tag set.

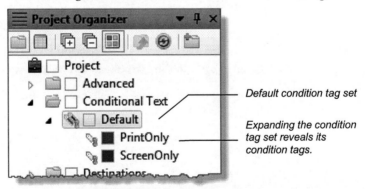

Default condition tag set

Expanding the condition tag set reveals its condition tags.

3. Double-click the condition tag set you want to add tags to. The Condition TagSet Editor opens, showing existing tags for the tag set.

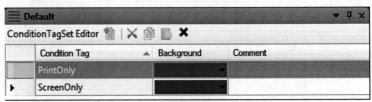

The default condition tag set contains two condition tags: "PrintOnly" and "ScreenOnly." Each condition tag has a unique color that highlights the content tagged with it.

4. Add or change tags as described in this table:

To ...	Do this ...
Add a new tag	▪ In the Condition TagSet Editor's toolbar, click **New item** . A new row appears, and Flare assigns a temporary name.
Rename a tag	▪ Select the tag's row and press **F2**. ▪ Select the existing name and type a new name for the tag. ┌─────────────────────────────────┐ │ ***Note*** — Renaming a tag changes its name │ │ wherever you've already used it. │ └─────────────────────────────────┘
Change a tag's color	▪ Click the Background drop-down arrow and select **Pick Color**. The Color Picker dialog opens. ▪ Select a color and click **OK**. (Only you will see the color; it doesn't appear in output.)
Add comments to a tag	▪ Click in the tag's **Comment** field. ▪ Press **F2** and type the comment. (Comments don't appear in output.)

5. When you're done adding or changing tags, click **Save All** to save your work.

After creating condition tags, you can apply them to your content.

APPLYING CONDITION TAGS

Flare provides two ways to apply a condition tag to content (text, images, table rows, etc.) in the XML Editor. You can apply a condition tag to:

▪ Some of the content within a block

▪ An entire block of content

If **Hide/show Conditional Indicators** 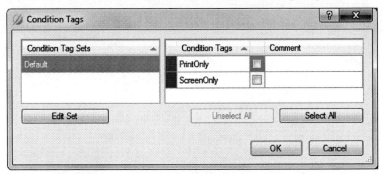 is selected on the XML Editor's bottom toolbar, the text that is marked with a condition tag is highlighted in color. Each condition tag is assigned a unique color.

> **Note** — Before you can apply a condition tag, you must create it. See the previous topic.

▶ **To apply a condition tag to content within a block:**

1. Select the content you want to apply the condition tag to.

2. Select **Home** tab → **Conditions** (in the Attributes group).

3. Select the condition tag set that contains the condition tag you want to apply.

> **Tip** — Alternatively, you can expand the condition tag set in the Project Organizer and then drag and drop a condition tag onto the selected text.

4. Select the checkbox for the condition tag you want to apply, and click **OK**. Flare applies the condition tag to the selected content.

   If **Hide/show Conditional Indicators** is turned on, the content is highlighted with the condition tag's color.

   If span bars are visible, they show that content has been tagged with a condition tag.

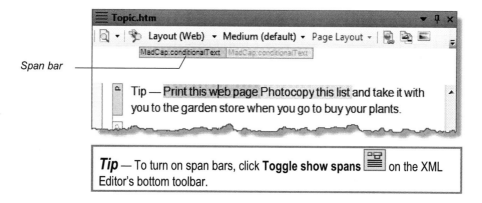

Span bar

Tip — To turn on span bars, click **Toggle show spans** on the XML Editor's bottom toolbar.

▶ To apply a condition tag to an entire block of content:

1. If not in view, show the tag bars (click on the XML Editor's bottom toolbar).

2. Right-click the tag bar for the block you want to apply the condition tag to, and select **Conditions**.

3. In the Condition Tags dialog, select the **Condition Tag Set** that contains the condition tag you want to apply.

4. Select the checkbox for the **Condition Tag** you want to apply, and click **OK**.

Tip — Alternatively, you can expand the condition tag set in the Project Organizer and then drag and drop a condition tag onto the tag bar.

Flare applies the condition tag to the entire block and highlights its structure bar with that condition tag's color. If **Hide/show Conditional Indicators** is turned on, the text block is also highlighted with the condition tag's color.

The tag bar is highlighted with condition tag color.

DocType: guide, because gardening is our joy and our passion, and we want to share our collective knowledge with other gardeners.

Feel free to photocopy the list of perennials so you can take it with you to the garden store. (It's easier than bring this complete book.)

We can inspire you to try new plants or designs, and maybe help you ...

Condition tag applied to entire text block

Filtering by condition tags in the XML Editor

If you've created and applied several condition tags to content in a topic and turned on conditional indicators, looking at your topic in the XML Editor can be like looking at a rainbow. It can be difficult to see how the content will look when generated. Of course, it's helpful to preview the content (with the "Preview as primary target" button), but filtering the content by condition tag allows you to edit your topic while viewing it as it will appear when generated.

▶ To filter by condition tags:

1. With the topic open in the XML Editor, make sure condition tags are applied to content as you want them, as in this example.

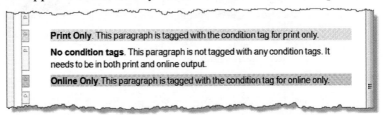

2. Click **Select the conditional expression to apply to the document** in the XML Editor's top toolbar. The Conditional Text dialog opens.

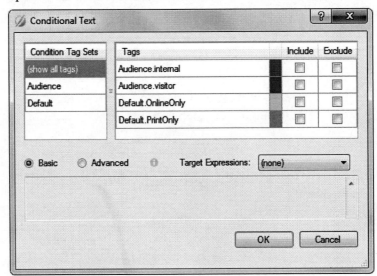

3. Either select the condition tags to exclude or open the Target Expressions list and select a target whose conditions you want to apply. The Conditional Text dialog is updated to reflect that target's Include and Exclude selections.

4. Click **OK**.

In our example, here's the result if we excluded the PrintOnly tag:

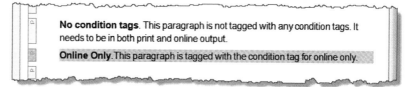

> **No condition tags**. This paragraph is not tagged with any condition tags. It needs to be in both print and online output.
>
> **Online Only**. This paragraph is tagged with the condition tag for online only.

And here's what we'd see in the XML Editor if we excluded the OnlineOnly tag:

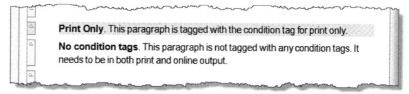

> **Print Only**. This paragraph is tagged with the condition tag for print only.
>
> **No condition tags**. This paragraph is not tagged with any condition tags. It needs to be in both print and online output.

UNDEFINED CONDITION TAGS

When using condition tags, you can inadvertently end up with undefined condition tags. This occurs if you apply a condition tag to content in a topic (or snippet), exclude or include the condition tag in a target, and then delete the condition tag from its condition tag set.

For example, suppose you create a condition tag called "Hidden," apply it to a text block in a topic and then exclude it in a target.

Figure F-1:
A condition tag excluded in a target

Target Editor	Build	View	Publish

General	Condition Tag Sets	Tags	Include	Exclude
Conditional Text	[show all tags]	Hidden		☑
Variables	Audience	OnlineOnly		
Publishing	Default	PrintOnly		

Suppose you then delete the condition tag from its condition tag set. Flare only removes it from one place—from the condition tag set. It does not remove it from other project files (like topics, snippets, and targets). So you can have references in your project to a condition tag that no longer exists. In topics and snippets, Flare highlights content that has undefined condition tags with gray shading, and the topic still contains the XML code for the condition tag.

You might not even be aware this situation exists until you open a target in which that condition tag was excluded or included. Undefined condition tags are shaded on the Target Editor's Conditional Text tab.

Figure F-2:
Undefined condition tag in the Target Editor

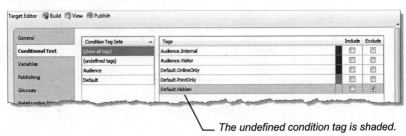

The undefined condition tag is shaded.

If you see "(undefined tags)" listed under Condition Tag Sets, you know you have at least one undefined condition tag to fix.

> **Important** — Flare flags undefined condition tags in the Target Editor only if they affect the open target. If a condition tag is applied to content but never specified in a target, the Target Editor would not be aware of it.

Fixing undefined condition tags

▶ **To fix an undefined condition tag:**

1. Open the target with the undefined condition tag.

2. Clear the condition tag's Include and Exclude checkboxes.

3. Click **Save All** to save the target.

4. Use the Internal Text Editor to open any topic or snippet to which you've applied that condition tag and manually remove the code (To open the Internal Text Editor, see Step 2: Learn the XML Editor, Task 3 on page 80).

> **Tip** — A faster alternative is to add the condition tag back to the condition tag set it was removed from, and then unapply it everywhere you used it. Make sure it exactly matches the original tag (spelling, spaces, upper and lower case, etc.).

USING SNIPPETS

Snippets are units of content that you create when you need to include the same content in more than one topic. They're a perfect example of reusing content. Snippets are not standalone content; they are meant to be inserted into topics (and templates).

The beauty of snippets is maintenance. You change *only* the snippet; Flare updates it everywhere the snippet is used. Done!

Unlike variables, which contain only a few words or numbers, snippets can contain any amount and any type of content—even images and tables.

Each snippet is stored in the Content Explorer's Resources\Snippets folder as a separate file with an ".flsnp" extension. You can share snippets with others, receive them from others, and use them in other projects—for even more content reuse!

CONDITIONAL SNIPPETS

Just like other content, you can apply a condition tag to a snippet so that it's included or excluded from targets.

You can also create **snippet** conditions, which are condition tags you can apply to content within snippets to customize the snippet for certain topics. For more information, search on "snippet conditions" in the Flare Help system.

SNIPPET FORMATTING

Like other content, snippets can be formatted with styles (or local formatting).

CREATING SNIPPETS

There are two ways to create snippets:

- From scratch
- From existing content

Creating snippets from scratch

Use the following procedure to create a snippet from scratch by
using a template. You don't need to have a topic open to do this.

▶ To create a snippet from scratch:

1. Select **Project** tab → **New** arrow → **Add Snippet**.

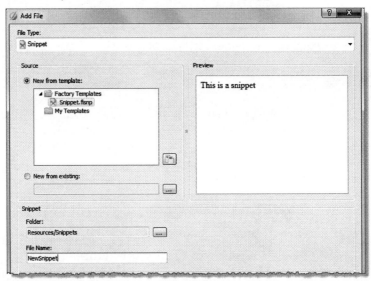

2. Fill in the fields on the Add File dialog:

Option	Description
New from template	Folders that contain templates used to create snippets. You can select: • (Recommended) **Factory Templates** to choose a template provided with Flare, or • **My Templates** to choose one of your own snippet templates, or • **Manage Templates** ⬚ to select a template from the Template Manager. (See "Using the Template Manager" on page 72.)
New from existing	Existing snippet that you can use as a starting point and change as needed. Click ⬚ to select an existing snippet.

Option	Description
Preview	A preview of the selected snippet template.
Folder	(Recommended) If this field does not show Resources\Snippets, click [...] and select (Resources) **Snippets** for the folder. Create a Snippets folder first if needed.
File Name	The file name for the snippet. (Type a name you'll easily recognize later.)

3. Click **Add**. Flare creates the snippet and adds it to the Resources\Snippets folder in your project's Content Explorer.

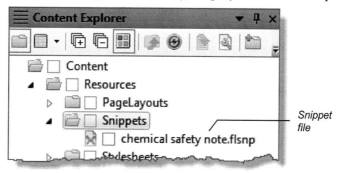

Snippet file

The new snippet opens in the XML Editor.

Placeholder text

4. Click in the XML Editor and type the text you want the snippet to contain. (Don't forget to replace the placeholder text.)

   Add other content as desired, such as tables, lists, and images.

5. Format the content as you would for a topic by applying styles, inserting links, etc.

6. Click **Save All** 🖫 to save your work.

   You can now insert the snippet you created into any topic in your project. See "Methods for inserting snippets" on page 357.

Creating snippets from existing content

If you have existing topic content that you need to reuse in other topics, use the following procedure to turn that content into a snippet.

▶ **To create a snippet from existing content:**

1. Open the topic that contains the content you want to turn into a snippet. For example, suppose you want to create a snippet for the "Important" note in the following topic.

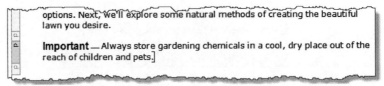

2. Place your cursor anywhere in the text block that contains the text you want to make into a snippet.

3. Right-click the text block's tag bar (left) and select **Create Snippet**. The Create Snippet dialog shows the text of the block your cursor is placed in.

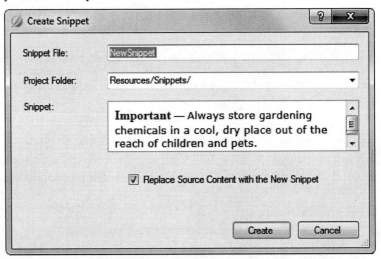

4. In the Snippet File field, type a meaningful name for the snippet (e.g., "chemical safety note").

> ***Important*** — Leave the Project Folder set to "Resources/Snippets."

5. To replace the selected text in the topic with the new snippet, select **Replace Source Content with the New Snippet**.

6. Click **Create**. Flare creates the snippet and copies it to the Resources\Snippets folder in your project's Content Explorer.

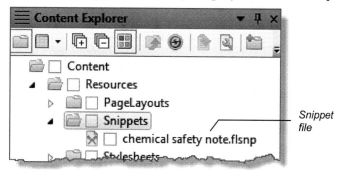

Snippet file

If you selected Replace Source Content … in Step 5 above, Flare replaces the source content with the new snippet. If markers are turned on, the snippet is surrounded by brackets in the topic.

Brackets around a snippet

Tag bar shows "MadCap Snippet Block."

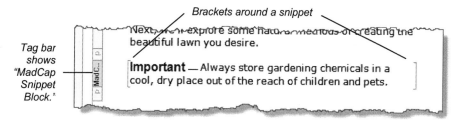

You can now insert the snippet you created into any topic in your project as described next.

> **Tip** — If you have MadCap Analyzer (a separate product), analyze your project for frequently used phrases, which are good candidates for snippets. Analyzer can turn those phrases into snippets and add them to your project automatically. For more information, see Analyzer's Help system.

METHODS FOR INSERTING SNIPPETS

Once you've created snippets, you can insert them into your topics:

- On a blank line, or

- Inside a text block that contains other text

You can even insert a snippet into a page layout header or footer.

Inserting a snippet on a blank line

If you insert a snippet on a blank line in a topic, it's inserted as a block and no other content can be added to that block. Any styles and formatting applied to the snippet are preserved.

> **Tip** — If you want the snippet to be part of a text block that contains other text, type the other text *before* inserting the snippet.

Inserting a snippet inside a text block with existing text

When a snippet is inserted into a text block that has existing text:

- The snippet inherits the formatting of the text block in which it's inserted.

- If the snippet contains multiple blocks, it becomes one continuous line of text.

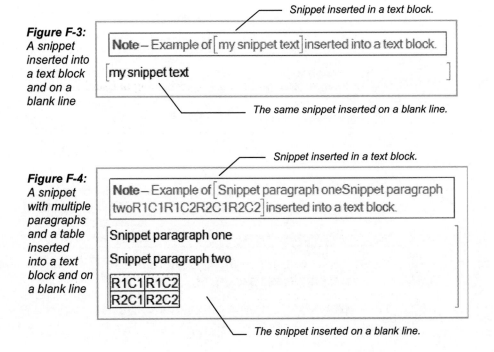

Figure F-3:
A snippet inserted into a text block and on a blank line

Snippet inserted in a text block.

Note— Example of [my snippet text] inserted into a text block.

[my snippet text]

The same snippet inserted on a blank line.

Figure F-4:
A snippet with multiple paragraphs and a table inserted into a text block and on a blank line

Snippet inserted in a text block.

Note— Example of [Snippet paragraph oneSnippet paragraph twoR1C1R1C2R2C1R2C2] inserted into a text block.

Snippet paragraph one

Snippet paragraph two

| R1C1 | R1C2 |
| R2C1 | R2C2 |

The snippet inserted on a blank line.

INSERTING SNIPPETS

Use the following procedure to insert a snippet into a topic or page-layout frame.

▶ **To insert a snippet:**

1. Place your cursor where you want to insert the snippet and click **Insert a snippet** ⊠. The Insert Snippet Link dialog opens.

2. Select the snippet you want to insert and click **OK**.

3. Click **Save All** 🖫 to save your work.

> **Note** — You can also insert a snippet by dragging it from the Content Explorer to a place in the active topic.

CHANGING SNIPPETS

If you change a snippet, Flare automatically makes the changes in all topics where you've inserted that snippet.

▶ **To change a snippet:**

1. Open the snippet you want to change by using one of these methods:

   - Open the Resources\Snippets folder (or the folder it's stored in) in the Content Explorer and double-click the snippet you want to change.

   - Right-click the snippet in a topic where you've inserted it and select **Open Link**.

2. In the XML Editor, change the snippet as desired.

3. Click **Save All** 🖫 to save your work.

The changes automatically appear everywhere that snippet is inserted.

USING VARIABLES

A **variable** holds information that may change. Variables are useful for short pieces of content, such as a few words or a number. You can insert variables in topics, master pages, page layout frames, and snippets—in short, wherever you create content.

> **Note** — You can also add variables to TOC entries, browse sequence entries, and links by adding the variable syntax manually. If interested, search on "About Variables" in the Flare Help system.

When you create a variable you assign it a default definition. When you set up a target, you can override the default definition for that target only. You can vary a variable's definition by changing the definition of the variable in the target *before* building output.

AN EXAMPLE

Suppose you want to place a version number in several places in your output. To do so, you'd create a variable for version number, give it a definition, and insert it wherever you want it used.

Later, if the version number changes, you just update the variable. When you build your output, the new value is automatically used wherever you inserted the variable.

CONDITIONAL VARIABLES

Just like other content, you can apply a condition tag to a variable so that it's included or excluded from targets.

VARIABLE FORMATTING

Variable content can be formatted, either locally or with styles.

VARIABLE SETS

Flare stores variables in sets, and each set can contain many variables. Out of the box, Flare includes three variable sets:

- Heading

- Variables

- System

> **Important** — You can insert variables from all three sets, but you can change only "Variables" by adding more variables to it or by changing its variables. One variable set might be adequate for you, but you can add more variable sets if desired. Search on "about variables" in the Flare Help system.

A variable has two main parts—a *name* and a *definition*. (The comment is optional.)

Figure F-5:
Default variables

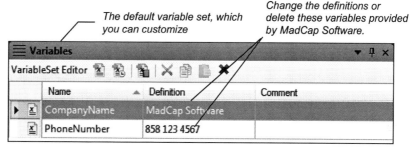

TYPES OF VARIABLES

Flare contains these kinds of variables:

- **User-defined**, which are the ones you add to the "Variables" set or to another variable set that you create.

- **System**, which includes variables such as page number, date, and time.

- **Heading**, which are heading styles h1 through h6 (useful for displaying heading text in running headers and footers in print output).

> **Note** — If you create print output in PDF, XPS, or XHTML format, you can use heading variables to show headings and terms in the glossary and index.

INSERTING VARIABLES

Use the following procedure to insert a variable into the active topic (snippet, or page-layout frame).

▶ **To insert a variable:**

1. Open the applicable topic, snippet, or page-layout frame. Place your cursor where you want to insert the variable and click **Insert a variable** .

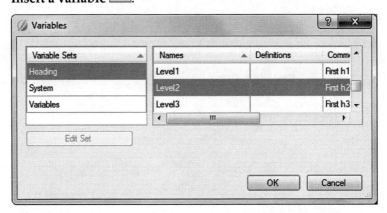

2. Select the desired variable set from the list on the left. The set's variables are shown on the right.

3. From the list on the right, select the variable you want to insert.

4. Click **OK**. The variable is added to the topic (snippet, or page-layout frame). If markers are turned on, you'll see brackets around the variable. If variable names are turned on, you'll also see the variable name.

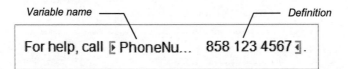

If markers are *not* turned on, you'll see only the variable's value.

For help, call 858 123 4567.

> *Tip* — To turn on markers, click the arrow on the **Show tags** [icon] button (XML Editor toolbar), and select **Show Markers**. To turn on variable names, click **Show Variable Names**.

6. Click **Save All** [icon] to save your work.

> *Tip* — To quickly insert a variable from the "Variables" set, do this: in the Project Organizer, expand the **Variables** folder, expand the **Variables** set, and drag the desired variable to the active topic.

HIGHLIGHTING VARIABLES

When you're viewing content, you can easily distinguish variables from other content if variable highlighting is turned on.

Figure F-6:
Highlighting
turned on

For help, call 858 123 4567

▶ To toggle highlighting on or off:

- Click the arrow on the **Show tags** [icon] button and select **Highlight Variables**.

ADDING AND CHANGING VARIABLES

You can do any of the following in your own variable sets:

- Add new variables

- Rename variables

- Change a variable's definition (its value)

- Delete a variable from the set

- Add comments

If you change a variable's definition after inserting the variable into topics, Flare automatically changes the result in those topics.

▶ To add or change variables:

1. Open the Project Organizer and expand the **Variables** folder.

> *Note* — Only user-defined variable sets are listed, since you cannot change the System or Heading variable sets.

2. Double-click the variable set you want to change, such as Variables. The VariableSet Editor (Figure F-5) opens.

3. Add or change variables as described in this table:

To ...	Do this ...
Add a new variable	▪ In the VariableSet Editor's toolbar, click **New item** 📋. A new row appears, and Flare assigns a temporary name. ▪ To change the temporary name, click it, type a new name, and press **ENTER**. ▪ To enter a default definition, click in the Definition field, press **F2**, type the definition, and press **ENTER**. (If you'll be overriding the variable's definition in the target, type a default value that is generic.)
Rename a variable	▪ Click the name and press **F2**. ▪ Select the existing name and type a new name. > *Note* — Renaming a variable changes its name wherever that variable is used.
Change a variable's definition	▪ Click in the Definition field for the variable you want to change and press **F2**. ▪ Select the existing definition, type a new definition and click **OK**.
Add a comment	▪ Click in the variable's Comment field. ▪ Press **F2** and type a comment. (Comments don't appear in the output.)

4. Click **Save All** 🖫 to save your work.

USING GLOBAL PROJECT LINKING

Global project linking is a method for reusing content in which common content is stored in a centralized global project and used in any number of other Flare "child" projects. For example, you might use a global project to store company information or standard terminology used by many of your company's products or documents; and each product might have its own Flare project.

You'll maintain the global content in the global project only, not in the child projects. Your child projects link to the global project and import some or all of its content.

WHAT SHOULD A GLOBAL PROJECT CONTAIN?

The decision about what the global project should contain is up to you and depends on the design of your content. Examples of good candidates for a global project are company logos, copyright information, company contact and customer support information, stylesheets, file status tags, snippets that contain warnings or messages, and condition tags.

This topic touches on the mechanics of setting up and using this feature in Flare. The more challenging skill involves designing the structure of your content across multiple projects for optimal content re-use. That skill is not within the scope or purpose of this book, but you might find some useful tips about it by talking with colleagues or attending professional seminars.

YOUR TASKS

To link a global project to one or more child projects, you'll need to complete these tasks:

- **Planning and design**. Decide what content the global project and child projects will contain. Decide what specific global content you want to include in (or exclude from) each child project.

- **Create the global project** and its content. (You can change the global content at any time and re-import it into your child projects.)

- **Create your child project(s)** and their content.

- **Set up an import file in each child project.**

- **Import the global content.**

- **Use imported content as you would in any individual Flare project.** (For example, you can include global topics in your TOC, or global snippets in your topics; or specify global page layouts in your targets.)

- **Build the output** for your child projects as you normally would.

The rest of this topic discusses how to set up the import file in your child projects and import global content.

▶ To set up a global project import and import content:

1. Make sure that the Flare project in which to import content is open with the Project Organizer in view.

2. In the Project Organizer, right-click the **Imports** folder and select **Add Flare Project Import File** from the menu. The Add File dialog opens.

3. If not already selected, select **New from template**. Select **MyProjectImport** under the **Factory Templates** folder or use one of your own templates from the **My Templates** folder.

4. Type a File Name. (Flare will add an extension of .flimpfl.)

5. Click **Add**. The File Name you typed is listed in the Project Organizer's Imports folder and the Import file opens in the middle pane.

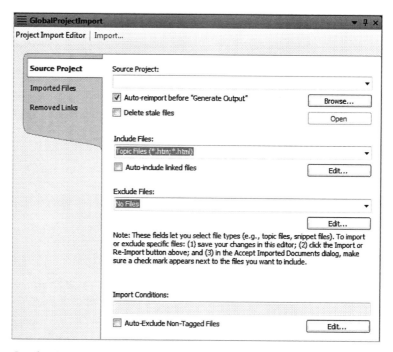

6. On the **Source Project** tab, do the following:

a. If you want Flare to incorporate changes from your linked project each time you build output, make sure that **Auto-reimport before "Generate Output"** is checked.

> **Note** — If you don't select this option, you can manually re-import global project content at any time by opening the Project Import Editor and selecting **Import**.

b. Click **Browse**, locate your source project (the global project), and select it. (You must select the project file, which has an extension of ".flprj")

> **Note** — The Include Files field is required. All topic files (*.htm and *.html) are included by default, but you can change the file types you include. See the next step.

7. Select other options on this tab as desired.

To ...	Do this ...
Delete previously imported files that have been removed from the global project.	Select **Delete stale files**. (The files are deleted the next time the global project is re-imported.)
Open the global project in another instance of Flare	Click **Open**.
Import all files from the global project	Click the down arrow to the right of "Include Files" and select **All Files (*.*)**
Import a specific file type (topic, snippets, stylesheets) from the global project	Click the down arrow to the right of "Include Files" and select the desired file type.
Include or exclude more than one type of global project file	Click **Edit** (to the right of "Include Files" or "Exclude Files"). In the Import File Filter dialog, click **Add**. Select the desired file type and click **OK**. Repeat this step to add another file type (or add a file name pattern, such as *.fl* to import all files whose extensions begin with ".fl").
Automatically import all files that are directly or indirectly linked to files you have chosen to include	Select **Auto-include linked files**.
Exclude or include files tagged with a specific condition tag	Click **Edit** (to the right of "Import Conditions") and select the checkboxes for the condition tags you want to exclude or include.
Exclude files that are not tagged with a condition tag	Select **Auto-Exclude Non-Tagged files**.

8. Click **Save All** to save your import settings.

9. If you want to import the content now, proceed to Step 10; otherwise, close the Project Import Editor.

10. Select **Import** (under the tab name). The Accept Imported Documents dialog lists the documents to be imported (on the left) and a preview of the currently selected document (on the right).

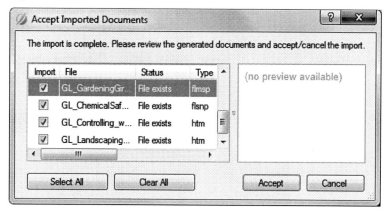

> **Notes** —
>
> To exclude a specific file, clear its checkbox.
>
> When you re-import, Flare shows "Source is Newer" for the status of any global content that has changed since the last import.

11. Click **Accept** to import the files.

The files are added to your Flare project in the same structure as they are found in the global project.

In the following example, the folders that begin with the word "Global" came from our global project. (The word "Global" is this author's convention; it was not assigned by Flare.)

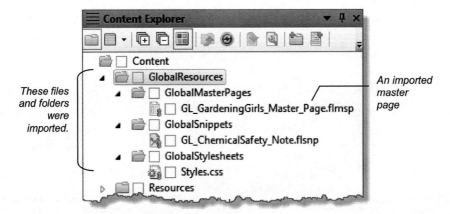

These files and folders were imported.

An imported master page

12. Close the Project Import Editor.

Appendix G: DITA Import and Export

In this chapter …

> Import DITA content
> Export to DITA

OVERVIEW

In this appendix you'll learn how to:

- import DITA content into a Flare project

- export Flare content to DITA

You can import DITA and DITAMAP files. When Flare imports DITA content, it converts it to XHTML format.

ABOUT IMPORTING

You can import DITA content into Flare:

- By creating a Flare project and then importing the content, or

- By importing content and creating the Flare project simultaneously.

This appendix describes only the first import method.

Flare lets you link your imported topics to the DITA source files from which they were created. If you link your content, you'll update it when needed in your source files and then update your Flare project by re-importing the content.

When source and destination files are linked, you can re-import the content at any time or have Flare automatically check for updates to the source. You would then use Flare as the "publishing engine."

ABOUT CONDITION TAGS

There are two scenarios that affect condition tags:

- **Import** — Conditions created in your DITA documents, using DITA conventions, will be retained by Flare.

- **Export** — Condition tags you create in Flare are lost when you export to DITA unless you used DITA conventions for creating the condition tags.

THE IMPORT PROCESS

Importing content from DITA files into Flare is a two-part process:

- First, you'll **set up the rules** for importing the content. This involves telling Flare the decisions you made about importing, such as if you want to link your Flare topics to source files.

> **Note** — Import rules are stored in a Flare import file, which is saved in the Imports folder of the Project Organizer. For DITA files, the file's extension is .flimpdita.

- Next, you'll **import the content** into your project, using the import rules.

Recommendation

Before you import *all* your content files, set up the import file and try importing a few sample files. Revise the import settings in your Flare import file if necessary until the imported content is correct. It might take a few test imports to decide exactly how you want to set it up.

> **Tip** — You can change a Flare import file from the **Project Organizer**. Simply open the **Imports** folder and double-click the name of the Flare import file you want to change.

CHOICES FOR MAINTAINING CONTENT

Before you import DITA content, you'll need to decide where you will maintain it. You have two choices:

- **Option 1** — Use Flare to maintain your content after import. You will import your content just once and maintain it in Flare after that.

- **Option 2** — Use the source application to maintain your content after import. With this option, your Flare topics will be linked to the source files from which they were created, and **you will not change your topics in Flare.**

> ### DECISION TIME!
>
> If you choose Option 2, select one of these options:
>
> ✓   Have Flare check your source files and remind you when they
>   have changed. Then it's up to you to update your Flare topics by
>   re-importing your source files.
>
> ✓   Have Flare check your source files for changes when you build
>   the output, automatically re-import them, and update the
>   corresponding Flare topics before building the output. This
>   option is called **Easy Sync**.

Use this chart to help you decide the right options for you.

Table G-1:
Options for
maintaining
content

Choose ...	When ...
Option 1: Maintain content in Flare	You don't need to keep the source files current.
	Changes are made by only one or two people (who have access to Flare).
Option 2: Maintain content in source application	Some of the people editing content have the source application, but not Flare.
Easy Sync (available with Option 2)	You make frequent changes to your content.
	Changes are made by many people.

About Easy Sync

With Easy Sync, you don't have to guess if and when your content
has changed. All changes to the source files will be incorporated
before the Flare output is built.

> **Important** — When you use Easy Sync, *don't change your topics in Flare!*
> They will be lost with the next automatic re-import.

You can change your mind after importing the content

You can easily switch between linking your files and not linking
them by using the "Link Generate Files to Source Files" checkbox on
the Source Files tab in the Import Editor. If you unlink the source
files, you must then begin updating your content with Flare instead
of with your source application.

IMPORTING DITA FILES

You can import DITA files that were created with any DITA application. You can import DITA files (.dita extension) or a DITAMAP file (.ditamap extension). If you import a DITAMAP file, the files it references are imported also. Each DITA file becomes one Flare topic when imported.

DITA files contain DITA elements (tags), which Flare converts to HTML tags in your topic files when it imports the content. Flare also creates an import stylesheet and makes a style class for each element in your DITA files.

EXAMPLES

- The DITA element <title> is converted to <h1 class="topictitle"> and a style class of "h1.topictitle" is added to the import stylesheet.

- "Resourceid" elements are converted to context-sensitive Help IDs.

- The "audience" attribute is converted to a condition tag set. For example, "audience='visitor'" is converted to a condition tag set called "audience" with a condition tag called "visitor."

BEFORE IMPORTING DITA FILES

DECISION TIME!

Before you import DITA content, decide:

✓ Do you want to import all files into one folder?

✓ Do you want Flare to preserve element IDs when it converts your DITA content? (important if you want to export the imported content back to DITA)

✓ Will you maintain the content with Flare or with an external application?

HOW TO IMPORT CONTENT FROM DITA FILES

Follow these instructions to import content from a DITA document into a Flare project. This procedure includes instructions for creating the DITA import file *and* importing the content.

▶ To import content from DITA files:

1. Make sure that the Flare project to which you want to import content is open with the Project Organizer in view.

   > **Note** — To import DITA files into a new project instead, select **File** tab → **New Project** → **DITA Document Set**, and follow the directions in the import wizard.

2. If you have previously imported DITA documents into this project, skip to Step 3, next.

   If you have not previously imported DITA documents into this project, you must create a Flare import file to store your import settings. Do the following:

   a. In the Project Organizer, right-click the **Imports** folder.

   b. Select **Add DITA Import File** from the menu.

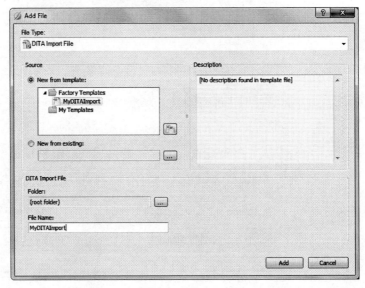

   c. Do one of the following:

To ...	Select ...
Use a Flare template	**MyDITAImport** in the Factory Templates folder
Use your own template	The template in the My Templates folder
Create an import file from an existing one	**New from existing,** browse for and select the import file

   d. Type a File Name. (Flare will add an extension of .flimpdita to the import file.)

   e. Click **Add**. The File Name you typed is listed in the Imports folder and the DITA Import Editor opens.

   f. Skip to Step 4 below.

3. If you have previously imported documents into this project, expand the **Imports** folder and double-click the Flare import file you want to use for this import. The DITA Import Editor opens.

4. On the **Source Files** tab, do the following:

   a. Click **Add Files** 🞤 and select the DITA documents you want to add. (You can choose DITA files or one DITAMAP file.)

> **Note** — You can add only one DITAMAP file to a Flare import file.

   b. If you want to update your content from Flare instead of from the source application after import, clear the **Link Generated Files To Source Files** checkbox. (See "Choices for maintaining content" on page 373 for options.)

> **Note** — If your imported topics are linked to your DITA source files, Flare displays a link icon 🔗 on the XML Editor tab next to a topic's file name. (If you are using source control, the source control icons appear instead.)

c. If you've selected multiple DITA documents to import, you
    can change the order in which they're listed by clicking
    Move Up ⬆ and **Move Down** ⬇.

> **Note** — The document order shown here determines the topic order
> in the Flare TOC.

5. If you want Flare to incorporate changes from your linked DITA
    documents each time you build your Flare output, do the
    following:

    a. Verify that the **Link Generated Files To Source Files**
        checkbox (Source Files tab) is checked.

    b. Click the **Options** tab, then select **Auto-reimport before
        'Generate Output'**. (This feature is called "Easy Sync" in the
        Flare Help system.)

6. *(Optional)* Set other options on the Options tab as desired:

To ...	Select this option ...
Store all imported DITA files including the cascading stylesheet in one folder in the Content Explorer.	Import all Content files to one folder
(If not selected, Flare puts the topic files in a Contents folder and the CSS under Stylesheets.)	
Preserve element IDs along with DITA content. (Needed only if you might create DITA output from the imported topics.)	Preserve ID attributes for elements

7. To specify how styles are handled, click the **Stylesheet** tab.

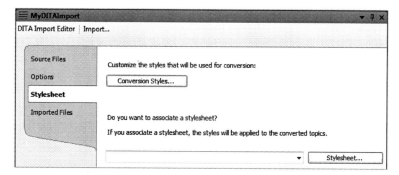

Complete the following tasks:

a. (*Optional*) Select a stylesheet to apply to the imported DITA topics. Either select the stylesheet from the list or click the **Stylesheet** button and browse for it.

b. (*Optional*) To specify the style properties (font, margins, borders, padding) for the style classes in the import stylesheet Flare creates, click **Conversion Styles**. The DITA Import Styles Editor opens.

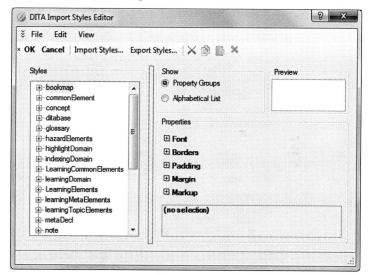

c. Set the properties for DITA elements as desired.

8. Do one of the following:

- If you want to import the content now, proceed to Step 9, next.

- If you don't want to import the content now, save your work, then close the DITA Import Editor.

9. Select **Import** (under the tab name).

Click here to import the files.

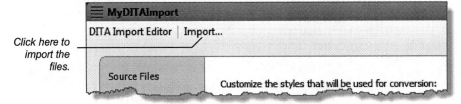

Click **Yes** when prompted to save changes to the Flare import file.

The Accept Imported Documents lists the documents to be imported (on the left) and a preview of the currently selected document (on the right).

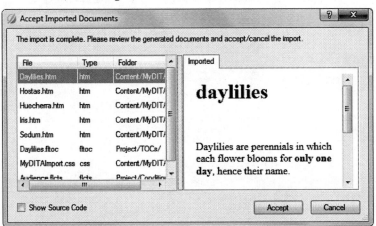

10. If you're satisfied with how the topic previews look, click **Accept** to import the files. The files are added to your Flare project.

11. Close the DITA Import Editor.

WHERE ARE MY IMPORTED TOPICS?

After you accept the imported topics, Flare places them in a Content Explorer folder that is named the same as the DITA import file you created.

Figure G-1:
Where Flare stores your imported DITA topics

Imported topics

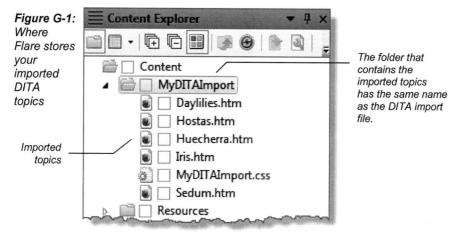

The folder that contains the imported topics has the same name as the DITA import file.

WHERE ARE MY DITA TOPIC TYPES?

During a DITA import, Flare tags each topic as a generic "topic" as opposed to a DITA concept, task, or reference. After import, *you must manually change each file to the appropriate DITA topic type if you intend to export your content back to DITA.* You can change your files in Flare only if they are not linked to their source files; otherwise your changes will be overwritten when the content is reimported.

EXPORTING TO **DITA**

You export to DITA by creating a target, building the target, and distributing the output. The output is DITA code, not published output. It has no formatting.

Before you begin exporting to DITA, make sure you have done the following:

- **Create your project**. Any Flare project can be exported to DITA. To create a project, see "Creating a Flare project" on page 47. To import DITA content, see "Importing DITA files" on page 375.

- **Create and format your content**. Create content and format it as you would for any other output as described in Step 2: Learn the XML Editor, and Step 3: Develop Content.

  > **Note** — Flare conditions are lost when you export to DITA unless you created your conditions using DITA conventions.

- **Add navigation aids**. Use Step 4: Create Navigation Aids, to add links and create index entries for navigation.

KEEPING TRACK OF *DITA* EXPORTS

To make it easier to track various targets and types of output, I've created a Target Settings form (see Appendix A). As you create more targets, you'll find it very helpful to record the names of the Flare project files each target uses.

THE BASIC STEPS

Here's a list of the steps you'll take to export to DITA:

- Create a TOC. See "Creating a Table of Contents" on page 164.

- Add index keywords in topics. See "Creating index entries" on page 188.

- Add navigation aids (such as text hyperlinks, cross-references, or relationship tables).

> **Note** — When developing DITA content, you may want to use relationship tables—a type of navigation aid that organizes related topics by category. (Although relationship tables are commonly used with DITA, you don't need to create DITA output to use them.) To learn about them, search the Flare Help system for "relationship tables."

- Set up your target.

- Build your DITA output.

- Test and troubleshoot.

- Distribute your DITA output.

SETTING UP YOUR DITA TARGET

After you've finished creating the content, TOC, and index keywords, you'll set up a DITA target.

▶ **To set up a DITA target:**

1. In the Project Organizer, expand the **Targets** folder and double-click the target you want to set up. (To add a target, see page 65.)

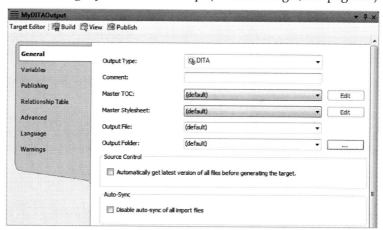

2. Click the **General** tab.

3. When you created your project, you should have selected DITA as the Output Type. If you didn't, select it now.

4. In the Master TOC field, select the desired TOC for this target. The TOC is used to create the DITAMAP file.

5. In the Master Stylesheet field, select the stylesheet used to apply styles to this target. If you select **default**, the Styles stylesheet will be used with this target.

6. Type a name for the Output File (the DITAMAP file) or leave it set to default. (If left as default, "Ditamap.ditamap" is used for the DITAMAP file name.)

> **Best Practice** — Don't forget to record the name of the target, the TOC, and the Output File on the Target Settings form in Appendix A. You'll need to remember its name when you distribute your output.

7. *(Optional)* If you want to obtain the latest version of your project files from your source control application, select **Automatically get latest version of all files before generating the target.**

8. *(Optional)* If you want to disable Easy Sync (chosen during a DITA import), select **Disable auto-sync of all import files.**

9. *(Optional)* If you are using variables in your topics, click the **Variables** tab to change the value of variables for this target only.

10. Click **Save All** 💾 to save your work.

BUILDING *DITA (CODE) OUTPUT*

When you build your DITA output, a DITAMAP file is created that contains links to multiple DITA files. XHTML tags in your topics are converted to DITA elements.

▶ **To build DITA output:**

1. In the Project Organizer, under Targets, right-click the desired DITA target and select **Build 'target name'** from the menu.

    A Build Progress window opens as Flare builds the output according to the selections you made. If your project is large, this might take several seconds.

2. Click **Yes** to view the DITA output when prompted. Flare opens your DITAMAP file in a DITA application such as structured FrameMaker or in a text editor.

Here's a DITAMAP file created from Flare and shown in FrameMaker.

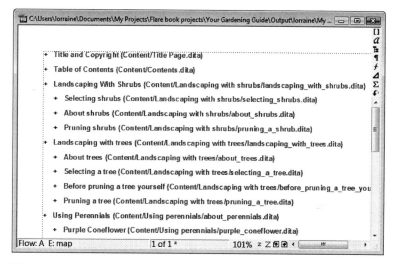

Here's the same DITAMAP file open in a text editor.

```
<?xml version="1.0" encoding="utf-8"?>
<!DOCTYPE map PUBLIC "-//OASIS//DTD DITA Map//EN" "map.dtd">
<map>
    <topicref href="Content/Appendix B - Shrubs/lilacs.dita" navtitle="Lilac" />
    <topicref href="Content/Appendix B - Shrubs/viburnum.dita" navtitle="Viburnum"
    <topicref href="Content/Appendix B - Shrubs/hydrangea.dita" navtitle="Hydrangea
    <topicref href="Content/Using perennials/purple_coneflower.dita" navtitle="Purpl
    <topicref href="Content/Appendix B - Shrubs/burning_bush.dita" navtitle="Burning
    <reltable>
        <relheader>
            <relcolspec type="concept" />
            <relcolspec type="task" />
            <relcolspec type="reference" />
        </relheader>
        <relrow class="Trees">
            <relcell>
                <topicref href="Content/Landscaping with trees/about_trees.dita" />
            </relcell>
            <relcell>
                <topicref href="Content/Landscaping with trees/selecting_a_tree.dita
                </topicref>
                <topicref href="Content/Landscaping with trees/pruning_a_tree.dita"
            </relcell>
            <relcell>
```

TESTING AND TROUBLESHOOTING

When you build the DITA output, Flare checks it for errors. During a build, errors will be listed in the Build Progress window.

One of the most common types of errors is broken links. This and other problems are described in Appendix E: Troubleshoot, which starts on page 327, along with information about using the internal analyzer that comes with Flare.

When you make any changes to your content, remember to re-build your output.

> **Best Practice** — After building DITA output, always test it in a DITA application to verify that your links connect to the correct content.

DISTRIBUTING EXPORTED DITA OUTPUT

Distributing exported DITA output is very similar to the methods used for online output. For details, see Step 5B: Create Online Output.

To distribute your exported DITA output, you must supply:

- The name of the DITAMAP file. See "Setting up your DITA target" on page 383 for details.

- Your output folders and DITA files (the files with a ".dita" extension).

> **Note** — You distribute only *output* files; you don't distribute your project's source files (the files contained in the Content folder under your project name).

Where are the project's output files?

Here is where you can find your project's output files if you use the default locations for storing your project files.

In Windows Explorer, open the **My Projects** folder in the **Documents** folder. The output files for each target are located in the Output folder under your project name.

> Example:
> Documents\My Projects\Gardening Girls\Output\<user name>\<target name>

About the DITAMAP file

You can find the DITAMAP file in the following folder (if you accepted the default project location when you created your project):

My Projects\<project name>\Output\<user name\<target name>

A FEW CAVEATS ABOUT EXPORTING TO DITA

After you export to DITA, you may have some cleanup to do. Be sure to account for these tasks when you plan your project:

- **In DITA output, all condition tags you created *in Flare* are los**t. You must manually re-create them in your DITA output. Consider using DITA conventions for your condition tags *before* you export DITA content, in which case Flare *will* create the condition tags when you build DITA output.

- **Flare does not create context-sensitive topic IDs in DITA output**. For example, if Topic 1 has an ID of 1000 and is mapped to topic ID_Topic_1, the topic ID will be missing after you create DITA output. You must manually add context-sensitive topic IDs to all applicable topics after you create your DITA output.

Appendix H:
Create EPUB
Output

In this chapter ...
➤ Learn what you can and cannot include in an EPUB document
➤ Set up an EPUB target
➤ Build EPUB output
➤ Create MOBI output

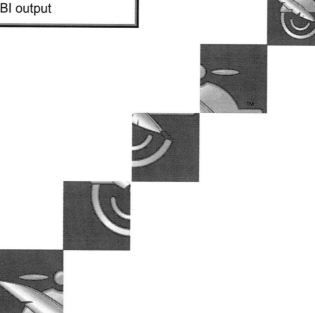

OVERVIEW

In this appendix, you'll learn how to build EPUB® output, a standard format for digital books (ebooks) that can be read on various platforms. Although similar in structure to print books, EPUB is meant to be viewed electronically. EPUB format was developed and is maintained by the International Digital Publishing Forum (IDPF).

Because the EPUB standard must support many different devices, the formatting of content is more basic than with output designed to be printed. For example, some print output features are not easily supported, like wrapping text around images ("object positioning" in Flare) and columns. (See "What you can't include" on page 392 for the list of features not supported.)

The content in your EPUB ebook is **reflowable**, which means that the amount of content shown on a page is fluid, not fixed. What you see will vary with the ebook reader and with the size of the text (which you can change on most e–book readers). The content always fills the reading space available on a device (or the window size if you're using an e-reader application on a computer).

> **Note** — Although dynamic pagination and resizing are part of the EPUB specification, results may vary with different ebook readers. Support for these features is not guaranteed with all ebook readers.

Flare automatically embeds the fonts you use in your EPUB output so even if a reader does not have the fonts you used, your ebook will look the same on all readers.

Ebooks typically include metadata—data about the ebook such as title, author, and an identifier (like an ISBN). Flare allows you to enter metadata in your EPUB target.

BEFORE CREATING EPUB OUTPUT

Before you create EPUB output, you should do the following:

- **Create your project**. You can build print output from any Flare project. To create the project, see "Creating a Flare project" on page 47.

- **Create and format your content**. You create and format content for print output as you would for any other output as described in Step 2: Learn the XML Editor, and Step 3: Develop Content.

- **Add navigation aids**. Use Step 4: Create Navigation Aids, to add cross-references, links, and index entries.

- **Add an EPUB target**. If not, add the target. See "Adding a target" on page 65.

WHAT YOU CAN INCLUDE IN AN EPUB DOCUMENT

> **Note** — For the complete list, see the Output Type Comparison Table in the Flare Help topic "About EPUB Output."

FRONT AND BACK MATTER

Your EPUB output can contain any of these document parts:

- glossary
- index
- list of elements, concepts, and endnotes
- TOCs and mini-TOCs

CONTENT

In addition to text, EPUB also supports these features:

- audio and movie files. (Not all e-readers support this.)
- auto-numbers
- equations marked up with MathML

- footnotes

- images (including SVG) and image hyperlinks

- lists

- output in right-to-left and left-to-right languages

- QR codes

- snippets and variables

- tables, including captions. (Not all e-readers support this.)

NAVIGATION LINKS

- cross-references

- index links

- relationship tables

- text hyperlinks

WHAT YOU CAN'T INCLUDE

The following features are not available—either because they are not applicable to ebooks, because they are not supported by the current EPUB standard, or because they are a function of ebook readers (not the EPUB standard).

- breadcrumbs

- drop-down and expanding text

- object positioning

- page layouts, master pages, page numbers. Since content is reflowed to fit the reading device, these features do not apply.

- search features. (Some ebook readers have their own search feature.)

- text boxes

- text redaction

CREATING AN EPUB DOCUMENT

To create an EPUB document, you'll need to create and set up an EPUB target, then you'll need to build the output.

▶ To set up an EPUB target:

1. Create a TOC that includes the topics to be printed in the desired print order. See "Creating a Table of Contents" on page 164. Flare uses this TOC as an outline when building the output.

> ***Important*** — If you are using auto-numbers, you must specify chapter breaks for each chapter in the TOC. For more information about specifying chapter breaks, see Task 7 in Step5A, "Create Print Output." (Although page layouts don't apply to EPUB, it is okay if they are specified in the TOC you use for EPUB.)

2. Add a new target and select **EPUB** for the Output Type. (See "Adding a target" on page 65 for more information.)

3. Click the **General** tab.

4. In the Master TOC list, select the TOC to use as an outline.

5. In the Master Stylesheet field, select the stylesheet to apply to this target. If you select **default**, the Styles stylesheet will be used with this target.

6. (*Optional*) To exclude content tagged with a condition tag, click the **Conditional Text** tab. Select the checkboxes for the condition tags you want to exclude from your output.

> ***Important*** — Unless excluded, all content tagged with a condition tag *is automatically included* in output.

7. (*Optional*) If you want to change the definitions of variables for this target, click the **Variables** tab and change values as desired.

8. Click the **EPUB Options** tab.

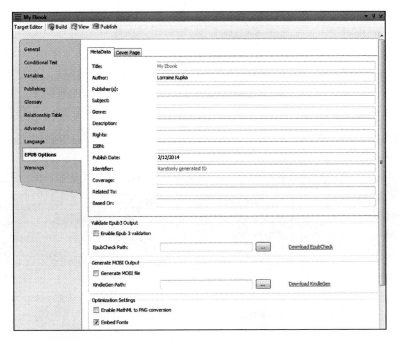

9. On the MetaData tab, fill in the desired metadata. (If you don't enter an identifier, Flare generates one for you.)

> **Note** — To validate your EPUB3 output for use in online stores, see "Specifying EPUB Options" in Flare's help system.

10. On the Cover Page tab, click the browse button to the right of "Image Location" to select an image for the cover of your ebook.

11. Click **Save All** to save your work.

▶ To build an EPUB target:

1. In the Project Organizer under **Targets**, right-click the target you just set up and select **Build <target name>** from the menu.

    Flare builds the output according to the selections you made. If your project is large, this might take several seconds.

2. When asked if you want to view output, do one of the following:

    ▪   Click **Yes** to view output in your default EBUB reader.

- Click **No** to choose a reader. In the Build Progress window, click the arrow to the right of **View Output** and select the desired reader from the list.

CREATING **MOBI** OUTPUT

Amazon Kindle devices do not support the ebook format ".epub". Instead they use Amazon's own ebook format—MOBI (which has a .mobi file extension). With Flare you can create ebooks in MOBI format for use on an Amazon Kindle or with Kindle reader apps.

You'll create MOBI output by using a Flare EPUB target. The same target generates your ebook in both EPUB and MOBI formats. But before you can build the MOBI output, you have to complete a few tasks in the Flare Target Editor and at Amazon's KindleGen website. Here's what you need to do:

▶ To build MOBI output:

1. Open your EPUB target (or create a new one) and click the **EPUB Options** tab.

2. In the Generate MOBI Output section, select the **Generate MOBI file** checkbox, then click **Download KindleGen**.

    The Amazon KindleGen website opens. KindleGen will convert your files to Kindle format, which you then download to your computer.

3. On the Amazon webpage, accept the terms of use and click the applicable download link (for Windows, MacOS or Linux) to download the converted file in zip format to your computer.

4. Extract the downloaded file and note where the file is located.

The remaining tasks are completed in Flare.

5.   In the Target Editor's EPUB Options tab, click ⌷⋯⌷ (next to the
     KindleGen Path field).

6.   Navigate to the folder on your computer where you extracted
     the zip file you downloaded from the Amazon KindleGen
     website.

7.   In the Open dialog, double-click the **kindlegen.exe** file.

8.   Click **Save All** 💾 to save your work.

9.   Build the EPUB target.

Flare creates both a MOBI file and an EPUB file in the output folder.
You can view the MOBI file on a Kindle or Kindle reader app.

DISTRIBUTING EPUB OUTPUT

EPUB output is saved in a single file. The EPUB or MOBI file is the
only file you need to distribute.

When you're ready to distribute your output, you'll find it in a folder
under your project's Output folder. By default, the file is in a folder
named for the target used to build output.

VIEWING EPUB OUTPUT

To view EPUB output, you need either an ebook reader (like Kindle
or Nook), a tablet app (like iBooks), or an e-reader application (like
Calibre or EPUBReader, a Firefox add-on). There are several free
EPUB viewers available for download from the Internet.

Figure H-1:
EPUB
output
in an
Ebook
Viewer

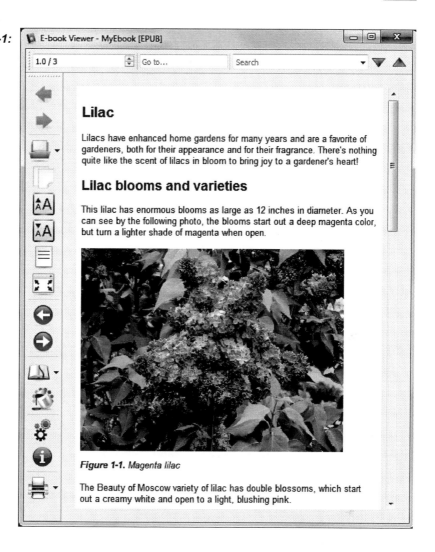

Figure 1-1. Magenta lilac

Appendix I:
The Next Step

In this chapter ...
➤ Advanced features to explore

NOW IT'S UP TO YOU

At this point, you've learned enough about Flare to complete your first project, and you might want to know a bit about which features to try next.

Flare is a powerful tool for topic-based authoring, with many options to explore. Table I-1 gives you a brief description of some of the features you might want to learn about on your own. Consult the Flare Help system for detailed information.

Table I-1:
Flare
features to
explore

With this feature …	You can …
Auto-numbering	■ Number content (paragraphs, chapters, sections, and volumes) automatically and include the number in table, figure, and page numbers.
Annotations and track changes	■ Insert comments and notes in topics. ■ Track your changes in the XML Editor
Batch targets / scheduling	■ Build multiple targets in one step. ■ Schedule the building of a batch of targets.
Movies	■ Launch MadCap Mimic right from Flare. ■ Add links to movies created in MadCap Mimic, Adobe Flash, Windows Media, or Apple QuickTime. ■ Change and preview movies.
Topic review and contribution	■ Email topics for review. Reviewers add annotations and return comments to you. ■ Accept reviewers' comments and add them to the source file. ■ Add topics created by others to your project.
Mini-TOCs (print output)	■ Create mini-TOCs for chapters (by inserting a mini-TOC proxy into each topic that begins a chapter).
Footnotes	■ Add footnotes to your topics.
Widows and orphans	■ Define widow and orphan settings with styles.

Table I-1:
(Cont.)

With this feature ...	You can ...
Templates	▪ Jumpstart your project by using one of Flare's many types of project templates for creating online output, online and print from the same project, and various types of print documents.
Project properties	▪ Use the Project Properties dialog to specify the project's master TOC, master stylesheet, master page layout, spell-check language and source control application (**Project** tab → **Project Properties**).
Window, topic and editor manipulation	▪ Float windows and editors to move them where you need them. ▪ Attach windows to the sides, top, or bottom of the workspace by docking them.
Custom layouts	▪ Open and position Flare windows per your needs. Then save the layout as a configuration. ▪ Create multiple configurations for different needs.
Manage recent project list	▪ Select **File** tab → **Manage Recent Projects**. (You can change the project list that appears on the Start Page and Recent Projects list.)
Text boxes	▪ Insert a box into a topic and add content to it. ▪ Position a text box as desired.
Complex conditional expressions	▪ Use the Advanced section on the Target Editor's Conditional text tab to create complex conditional expressions that include or exclude the exact combination of conditions you need when you build a target.
Object positioning	▪ Position objects, such as images and text boxes, exactly where you want them (object positioning must be enabled).
Hyphenation (print output)	▪ Specify if hyphens will be used at the end of lines.
"List of" proxy	▪ Create a linked list of various types of elements in your output, such as tables or images.
Smart quotes	▪ Set a global option to use smart quotes when you create or edit content.

Table I-1:
(Cont.)

With this feature ...	You can ...
Find and Replace	■ Quickly find and replace text in the open topic, in all topics, or in project files.
Page and column break icons (Print Layout mode)	■ Determine where page / column breaks or widow / orphan control have forced a paragraph to move to another page (icons appear in the text margins).
	■ Open the paragraph properties (by clicking a page or column break icon).
Advanced index options	■ Add index terms automatically rather than inserting index markers manually.
	■ Exclude index entries from searches (by default, index entries are included in searches).
	■ Link index entries to other index entries ("see" and "see also" links).
Crop and registration marks	■ View crop and registration marks in the Page Layout Editor, and print them in PDF output. (See the Target Editor's PDF Options tab.)
Slideshows	■ Display content as a slideshow.
CMYK	■ Enable CMYK (a color model used by graphic designers and professional printers) in PDF output
	■ Convert RGB Colors to CMYK.
Compare files for differences	■ View differences between a project file and its older backup file. (Search for 'backups" in the Flare's Help.)
Export projects	■ Export all or part of a Flare project.
Equation Editor	■ Create equations and insert them into your topics. (Math Markup Language is used.)
Pulse—socially enabled output (*an optional feature sold separately from Flare*)	■ Communicate with and receive feedback from your users about your online output. Pulse provides an alternative to MadCap Feedback and can be used with WebHelp, HTML5, and DotNet Help outputs.
Adding multiple variable definitions	■ Add multiple definitions for variables. When you override a variable's definition in the Target Editor, you can select from all of its definitions.

Index

A

accessibility, options for, 234, 241
accordion bars, 24
active panes, 22-23
active topics, 67, 93
addresses (e-mail and websites), creating text hyperlinks to, 174
Adobe AIR, 16, 245
Adobe FrameMaker. *See* FrameMaker
Adobe Portable Document Format. *See* PDF output
advanced Flare features, 400
alias files, 315, 317
   adding to a project, 320-21
   setting up, 321-24
A-links, 173
Amazon Kindle output, creating, 395
Analyzer, external. *See* MadCap Analyzer
analyzers, internal, 33
analyzing projects, 334
Apache Subversion, 52
appearance of online output, 252, 253
ASCII characters, inserting, 305
audio links, 173
authoring, traditional vs. topic-based, 10
auto-numbering, 400
Auto-reimport before 'Generate Output' option, 287, 378
AutoSuggestion, 78, 99-100

B

backups, project, 50
bars
   accordion, 24
   span, 88

bars (*continued*)
   span and tag, 95-98
basic tasks for Flare projects, 41
batch targets, 400
best practices
   avoiding unlinked TOC items, 330
   backing up projects, 50
   building output, 256
   creating targets, 12
   deleting pages from page layouts, 221
   embedding images in Word documents, 203
   importing FrameMaker books, 293
   inserting markers in source files, 294
   limiting number of open topics, 94
   naming projects, 38
   naming TOCs, 214
   preventing extra lines in print output, 177
   recording target names, 384
   remembering master page names, 251
   saving errors in logs, 332
   saving projects, 67, 94
   sizing images, 128
   testing DITA output, 386
   testing links, 258
   typing spaces between words, 56
   using page layouts, 237
   using styles, 86
blocks, described, 82
body frames, 240
bookmarks
   described, 172
   inserting and linking to, 177-80
   troubleshooting, 336

bookmarks (*continued*)
    viewing markers for, 98
Borders tab, Insert Table dialog, 161
breadcrumbs, in online output, 250
broken links, 328-30, 333
browse sequences, 250
build errors, troubleshooting, 331
building output, 12
    DITA, 384
    EPUB, 394
    online, 256
    print, 235
    scheduling, 400
bulleted lists, creating, 110-12

C

callouts, how imported from Word, 284
Capture, adding screen captures to topics
    from, 127
cascading stylesheet (CSS), 142, 149
cells, cutting and pasting, 123
changes, saving, 66
chapter breaks, 230
characters, ASCII, 305
checking spelling, 60-64
CHM files, importing to Flare, 302
classes, style, 149, 154
closing, files, 68
columns
    cutting and pasting, 123
    deleting, 120
    inserting, 120
    moving, 122
    resizing, 121
combining lists, 116-17
commands, cross-references, 180, 186
compiling. *See* building
concept links, 173
condition tag sets, 346
condition tags
    applying to snippets, 353
    applying to variables, 360

condition tags (*continued*)
    creating and applying, 344-49
    DITA, 372
    filtering while editing, 350
    highlighting tagged content, 307
    in topic preview, 58
    selecting in online targets, 255, 393
    undefined, 351
content. *See also* text
    applying condition tags to, 347
    creating snippets from, 356
    described, 54
    excluding from output, 345
    formatting, 85-91, 141-57
    from DITA, maintaining, 373
    from Word or FrameMaker,
        maintaining, 281
    importing Word and FrameMaker
        files, overview, 274
    single-sourcing, 344
Content Explorer, 24, 26
Content Reviews worksheet, 267
Content Structure and Management
    worksheet, 268
context-sensitive help, 314
    alias files, 320-21
    described, 14
    header (map) files, 318-20
    tasks for creating, 317
    testing, 325
converting, tables to text and text to
    tables, 122
copying
    page layout frames, 225
    text into topics, 105, 310
cross-references, 172
    advanced features, 188
    changing, 184-86
    commands, 180
    inserting in topics, 180-88
    updating manually, 187
    vs. text hyperlinks, 180

CSS (cascading stylesheet), 142, 149
cursors
    types in XML Editor, 308-9
    viewing in XML Editor, 82-83
custom layouts, 401

D

default stylesheet, 89, 147
deleting
    breadcrumb trails, 250
    index keywords, 195
    markers, 195
    pages from page layouts, 221
    rows and columns, 120
    text, 310
    topics, 106-7
dictionaries, adding terms to, 64
disability laws, compliance with, 241
distributing output, 12
    online, 259-61
    print, 203-5
DITA (Darwin Information Typing
    Architecture, 18
    exporting from Flare to, 382-87
DITA content, importing, 375-81
DITA output
    building, 383-84
    publishing, 386
    testing, 386
DITAMAP files, 377, 387
dividing source files when importing, 279
document formats
    online, 14
    print, 13
DotNet Help, 16, 246
drawing objects, importing
    from FrameMaker, 293
    from Word, 283
drop-down text, 173
Dynamic Help window, 77

E

Easy Sync, 282, 374
ebooks, creating, 390
Eclipse Help, 246
editing
    content with the Text Editor, 80
    page layout frames, 223, 240
    skins, 252
Editor tabs, 27
e-mail addresses, creating text hyperlinks
    to, 174
embedding images, 203
entering, index keywords, 188
EPUB, 390
    creating a target for, 393
    distributing and viewing, 396
error log, opening and saving, 332
errors
    analyzing, 333
    building output, 331
excluding, content from output, 257, 345
expanding text, 173
exporting from Flare to DITA, 382-87
Extensible Markup Language (XML), 76
external Analyzer. *See* MadCap Analyzer
external links, 172
external resources, 38

F

file extensions, for online Output File, 261
file tagging, 337-40
files
    closing, 68
    saving, 66
fixing
    broken links, 333
    unlinked TOC items, 331
Flare editors, 27
Flare workspace, 22
footer frames, 241
footers, adding
    to online output, 251

footers, adding (*continued*)
  to print output, 223
footnotes, 400
formats, for previewing topics, 57
formatting
  content, 141-57
  cross-references, 184-86
  images as thumbnails, 135
  indexes for print output, 197
  snippets, 353
  tables, 143, 145-46
  text, 85-91
  text for redaction, 155
  variables, 360
  with styles, 142
FrameMaker, importing content to Flare
  from, 276, 292-302
frames, copying, 225

G

General tab, Insert Table dialog, 158
generating. *See* building
global project linking, 344, 365-70
graphics. *See* images
grid lines, displaying, 118

H

header (map) files, 314-15, 317
  adding to a project, 318-20
  contents of, 318
header frames, 241
headers, adding
  to online output, 251
  to print output, 227
heading variables, 361
Help format, selecting, 15
Help systems, 13, *See also* online ouput
  context-sensitive, 14, 314
  creating, 244
  vs. knowledge bases, 14
highlighting variables, 363
hotspots. *See* links

HTML Help, 16, 246
HTML5, 15, 245, 255
hyperlinks. *See* links
hyphenation, 401

I

image formats, 124, 128
image hyperlinks, 172
image problems, 331
images
  adding to topics, 124-31
  changing, 125
  embedding in Word ouput, 203
  importing from Word, 283
  resizing, 128-31
  showing as thumbnails, 131
  where stored, 125
import file, 279
imported topics, where stored
  DITA, 381
  FrameMaker, 301
  Word, 291
importing
  CHM files, 302
  DITA to Flare, 372, 375-81
  documents and projects, 274
  FrameMaker documents, 276, 292-302
  segmenting one document into
    multiple topics, 279
  styles, 280
  tasks, 278
  Word documents, 276, 283-92
  Word or FrameMaker files
    maintaining, 281
    overview, 274
index
  creating for print output, 213
  creating keywords for, 188
  formatting for print output, 197
index entries, in online and print output,
  196

Index Entry mode, 188
    adding keywords in, 189
    when to use, 189
index keywords, 188-99
    adding, 188-94
    changing and deleting, 195
index markers, viewing, 195
index options, advanced, 402
index proxy, 215
Index window, 188
    adding keywords in, 191
    when to use, 189
inline formatting, 85, 142, *See also* local
    formatting
input. *See* source content
Insert Table dialog, 158
    Borders tab, 161
    General tab, 158
inserting
    images, 126
    links to bookmarks, 179
    QR codes, 139
    rows and columns, 120
    snippets, 357-59
    variables, 362
internal analyzer, 33, 333
Internal Text Editor, opening active
    topics in, 305

J
Java Runtime Environment, 245
    and WebHelp AIR, 16

K
keywords, 188-99
    adding, 188-94
    changing and deleting, 195
k-links (keyword links), 173
knowledge bases, 14, 244

L
layout modes, 91
layouts, 401
learning Flare, tips for, 6-8
left pane, 24
lines, removing from TOCs and indexes,
    236
Link Generated Files to Source Files
    option, 286, 377
Link Viewer, checking links in, 108
linking
    imported topics to source files, 286
    page layouts to TOC items, 230
    topics to TOC items, 168
linking to
    bookmarks, 179
    external files and topics, 175
    topics and websites, 174
links, 172
    broken, 328-30
    checking, 108
    creating text hyperlinks, 173-76
    deleting, 106
    inserting related topics, 176-77
    testing, 180
    types of, 172
list actions, 113
list-of proxy, 401
lists
    changing, 112
    creating, 110-12
    merging, 116-17
    rearranging, 113
    re-numbering, 114-16
    sorting, 114
    types of, 109
local formatting, 85
    applying, 144
log files, opening, 332

M

MadCap Analyzer, 33, 333
MadCap Capture, adding screen captures
    to topics from, 127
MadCap Mimic, 400
MadCap:xref style, 181
maintaining content after importing, 281
map (header) files, 314
markers
    deleting, 195
    viewing, 98, 195
master pages
    adding to projects, 251-52
    vs. page layouts, 237
master TOC, 165
mediums, 93, 181, 240
menus, structure bar, 97
merging
    lists, 116-17
    tables, 123
Microsoft SharePoint, 38
Microsoft Word. *See* Word
middle pane, 23, 27
Mimic. *See* MadCap Mimic
mini-TOCs, 400
    adding to online output, 251
MOBI, creating output for, 395
mobile formats. *See* WebHelp Mobile
modes for viewing topics, 91
movie links, 173, 400
moving
    rows and columns, 122
    text within topics, 310-11
multi-channel publishing, 344
multi-level lists, creating, 111

N

navigation aids
    breadcrumb trails, 250
    browse sequences, 250
    cross-references, 180-88
    described, 10

navigation aids (*continued*)
    indexes, 188-99
    links, 172
    TOCs, 164-71
numbered lists, creating, 110

O

object positioning, 401
objects (drawing), importing from Word
    to Flare, 283
online documents, types of, 13-15
online output, 244
    adding and editing, skins, 252
    adding headers and footers to, 251
    adding master pages to, 251
    basic steps for creating, 249
    building, 256
    cross-references in, 181
    distributing, 259-61
    excluding topics from, 257
    publishing, 259
    setting up targets for, 253-56
    showing breadcrumbs in, 250
    testing and troubleshooting, 258
    types of, 245
opening
    a TOC in the TOC Editor, 168
    active topics in the Text Editor, 80, 305
    build log files, 332
    file from Project Organizer, 25
    Link Viewer, 108
    Project Organizer, 25
    projects, 53
    Properties dialog for TOC items, 169
    TOCs, 30
    topics, 59
        from a TOC, 169
ordered lists, 110
output
    described, 11
    Help formats Flare can create, 14
    types of, 13

Output File, described, 261

P

page buttons, 239
page frames, 239
page layouts, 236
  adding to a project, 219
  deleting pages from, 221
  frames, 239
    body, 240
    copying, 225
    header and footer, 241
  linking to TOC items, 230
  templates for, 219, 237
  vs. master pages, 237
pages
  deleting from page layouts, 221
  master, 237, 251-52
  navigating, 306
  types of, 238
paragraphs, 82, *See also* blocks
paratext command, 183
pasting, text into topics, 105, 310
PDF output, 204, 206
Perforce, 50
pictures. *See* images
placeholder topics, creating, 213
planning projects, 36-39
planning worksheets, 263
previewing, topics, 57-59
primary targets, 12
print formats, available with Flare, 13
Print Layout mode, 29, 91
print output
  adding page layouts, 219
  appearance of index entries in, 197
  before creating, 205
  building, 235
  creating a simple PDF document, 206
  creating placeholder topics, 213
  creating topic outlines, 216
  cross-references in, 181

print output (*continued*)
  customizing footers, 223
  customizing headers, 227
  deleting pages from page layouts, 221
  formatting indexes, 197
  FrameMaker, 203
  front and back matter, 208
  linking page layouts to TOC items, 230
  overview, creating a complex
    document, 208
  PDF, 204
  setting print targets, 233
  table of contents, creating, 213
  types created by Flare, 202
  Word, 203
  XHTML, 205
  XPS, 204
print targets, setting, 233
problems
  in projects, 328
  with images, 331
Project Conventions and Documentation
  worksheet, 268, 269
project files, caution about deleting, 329
Project Organizer, 24-25
project output files, locating, 260
Project Properties dialog, 401
projects
  adding targets to, 65
  adding topics to, 53-57
  analyzing, 333
  backing up, 50
  binding to source control applications,
    50-53
  creating, 48-53
  described, 54
  linking, 365-70
  opening, 53
  planning, 36-39
  reporting information from, 340
  saving, 94
  templates, 71

projects (*continued*)
    tracking development of, 337
    troubleshooting, 328
    worksheet for starting, 269
Properties dialog, opening, 169
proxy, 213
    breadcrumbs, 250
proxy styles, 236
pseudo classes, 150
publishing, 12
    DITA output, 386
    online output, 259

Q

QR codes, inserting, 139
quality of images, 128
Quick Character, 140

R

raster (bitmap) images, resizing, 128
rearranging
    lists, 113
    TOC items and books, 171
redaction, marking text for, 155
related topic links, 173, 176-77
relationship tables, 173
removing pages from page layouts, 221
renaming TOCs, 171
re-numbering, lists, 114-16
reports, 340
resizing
    images, 128-31
    rows and columns, 121
Resources folder, contents of, 26
Resources\Images folder, 125
responsive output, 245, 248
reviewing content, choices for, 267
ribbons and toolbars, 31-33
right pane, 23, 31
roadmap, for getting started with Flare, 39-45

rows
    cutting and pasting, 123
    deleting, 120
    inserting, 120
    moving, 122
    resizing, 121
rulers
    changing units of measure for, 102
    showing and hiding, 101

S

Save All vs. Save, 94
saving
    documents, 68
    errors in logs, 332
    FrameMaker output in a single file, 203
    projects, 66, 94
scheduling, builds, 400
screen captures, adding from Capture, 127
searches, excluding topics from, 257
See Also links, 173
selecting
    rows and columns, 119
    text, 84, 309
sequence numbers, assigning to lists, 112
sequences, browse, 250
setting the default Quick Character, 140
setting up
    alias files, 321-24
    target for output
        DITA, 383-84
        online, 253-56
        print, 233
SharePoint, integration with, 38
shortcut controls, 173
shortcuts, 309-12
Show Markers, 195
single-level lists, creating, 110
single-sourcing, 344
    condition tags, 344-49

single-sourcing (*continued*)
    snippets, 353-59
    variables, 360-64
Skin Editor, 253
skins
    adding and editing, 252
    assigning to topics, 315
    described, 16
    selecting for targets, WebHelp Mobile, 255
snippet conditions, 353
snippets, 344, 353-59
    creating, 354-57
    formatting, 353
    inserting, 357-59
    using condition tags with, 353
sorting
    lists, 114
    tables, 124
sound (audio) links, 173
source content, 36
source control applications, binding projects to, 50-53
source files
    FrameMaker, inserting markers in, 294
    importing content from, 279
    linking imported topics to, 287, 296
    troubleshooting, 333
Source of Content worksheet, 264
spaces between words, 56
span bars, 96
    showing, 88
    toggling on and off, 97
special characters, adding to text, 140
spell check, 60-64
Spell Check window, 63
Start New Project Wizard, 48
Start New Project worksheet, 269
Start Page, 22, 77
status bar, 33
status reports, 340
structure bar menus, 97

structure bars, 95-98
style classes, 149
    adding, 154
style formatting, 85, 142
styles
    applying to text, 148
    applying to topics and tables, 146
    changing, 151
    cleaning up before importing content, 277
    customizing, 149
    formatting images as thumbnails with, 137
    importing, 280
    MadCap:xref, 181
    proxy, 236
    resizing images with, 131
Styles.css, 89, 141
Stylesheet Editor
    Advanced View, 153
    changing styles with, 151
    Simplified View, 152
stylesheets, 85, 146
    described, 142
    linking imported FrameMaker topics to, 298
    linking imported Word topics to, 288
    mediums, 93, 181
sub-keywords, adding to indexes, 192
Subversion, 52
switching topics, 93
symbols, adding to text, 140
system variables, 361

T

table cells, cutting and pasting, 123
table of contents. *See also* TOCs
    creating for print output, 213
    Word output, creating from Flare, 203
table stylesheets, 146
tables, 117
    converting to text, 122

tables (*continued*)
displaying grid lines, 118
formatting, 143
locally, 145-46
with styles, 146
Insert Table dialog, 158
inserting, 118
merging, 123
rows and columns
deleting, 120
inserting, 120
moving, 122
resizing, 121
selecting, 119
selecting, 119
sorting, 124
stylesheets, 146
tag bars, 95, 97
tags
condition
creating and applying, 344-49
described, 346
DITA, 372
filtering while editing, 350
highlighting tagged content, 307
selecting in targets, 255, 393
undefined, 351
described, 76
excluding text with, 345
file, 337
topic, editing, 80
viewing in the Text Editor, 80
XML, viewing in topics, 305
Target Settings form, 270
targets
adding to projects, 65
building
DITA output, 384
online output, 256
print output, 235
context-sensitive help, 325
described, 12

targets (*continued*)
planning worksheet, 270
primary, 12
setting up
DITA output, 383-84
online output, 253-56
print output, 233
tasks for importing, 278
Team Foundation Server (TFS), 50, 52
Template Manager, 69, 72
templates
creating, 68-72
managing, 72
page layout, 237
terms
adding to dictionaries, 64
adding to indexes, 188-94
testing
context-sensitive help, 325
DITA output, 386
links, 180
online output, 258
text. *See also* content
adding symbols and special
characters, 140
applying condition tags to, 347
converting to tables, 122
copying and pasting, 105, 310
deleting, 310
entering in XML Editor, 78
formatting, 85-91
locally, 144
with styles, 148
marking for redaction, 155
moving within topics, 310-11
selecting, 309
spaces between words, 56
spell check, 60-64
text blocks. *See also* text
described, 82
text boxes, 401
Text Editor, 80

text hyperlinks, 172
    creating, 173-76
text popups, 172
text redaction, 155
TFS (Team Foundation Server), 50, 52
thumbnails, showing images as, 131
TOC books, adding to a TOC, 169
TOC Editor, 30
TOC items
    adding along with topics, 171
    adding to a TOC, 170
    linking to page layouts, 230
    linking topics to, 168
    unlinked, 328, 330
    viewing properties of, 169
TOCs, 164-71
    adding books to, 169
    adding items to, 170
    adding topics to, 168
    created from Word import, 284
    creating, 164, 167
    creating topics and items
        simultaneously, 171
    expanding, 31
    imported, naming, 166
    linking, 166
    linking page layouts to topics in, 230
    master, 165
    naming, 214
    opening, 30, 168
        topics from, 169
    rearranging items and books in, 171
    renaming, 171
    troubleshooting, 329
    using as topic outlines for print
        output, 216
togglers, 173
toolbars
    XML Editor, 95, 304-8
topic files, deleting, 329
topic outlines, creating for print output,
    216

topic popups, 172
topic stylesheets, 146
topic tags, editing, 80
topic-based authoring, 10
topics
    active, 67
    adding along with TOC items, 171
    adding images to, 124-31, 126
    adding to projects, 53-57, 93
    adding to TOCs, 54
    assigning skins to, 315
    copying and pasting text into, 105
    creating simultaneously with TOC
        items, 171
    creating templates for, 68-72
    deleting, 106-7
    described, 53, 104
    excluding from online output, 257
    inserting bookmarks in, 177-80
    inserting cross-references in, 180-88
    inserting related topic links into, 176-
        77
    inserting tables in, 118
    moving text within, 310-11
    opening, 59, 169
    previewing, 57-59
    saving, 66, 94
    shortcuts for navigating, 312
    spell checking, 60-64
    stylesheets, 146
    viewing, 57-59
tracking project status, 337
traditional authoring, described, 10
troubleshooting, 328
    analyzing projects, 333
    broken links and unlinked items, 328-
        30
    build errors, 331
    DITA output, 386
    images, 331
    online output, 258
turning on markers, 195

Type of Output worksheet, 265
typing, spell checking while, 61

U

undefined condition tags, 351
    fixing, 352
units of measure, changing, 102
unlinked TOC items, 328
    avoiding, 330
    fixing, 331
    symbol in TOC Editor, 329
unordered lists, 110
updating cross-references, 187

V

variable sets, 360
variables, 344, 360-64
    adding and changing, 363
Variables set, 361
vector images, resizing, 128
viewing
    grid lines, 118
    index keywords, 195
    markers, 98, 195
    rulers, 101
    span bars, 88, 307
    tag bars, 307
    tags in the Text Editor, 80
    TOC item properties, 169
Visual Source Safe (VSS), 50, 52

W

Web Layout mode, 29, 91
WebHelp, 15, 245
WebHelp AIR, 16, 245
WebHelp Mobile, 15, 245
    skins, 17
WebHelp Plus, 16, 245
websites, creating text hyperlinks to, 174
widows and orphans, 400

Windows Explorer, deleting topic and
    project files from, 329
Windows Server 2003, 16
wizards, Start New Project, 48
Word
    importing content to Flare from, 276,
        283-92
    output, 203
words, spaces between, 56
worksheets, project planning, 263
workspace, 22
World Wide Web Consortium (W3C), 76
wrapping, index entries, 199

X

XHTML output, 205
XML (Extensible Markup Language), 76
XML Editor, 76
    adding keywords in Index Entry
        mode, 189
    adding topics, 93
    Auto Suggestion, 99-100
    creating text hyperlinks, 173-76
    cursors available in, 308-9
    described, 28-30
    entering text, 78
    formatting text, 85-91
    resizing images, 128-31
    rulers, 101
    selecting and manipulating text, 84
    shortcuts, 309-12
    structure bars, 95-98
    toolbars, 95, 304-8
    typing spaces, 82
    viewing cursors and text blocks, 82-83
    viewing layout modes, 91
    viewing markers, 98
    viewing tag and span bars, 97
XPS (XML Paper Specification) output,
    204